SPANISH ART

Printed and Engraved by
Herbert Reiach, Ltd., Eyot
Works, St. Peter's Square,
Hammersmith, London, W.6

Sto. Domingo de Silos, by Bartolomé Bermejo. 1474-77. Panel, 95¼ in. by 51⅛ in. (Prado)

BURLINGTON MAGAZINE MONOGRAPH–II

SPANISH ART

AN INTRODUCTORY REVIEW OF ARCHI-TECTURE, PAINTING, SCULPTURE, TEXTILES, CERAMICS, WOODWORK, METALWORK

BY

R. R. TATLOCK
ROYALL TYLER
SIR CHARLES HOLMES
H. ISHERWOOD KAY
GEOFFREY WEBB

A. F. KENDRICK
A. VAN DE PUT
BERNARD RACKHAM
BERNARD BEVAN
PEDRO DE ARTIÑANO

Published for The Burlington Magazine by

B. T. BATSFORD, LTD., 94 HIGH HOLBORN, LONDON

1927

This series of Monographs is produced by
THE BURLINGTON MAGAZINE, LTD.,
Bank Buildings, 16A St. James's Street,
London, and published for them by B. T.
BATSFORD, LTD., 94 High Holborn,
London. The sole agent for their sale in the
United States of America is E. WEYHE,
794 Lexington Avenue, New York.

CHINESE ART, the first monograph in the
series, published 1925, is now out of print.

Made and Printed in Great Britain.

CONTENTS

INTRODUCTION

TO see Spanish art steadily and to see it as a whole is admittedly difficult; success is achieved, as a rule, only by those who have mastered, at least in outline, the rest of European art history. For the art that has been proclaimed by a given generation as the last word, and discarded by the next as obsolescent, has often been tardily granted an asylum and a renewal of life in Spain. Spain appears to-day as the Tower of Babel within which resound the many languages of art, the echoes of culture after culture, alive, moribund and dead; tongues as dissimilar as the Arab, the Gothic, the Italian and the Flemish, co-mingle and contend within the four corners of the square Peninsula. Only the ear well accustomed to the local vernaculars of the rest of Europe can readily distinguish between them and the dialects native to Spain.

It is true that many have accomplished this feat, which, however, is or should be, but a means to an end. No ambitious art student can be content with a mere analysis of that kind. The first step, then, towards acquiring the materials for a synthetic study of the art of Spain, must be taken outside her borders. The next step consists in realizing that the multitude of towns and villages encompassed by Oviedo and Granada, Salamanca and Barcelona are, in terms of art history, an enormous melting pot. The final step must be to envisage Spanish art not only as a mere commentary on European culture, but as a special product of the race.

This has never yet been done, or if it has been done, no one has so far dared to translate such an experience into the written word. We must believe that the wooing of Spain will one day be consummated, but the bell ringers may still count on a term of slumber before they will be called to duty. In the meantime those of us who aspire to a complete understanding of what we instinctively feel to be a great and inspiring school, must, if we are quite frank, confess to some degree of bewilderment, a bewilderment intensified by the abundant evidence of how sharply the aloof Spanish temperament is marked off from those of her neighbours. It is as if, by some obscure law in psychology, the very individuality of her national character were compensated for by a confirmed habit of steeping herself in turn in every form of culture happening to come her way, with the result that, to the mind of the foreigner, Spanish art appears to be at one moment idiosyncratic and at another elemental.

A veteran among observant students of Spain and Spanish art assures me that to those who have the eyes to see, and the ears to hear, as well as a sufficiency of patience, there inevitably comes a day when Spain is really seen as an entity and when the whole complex of styles and schools represented, often in strangely modified but still recognizable forms, within her shores, fuse together in the mind as a delightful and unique experience. Accepting this, the great thing should be to go on and on until the transformation occurs; then and only then you may know Spanish art as George Borrow knew Spain.

It is our hope that the present book about Spanish art will help to accelerate some such process. The object of the book is, then, to encourage a closer and more intimate study of Spanish art, both on the part of those who know the country at first hand, and on that of students who have not yet done so. The plan on which it is built is a simple, but, we hope, an efficient one. It was suggested by our first and less ambitious experiment in book production, "Chinese Art," which is uniform with this volume.

It is a far cry from Chinese to Spanish art, but both that subject and this suffer from a dearth of good literature ; and it is our belief that the deficiency in either case is mainly due to the fact that no one writer can hope to deal with the whole material. One student has mastered the architecture, another the painting, and a third the sculpture of Spain. No one ventures to interpret the evidence as a whole. Therefore, we have adopted once more our former plan by enlisting the services of nine contributors, each of whom, we feel, may be relied upon for soundness of judgment and fullness of knowledge within the compass of his own special sphere of interest.

One day, we are confident, some individual author able to realize the subject as a whole will write such a book, but its appearance will not be accelerated if in the meantime we merely stand aside and wait for it. If " Spanish Art " turns out to be the forerunner of such a work, none will feel prouder than those who have co-operated to produce the essays and to collect the photographs which appear in the following pages.

To these contributors, I take this opportunity of offering my thanks for the patience and skill they have expended over many months in what has been a very arduous task. Many others besides the contributors themselves have most generously helped us. So much so, indeed, that it is impossible for me to acknowledge as I should like the many kindnesses that have been showered upon us in the course of our work. It is, however, impossible for me to forget to take this opportunity of acknowledging in public, as I have already done in private, the substantial help received from Dr. A. R. Pastor, Mr. O. M. Dalton and Mr. A. Van de Put, the last having compiled the valuable bibliography at the end of the book. For aid in obtaining photographs we are, as ever, indebted to Sir Robert and Lady Witt, as well as to the Spanish Travel Bureau, Mr. A. Kingsley Porter, Messrs. Salvat Editores, the Archæological Museum, Ghent, Señor Plandiura, Mr. E. Bendir, the Institutó de Valencia de Don Juan, the Montpelier Museum, the Fogg Museum of Art, M. D. Kelekian, Sir Herbert Cook, the National Gallery, Dublin, the Alte Pinakothek, Munich, Messrs. Lewis and Simmons. Mr. Lionel Harris kindly allowed us to use many photographs of examples of woodwork in his collection and, where no other owner's name appears under the plates in that section of the book, the object illustrated is in his collection.

R. R. TATLOCK,
Editor, " The Burlington Magazine "

ARCHITECTURE. *By Royall Tyler*

ALL Spanish building may be roughly divided into two classes: the products of native schools sprung from the soil, and the work of foreigners. The vicissitudes through which Spain has passed have handicapped the native builders, who have usually been less well equipped for the construction of great churches and palaces than their competitors from abroad. But the native builders, if they have lacked the patronage of princes and knowledge of the latest methods and styles evolved in Europe, have possessed what the foreigners lacked: an instinctive feeling for the local conditions—climate, light and habits of life—to disregard which is a heavy fault in architecture. Whatever fashion reigned among the religious orders, in cathedral chapters and at court, the native Spanish builders have put up the houses in which their countrymen have lived, and at times have set their hands to more ambitious tasks, but their creations, vigorous and full of character as many of them are, have been kept in the background while the places of honour have been given to Frenchmen, Flemings, Rhinelanders and Italians. However, the overpowering national sentiment of the Spaniard has not allowed the matter to rest there. His king or his bishop may have imposed an outlandish cathedral upon him, but he has managed to enlarge and embellish that cathedral to his own taste, without and within, until only the practised eye detects the foreign fabric and the whole is suffused with the local colour that pervades everything in Spain.

In practice, of course, there are many buildings that belong partly to one of these two main classes, and partly to the other. Mediæval churches were usually long in the making; very few can have been completed by foreign builders, and where Spaniards were employed local characteristics soon made their appearance. Also, the native builders themselves were to some extent influenced by technique and fashions in design brought in from abroad. However, in the main, the division holds good. The foreign schools failed, one and all, to strike root in Spain. Their adoption was determined not so much by artistic affinity as by political association; they held the field for a few years and died away. Meanwhile the Spaniards went on building houses and churches according to their own ideas of what houses and churches ought to be like, superficially modified by a foreign formula here and there.

The Moslem influence was a different affair from the passing European fashions which left many grand monuments in Spain and no lasting impression on the Spaniards. Several of the Spanish kingdoms were under Mohammedan rule for centuries, and long after the Reconquest a Moorish population continued to live side by side with the Christian in many Spanish cities. Moreover, when the Islamic conquerors first began building in Spain they made use of what they found on the spot, utilising in their mosques columns, capitals and window frames taken from Visigothic churches and palaces. Very little remains of what was made in the Moslem cities during the first century or two of Moslem rule, but that little [PLATE 6, B] and the rather more numerous vestiges in the lands that were then held by Christians are enough to show that for a long time after the Islamic conquest Christians and Mohammedans went on building in closely similar styles. Later, the divergences springing from the different character of the cult in the two communities, and their manner of life, became more and more marked. The mosque and the cathedral of the middle ages are far apart. But even then the domestic architecture of the greater part of Christian Spain has

3

much in common with that of the Moors. The smaller mosques, the synagogues and the churches built by Spaniards are full of evidences, not only in decoration but also in construction, of the existence of a common fund of Hispanic building lore which was drawn upon by Christian, Jew and Moor.

Thus, protruding from a mass of native Spanish architecture, we have on the one hand the French or Northern churches which belong to the history of European art, and on the other the very few surviving monuments which are part of the Moslem world. Most of the native architecture is Christian in the sense that it was built under Christian rule, but it is Spanish first, whether Christian or paynim.

The monuments falling into the main classes are not grouped together geographically. Side by side, in the cities of Castile, there may be seen examples of half a dozen foreign styles surrounded by other buildings of strongly Spanish character; indeed, all these phenomena may here and there be found collected together in one great church. With the exception of Catalonia, which is in every respect different from the other regions, there is no Spanish province where the big churches show sustained development from one generation to the next, and it would be vain to look for it in the more indigenous, popular buildings. Native Spanish architecture differs essentially from the European schools in the ends it pursues and the conditions in which it was produced; local diversity is its characteristic rather than the European tendency to concentrate upon the elaboration of highly perfected and disciplined formulæ. Few concerted movements of national or even provincial scope are discernible in it. At first sight, it is all incoherent variety; fundamentally its variants are at one in indifference to the problems of construction, plan and proportion that chiefly occupied the builders of the great European periods, and in absorption in ornament and detail. It expresses the scattering multitude of the Spanish people, as the forces of unification and discipline are expressed in the orderly and powerful erections of the foreign bishops and religious communities who undertook the task of schooling Spain into conformity.

Constant reference to political history, in Spain perhaps more than in any other country, is necessary in order to understand how the monuments came into being; many of the most celebrated of them owe as much to the country which they happen to adorn as the candles do to the Christmas-tree, though ingenious attempts have been made to explain how they grew there naturally.

THE VISIGOTHIC INHERITANCE.—Spanish nobles trace their descent from Visigothic ancestors; it seems that Spanish music owes its peculiar character to the Visigoths, and certain it is that under their rule architectural forms appear which were destined to be absorbed into the native Spanish stock and to be used for long centuries.

Not that the Roman remains in the Peninsula are negligible. There are the well-known aqueducts of Tarragona and Segovia, the bridge of Alcántara, the walls and theatre of Sagunto; but Roman architecture is almost as remote from Spain of the middle ages as are the megalithic or Cyclopean walls built of colossal unhewn blocks of stone, considerable portions of which still stand at Tarragona, lightly carrying Roman walls as a superstructure to crown them. The reminiscences of classical antiquity discernible in mediæval Spanish art have been passed through the sieve of Visigothic selection. Indeed, the Visigoths themselves, though they doubtless made use of such of the Roman buildings at Mérida, Seville and elsewhere as had survived the devastations of Franks, Suevi, Vandals and Alans, drew their plastic ideas from the Byzantine Empire and built in imitation not of the Roman monuments which they saw in Spain but of a style which had spread along the north coast of Africa. They were Christians (Arians) when Theoderic led them into Spain; they spoke Latin, and before the end of the sixth century had accepted the Nicene creed. They were deeply tinged with the tastes and fashions then current in the Empire.

Under the Visigoths, Spain had what it was not again to possess for a thousand years: a style of architecture and decoration extending over the whole Peninsula, which itself was united politically, with the exception of the Byzantine possessions on the southern part of the Mediterranean coast. Not only was Spain one artistic province, but that province was in easy communication with the rest of Christendom. The Visigoth state extended over the Eastern Pyrenees and across southern France as far as the Rhone, there joining the realm of the Ostrogoths. The north coast of Africa was Christian and, except during the hundred years' domination of the Vandals which was ended by Belisarius's victory over Gelimer, belonged to the Empire the capital of which was Constantinople. Byzantine and African influences were perhaps stronger on the Mediterranean coast and in the Balearic Islands, which were actually subject to the ecclesiastical authority of the Archbishop of Carthage, than in the Visigothic dominions. But we hardly know enough, as yet, of the art of the Peninsula from the fifth century to the eighth to say with assurance where provincial Byzantine ends and Visigothic begins.

Centuries of destruction, however, have not entirely obscured the character of Hispanic art in those days. We have not a little to guide us, and a good deal more will probably come to light when all the corners where Visigothic remains are likely to linger have been turned out. The late fourth-century silver disc of Theodosius, himself a Spaniard, in Madrid, may be taken as characteristic of the style in favour in Spain on the eve of the arrival of the Visigoths—and not in Spain only, but throughout the Empire. The seventh-century golden votive crowns and crosses found at Guarrazar near Toledo, the best of which, including one great crown with the name of the donor, King Reccesvinthus, are in the Cluny Museum in Paris [see Metalwork, PLATE 10, A], and the remainder in the Royal Armoury in Madrid, bear a priceless testimony to the Byzantine character of the sacred offerings made by Visigothic princes.

The provincial character was stronger in architecture than in small, portable works of art. Very few buildings, considerable portions of which date from the Visigothic period, now exist, and one of them, the baptistery (San Miguel) of Tarrassa in Catalonia, is a rough Byzantine construction on the Greek-cross plan rather than Spanish. What remains of the little San Juan de Baños de Cerrato, near the railway junction of Venta de Baños in Old Castile, opens quite different vistas. San Juan is a wooden-roofed basilica of a nave and aisles [PLATE 1, A], with round-headed arches of horse-shoe shape, and carved slabs with designs like those seen on the Visigothic crowns. It appears from excavation that the present building is only part of the original one, which had a differently disposed east-end and an external gallery running along one side of the nave.

San Juan de Baños's claims to be the building, the dedication of which by King Reccesvinthus in A.D. 661 is recorded by an inscription, have been contested, but its champions appear to have made their case, and the pre-Moslem-invasion Visigothic origin of a couple of other little churches: Santa Comba de Bande (Province of Orense) and San Pedro de la Nave (Province of Zamora), as well as the important ruins of Cabeza de Griego (Province of Cuenca) may also be accepted. Some of the columns and capitals in the Santo Cristo de la Luz at Toledo [PLATE 2, A] are of the same period. Moreover, the fragments from the Visigothic ducal palace at Mérida, now in the museum of that town, include the frame of a double round-headed horse-shoe window, with its little dividing shaft and capital. There is good reason for belief that the horse-shoe arch, which appears as a decorative motive on funeral slabs, supposed to be of Syrian origin and certainly pre-Visigothic, preserved in the Museum in San Marcos at León, was actually in use in construction in Spain before the Arab invasion. Although Spanish scholars quote Arabic writers who speak of the removal of architectural fragments from the Visigothic buildings of Mérida to adorn the great mosque of Córdova, it is perhaps going a little far to assert that Mohammedan architects first learnt to use the horse-shoe arch in Spain. Spaniards may well be content with showing that the Visigoths applied it independently of the Moslems.

Our knowledge of Visigothic architecture, fragmentary if derived only from the monuments which purport to date from before the Arab conquest, may be enlarged by study of the buildings erected in Asturias when the Christian monarchy began to reorganise its forces behind the protecting rampart of the Cantabrian Mountains. Alfonso II, who died after a reign of half a century in A.D. 842, built churches, parts of which survive in the Cámara Santa and Santullano at Oviedo, and his successors continued with San Miguel de Linio (or Liño) and Santa Maria de Naranco, which stand a few hundred yards apart on the hillside overlooking Oviedo; San Salvador de Priesca and San Salvador de Val-de-Dios in the region of Villaviciosa, and Santa Cristina de Lena near the railway between Oviedo and Leon. Consecration stones exist giving the date of Santa Maria as A.D. 848 and that of San Salvador de Val-de-Dios as A.D. 893. But by the end of the ninth century, the Christians had pushed their way south of the mountains into the great central plain and set up the kingdom of Leon, whereupon the little Asturian churches were abandoned to the obscurity which alone could preserve them.

Three types are represented among these monuments. What remains of Linio [PLATE 3] shows a plan which appears to have been a Greek cross inscribed in a square. Then there is a tiny basilica with nave and aisles, parallel square-headed apses and an external gallery (Priesca and Val-de-Dios). Finally we have a cell of rectangular plan, divided up internally by a screen (iconostasis, perfectly preserved at Lena, PLATE 4, A) carried on arches, and with compartments added on to the sides. At Naranco [PLATE 4, B], this rectangular structure was originally an open arcade, or possibly it is merely the external gallery of a vanished basilica; at Lena, the sides were always walled. Features that appear at Baños occur in these churches, as well as others, due in part to Carolingian influences, and in part to new fashions from Southern Spain. The horse-shoe arch is common, capitals, bases and the stone slabs that formed the screens and fill some of the windows are richly carved with designs among which those of the Visigothic votive crowns are repeated, together with scenes copied from consular diptychs (which, by the way, had ceased to be produced some three centuries before the Asturian churches were built, a circumstance that speaks for these churches' archaism). The lateral gallery found in the basilicas appears already to have existed at Baños; it is a feature which persists in native Spanish architecture throughout the middle ages. Flat, shallow buttresses strengthen the outer walls. Semi-circular stone vaults are used at Val-de-Dios, as well as a primitive sort of clustered pier formed by engaged columns applied to each face of the buttresses in the lateral gallery. The character of the masonry varies greatly, but here and there displays considerable accomplishment.

There is literary evidence to show that the Asturian churches, like those built by the Visigoths in the rest of Spain, were richly decorated inside with coloured marbles and mosaics. Remains of such decorations in the Oviedo churches were described by Morales as late as the sixteenth century, and it is conceivable that there may still be some vestiges left under coats of whitewash, a lavish use of which was long the one measure of preservation applied to these monuments.

While the reviving monarchy was continuing, on a tiny scale appropriate to its slender resources, the tradition inherited from the Visigoths, the bulk of the Christian population of Spain lived under Moslem rule. For a time, the Visigothic framework of society was little changed. The invaders were in a very small minority and the Christian cities were left to manage their affairs pretty much as they had done before. Gradually, however, the advantages enjoyed by Moslems induced numbers of native Spaniards to profess Islam ; feeling between the two communities grew bitter and, Christian thirst for martyrdom aiding, resulted in the persecutions of the ninth century, which drove many monks to seek refuge in the rising Christian states of the north and east. In the tenth and greater part of the eleventh centuries, the Mozárabes, as the Christians dwelling in the Khalifate were called, enjoyed another period of quiet, but the fierce puritan savages from Africa, Almoravides and Almohades, who invaded Spain in the later eleventh and twelfth centuries, expelled Christians and Jews and destroyed their places of worship, together with almost all the buildings put up by the civilised Moslems, whom the Almohades regarded as little better than infidels.

In the South where it was evolved, Mozárabe architecture has altogether disappeared ; nothing remains but a few inscriptions and other fragments. However, the refugees who fled to the Christian states at times of persecution, and doubtless travellers in more peaceful days, took with them a style which grew up in the great days of the Khalifate. This style sprang primarily from the Visigothic trunk which had also put out tardy shoots among the Asturian mountains, and which had certainly exercised some influence on beginnings at Cordova. But, living in the midst of a flourishing civilization which, in touch with the Byzantine centres, with Mesopotamia, Syria and Egypt, was rapidly working whatever elements it fancied into an art of its own, the Mozárabes had opportunities which their brothers in the north lacked, and turned them to such good account that their manner of building supplanted the old Asturian tradition and was adopted not only in the young Leonese kingdom but in Castile, Navarre, Aragon and Catalonia—wherever Christian states were forming. In the towns of these regions hardly more Mozárabe monuments remain than in Andalusia, for in the latter part of the eleventh century Spain was flooded with Frenchmen who rebuilt the more important churches in a powerful new style from across the Pyrenees. It is therefore probable that the work by which the Mozárabe builders would have preferred to be remembered has disappeared. However, in remote places, which had a brief hour of life between the ninth and the eleventh centuries and sank again into obscurity after the front had moved on southwards, there remain a good score of Mozárabe churches, and fragments from many more are preserved in Spanish museums.

The best preserved of the Mozárabe churches, all of them in formidably inaccessible places, are San Miguel de Escalada, San Cebrian de Mazote, Santa Maria de Melque, Santa Maria de Bamba, Santo Tomás de las Ollas, Santiago de Peñabla, Santa Maria de Lebena, San Millan de la Cogolla de Suso, and San Baudilio (or Baudel) de Casillas de Berlanga. Photographs, ground plans, drawings of mouldings and details, minute descriptions and, not least, accurate instructions as to how to reach them, may be found in Gómez-Moreno's work. Together with the manuscripts and portable works of art which may be studied in Madrid, and the Mozarabic rite which is still celebrated daily at Toledo and occasionally in Salamanca and Segovia, these buildings constitute perhaps the most curious and moving chapter in all the history of art in Spain. They record the contact between Spaniards of the two religions, which was maintained for a time, keeping Spain in touch with the most highly civilized centres of the Eastern Empire and of the Moslem world and supplying the Peninsula with a wealth of plastic ideas which appear to have been readily absorbed and therefore to have been less foreign to the Spanish genius than the Latin-European fare to which the Spanish palate has never grown entirely accustomed. Spaniards have often looked wistfully back towards those days as the time when they had a chance of creating a spiritual world of their own. However, it was not to be. Berber fanatics were no less determined to suppress the scandal of a tolerant, art-loving, Hispano-Arab civilization than were the monks of Cluny to oust the old Spanish liturgy in favour of the Roman, to rebuild every important church on French lines, in a word to organize Christian Spain on the European model and open it up to colonization.

Thus Mozárabe art was cut down in its prime, but enough remains copiously to illustrate its character. The old Visigothic stock was rejuvenated by many new elements from the Christian East and from the Islamic. The horse-shoe arch, both in ground plan and in elevation, constantly recurs. Churches are found with horse-shoe planned apses at the east and west ends of the nave, and even at the extremities of the transepts. Both these apses and the rectangular spaces over the crossing are sometimes covered with grooved but unribbed, as it were scalloped, stone vaults. Here and there, as at San Millan de la Cogolla de Suso, there are octopartite, square-ribbed vaults. At Berlanga, the corner ribs spring from squinches, and in the central lantern there is a system of parallel cross ribs, which was destined to live long in Spain. Semicircular, ultra-semicircular (or horse-shoe) and quadripartite (unribbed) stone vaults are often used where the space is a narrow one, broader spaces being roofed with wood. The type of basilica with an external lateral gallery, characteristic of the Asturian churches, persisted, as witness the fine example of San Miguel de Escalada [PLATE 5, A]. Masonry is occasionally of beautiful finish, but more often rough, at any rate in the surviving monuments which it would not be fair to take as typical of the style as a whole. Windows are small and frequently filled with pierced slabs. Bold, widely projecting and richly carved corbels of a form also found in the Mosque at Córdova support the roof beams in several of these churches.

Until late in the eleventh century, when the French invasion began, an ancient Spanish tradition continued to forbid representations in sculpture or painting of our Lord's life or passion, or indeed of any sacred subject except angels and cherubim. Carved decoration is chiefly reserved for capitals, imposts, corbels and above all the closure slabs of the iconostasis and the presbyterium. Capitals vary greatly in quality, though they are almost all of the acanthus type: the finest, like some from Sahagun, now in the León Museum, and those of San

Cebrian de Mazote, are of consummate accomplishment. The carving covering flat surfaces shows entrelacs and linear and leaf ornament, scrolls with birds and bunches of grapes. Human representations hardly ever occur in architectural sculpture, and animal forms are rare. In carved ivories, like the famous altar at San Millan de la Cogolla and the closely similar fragments of a cross in the Louvre [PLATE 6, A], they do appear, and on metal caskets there are reliefs of angels and of the emblems of the Evangelists. Whatever there may have been in the way of enriched pavements and wall mosaics has vanished; and in any case there was little marble or coloured stone in the regions where the surviving churches were built. Very curious frescoes depicting human beings and beasts are still to be seen at Berlanga.[1] The famous Cross of Victory at Oviedo has enamels of a high order. There are a few objects of rock-crystal and cut-glass.

Evidence of Eastern influence crops up at every step, both in the churches and, still more, in portable works of art and painted manuscripts such as the *Biblia Hispalense,* the *Biblia Complutense* and others in the Academy of History at Madrid, the fantastic birds, beasts and fishes in the margins of which strongly recall Byzantine fancies of the ninth century, though there is a difference in turn and twist, the meaning of which may be that the Spanish artist had seen Moslem-Egyptian imitations rather than Byzantine originals. The flat carving is often reminiscent of Egypt, Coptic and Arab, whence the rock-crystal chessmen at San Millan de la Cogolla must actually have come, like the engraved glass bottle at Astorga. The enamels in the Victory Cross may well be the work of Byzantine hands, though there is a local flavour about the animals, birds and fishes that appear in them, as there is a Mesopotamian feeling about the beasts on the Ewer of Charlemagne at St. Maurice d'Agaune, the enamels on which are rather like the Oviedo ones in quality, and probably of about the same period. Few if any remains of textiles that can definitely be called Christian of this period appear to exist; the Córdovese products, many of which must have found their way north, are very close to their Fatimide models. In ground-plan, the churches are often curiously like the Syrian or Armenian.

In general, it may be said that the Mózarabes received next to nothing from north of the Pyrenees, and that Córdova was the distributing centre from which imports from the eastern shores of the Mediterranean were passed on to them. Their art consequently became more and more permeated with Cordovese influence, though it should always be remembered that Córdova had also, at an earlier stage, taken a good deal from Christian Spaniards, so that there is a re-echoing which may well perplex the inquirer. If a few Christian monuments built or restored at Córdova under the Khalifate had only been preserved, we should know more than we do. Happily, the Christian conquerors of Andalusia did not make a clean sweep after the manner of the Almoravides and Almohades, and the Mosque of Córdova remains, together with the fragments found in the excavations of the palace of Azzahra [PLATE 6, B]. The mosaics of the Córdova mihrab [PLATE 1, B] are, it is well known, the work of Byzantines. In our penury of smaller works of art we may at any rate point to the bronze lampholders in the Museum at Granada, which almost exactly resemble a Byzantine polycandelon in the British Museum, and to the Spanish Moslem textiles in the Museum of Vich, in Catalonia, one of which recalls the design of the Byzantine shroud of St. Victor in the treasure of Sens Cathedral. It is not likely that the Cordovese would permit any Byzantine craftsmen they had the fortune to get hold of to waste their time working for the Christian states in the north. At any rate, nothing has been

[1] See note at the end of this article.

discovered as yet to prove that any Byzantine (or Syrian or Armenian) had any share whatever in building or decorating any surviving Mozárabe church. When Mozárabe art is looked at with eyes full of images of western Romanesque and pre-Romanesque, it seems so eastern that the beholder feels sure he could turn up any number of photographs of exactly similar capitals, closure slabs and transennæ from the other end of Christendom. But reverse the process, look first at Syrian and Byzantine work and then at Mozárabe, and it will be seen that except in a few portable objects the Spanish character of the whole Mozárabe corpus is as undeniable as is the fact that in those days Spain was artistically an Eastern province.

FRENCH INVASION AND SPANISH REACTION.—Europe, however, had an eye on the Peninsula, and was determined to bring it back into the Western fold. No sooner had the central power in the great French feudal states : Burgundy, Normandy, Aquitaine, grown strong enough to prevent each noble from fighting his neighbour, and the abounding energies that for a couple of centuries had been spent in domestic warfare were available for adventure abroad, than the Spanish crusades began. Charlemagne's expedition across the Pyrenees had never ceased haunting the minds of Frenchmen, and lived anew in the eleventh century *Chanson de Roland*, the epic of the long series of campaigns that did not end until the roads to Santiago de Compostela had been freed from the Moors and the crusading current had turned eastward towards the Holy Land.

Feeling their way southwards from the Cantabrian Mountains, making each step secure by building walled towns and the castles which gave Castile its name, the Christians do not seem to have met with very formidable resistance until they reached the Tagus. Fortresses like Turégano, and La Mota [PLATE 7, A] near Medina del Campo, walled towns like Avila [PLATE 7, B], Sepúlveda and Madrigal de las Altas Torres, though built later than the reconquest period, give a good idea of this border-land as it was in the middle ages. León had never greatly tempted the Moslem, and after the collapse of the Khalifate early in the eleventh century the new kingdom's expansion was chiefly retarded by its own inability to colonize reconquered provinces. In the later eleventh century the Cid actually took Valencia, on the south-eastern coast, and held it for years. After his death, the Moors took possession again.

In the Ebro valley the position was quite different. Aragon was the strongest Spanish Moslem state after the fall of the Khalifate, and the Ebro, which was then navigable, furnished an admirable shuttle-line of supply for a barrier thrown across the neck of Spain from the mountains of Navarre to the Mediterranean, shutting off the Christian states of the north-west from Catalonia and forcing the pilgrims to the shrine of St. James at Compostela to pass through the wild Basque country. The key of this barrier was Zaragoza, and its fall in 1118 put an end to the Moorish power in Northern Spain.

For the better part of a century, hosts of Frenchmen had been campaigning in the upper Ebro valley, attracted by opportunities for establishing themselves in newly-won lands, by indulgences and by prospects of looting the fabled riches of the Saracen. At the same time, the monks of Cluny were making themselves masters of the Spanish church. Alfonso VI of Castile had a French confessor, Bernard, who became Archbishop of Toledo and Primate of Spain ; by the close of the eleventh century, a Frenchman was named as a matter of course to each Spanish See as it became vacant and all Spanish religious houses were subject to Cluny. Alfonso VI married his daughter to Raymond of Burgundy, who colonized the Castilian cities with his compatriots. The royal house of Portugal was founded by a Burgundian. As the towns of the Ebro valley were won back they were given, entire or in part, to French lords, and French speaking parishes continued to exist for generations.

This irresistible flood of trans-Pyrenean influence, coinciding with the interruption of relations with the Moslem South caused by the supremacy in Andalusia of violently anti-Christian elements from Africa, looked for a time like making the architecture of the northern kingdoms as French as that of Burgundy or Poitou. The Santiago pilgrimage was a great enterprise managed by French ecclesiastical business men, but it was only one of many instruments used in the process of gallicisation to which Spain was submitted. There is no indication that Santiago itself, until a great church of the family of Conques and St. Sernin of Toulouse was built there late in the eleventh century, possessed any more art than the rest of Galicia, whose granite breast was not made to suckle architecture or sculpture. In imitation of Santiago, churches were built at Lugo, Orense, Tuy and elsewhere in Galicia, but their inferiority both in construction and in sculpture shows the poverty of the soil. The Romanesque churches that sprang up all over the Leonese, Castilian and Navarrese territories belong to an altogether different world from that recorded by Spanish monuments of a generation earlier, which were made by men whose eyes were turned towards Córdova and the East. The breach with the Spanish past is complete in the earlier Romanesque buildings, but as time passed the French flood began to subside and familiar features of the Spanish scene appeared once more.

Raymond of Burgundy brought Burgundian builders the most complete example of whose work is San Vicente at Avila [PLATE 5, B], a thoroughly Burgundian church with a great sculptured doorway [PLATE 8, A] in a western porch like those at Vézelay and Autun. The earlier churches at León, Salamanca, Toro and Segovia were built or begun by the same school.

Shortly after Raymond's time, however, western and south-western French influences got the upper hand; twelfth century architecture in Castile and León is shaped by them. The Burgundian barrel-vaulted nave with a clerestory and groined vaulted aisles gives way to a nave and aisles, the vaults of which spring from the same level, the aisles thus serving as supports for the central system, and domiform ribbed vaults also make their appearance, the change often taking place while a church is being built, as at Salamanca.

The twelfth century was not far gone before another wave from France broke over the Pyrenees, and the Cistercians brought in, if not a style of architecture, at any rate principles that were so generally applied as to give their abbey churches and the secular cathedrals influenced by them somewhat of a family air. As had happened in France, the rich sculptured ornamentation, that had grown so freely on doorways and capitals while Cluny was supreme, disappeared altogether from the Cistercians' own churches and was kept within stricter bounds in the others. Soaring bell-towers were no longer used, and church builders could excel only in harmonious proportion, the correct solution of vaulting problems, and exquisite but sober finish. The earliest Cistercian foundation in Spain, Moreruela in the Province of Zamora, is a ruin, but Veruela and Fitero in Navarre; Poblet, Santas Creus and Vallbona-de-las-Monjas in Catalonia, and Las Huelgas near Burgos make an imposing array, whilst the cathedrals of Tudela, Tarragona, Lérida, Sigüenza and El Burgo de Osma represent a school that was not actually in the hands of the order but was deferent to it. Now, Cistercian houses were building in Spain before the middle of the twelfth century, and for the next hundred years represented the most advanced architecture known to the Peninsula. It is characteristic of Spain that during all this time there was no development in the sense in which architecture was developing in France. Vault-building, the question which of all others occupied French architects of the period, remained where it was when the first Cistercians came. Whilst in France builders had no sooner learnt how to construct a vault on cross-arches, gathering the thrust into the four supports, than they took the further step that led to flying buttresses and the opening-out of side walls, in Spain they went on erecting massive walls and foregoing the main advantages of the ogival vaulting system : building Romanesque, in fact, until yet another wave from France brought to them the full-blown Gothic of the thirteenth century. These churches have great beauty and are excellently built. It is by no means to detract from their merit to point out how strikingly they illustrate a deep-lying difference between Spanish and French architecture.

Three cathedrals in Spain belong to the family of Notre Dame de Paris, Bourges, Chartres and Amiens. Bishop Mauricio of Burgos, previously Archdeacon of Toledo, passed through France on a diplomatic mission in 1221 and appears to have summoned the builders who started work soon afterwards on the cathedrals of Burgos and Toledo [PLATE 9, A and B]. The present fabric of León was doubtless begun a generation later. The three most celebrated of all Spanish churches have no forbears in the Peninsula, as their descent is not from Burgundy, or Auvergne, or south-western France, from which provinces Spanish Romanesque came, but from the Royal Domain. Nor did they have any lasting effect on the subsequent trend of Spanish architecture. Indeed, far from imitating them, the Spaniards have for centuries been employed in dressing them up in native Spanish garb in such a way as to disguise their original character [PLATE 9, B], and with considerable success except in the case of León where modern restoration has attempted to clear away the aftergrowth. Of all the monuments in Spain there are none more foreign to the Spanish genius than the cathedrals of Burgos, Toledo and León.

By the time they were begun, the Spanish *milieu* had assimilated the French colonists who, two centuries earlier, had taken a hand in the country's reconstruction. The energy with which the Spanish temperament mastered external elements has deeply marked the Romanesque churches that survive in the old cities of the northern kingdoms. Christian Spain and Moslem Spain had been for ever separated by the happenings of the eleventh and twelfth centuries, but when it came to absorbing Christian Spain into Western Europe the undertaking was soon shown to be hopeless and the absorbers were either rejected or themselves absorbed. Thus it is only natural that Spaniards should feel that their Romanesque architecture belongs to them ; although the French origin of the earlier examples cannot be disputed, there is hardly a Romanesque or Transitional church in Spain which has not in some significant respect been hispanolised. And the process has by no means been limited to the change, deformation rather than transformation, which unavoidably occurs when forms are reproduced, without being wholly understood or deeply felt, in different surroundings from those in which they first appeared. French forms often did suffer such deformation in Spain, but there was also a strain in Romanesque, especially the Romanesque of south-western France, which perhaps by reason of its kinship with the architecture of the Christian East was sufficiently congenial to the Spanish mind to stimulate collaboration—a statement which cannot be made of Ile-de-France Gothic.

An admirable illustration of the creative power displayed by Spain during this too brief period may be seen in the Salamantine group of churches, among which the twelfth-century cathedral at Salamanca is the best known as well as the most perfect, though Zamora, Toro and Benavente also stand high. Salamanca has a lantern of two open arcaded stories, carried on pendentives over the crossing, round within and polygonal with four flanking turrets without, with a vault supported by ribs carried on sixteen shafts which rise between the lights of the pierced stories: an architectural feature as beautiful as it is mysterious in origin. The rest of the church, and the detail of the lantern itself, have a strong air of Aunis and Saintonge, but in plan the lantern is much more like a Byzantine construction, though here again it is no mere matter of copying. The farthest it is possible to go, in this case, to meet French claims, is to admit that it would not be surprising if such a dome were met with in France, but the fact remains that there is nothing comparable with it in France, while in Spain it is characteristic of a school. There may be much in the suggestions of archæologists as to how the idea of this lantern reached Spain, but the important thing about it is that it cannot really be paralleled, as a work of art, outside the kingdom of León.

The Salamantine dome is the isolated creation of some man of genius, or of a school. Who knows? At any rate it cannot be said to be rooted in Spanish tradition. Romanesque building had not long been practised in Spain, however, before features began to reappear in it which had been familiar to the Mozárabes. Horse-shoe windows are used in the apse of Avila Cathedral. In the Ebro valley, ornamental brickwork of a Moorish character enriches bell towers and the outer walls of apses [PLATE 22, B]. Several of the twelfth-century churches at Segovia have an external arcaded gallery, or cloister, added on to one side of the nave in a manner reminiscent of the pre-Romanesque San Miguel de Escalada and Val-de-Dios, and which, it seems, follows a Visigothic example recorded in San Juan de Baños. Similar lateral galleries were built at Valladolid (Santa Maria la Antigua) at Las Huelgas near Burgos, and persisted much later, in advanced Gothic times, in Avila (San Vicente). There has always been a tendency in Spain to mask main lines, which it was the French builders' pride to display; the Spanish mind modestly recoiled from allowing the limbs of a church to show, as it did from leaving bare the stone of a statue of Our Lady. The statue was swathed in silk, and the church buried in out-buildings until the beholder often cannot tell from outside which is the East end and which the West. Inside the church, equally drastic steps were taken. Cathedral chapters built a second and snugger church for themselves within the other; by the end of the middle ages not a cathedral remained that had not had its choir stalls, or *coro*, moved west of the crossing and enclosed, like the choir proper, or *capilla mayor* as the Spaniards call it, in high walls to keep out draughts and indiscreet worshippers. As the nave west of the *coro* had no view of the high altar it became meaningless, and churches tended more and more to slough off western bays and to be square in plan. Cathedral congregations were obliged to gather in the transepts and crane their necks to see the altar. The great clerestory windows of churches in the Northern French style were walled up to keep out the sun and wind. Frequently, in later additions, the native Spanish strain comes out, as in the so-called Mozárabe chapel [PLATE 8, B] in the cloisters of Salamanca Cathedral, which, square below and brought to an octagon above by squinches across the angles, has a vault carried on parallel cross ribs, a device found in the mosque of Córdova, San Millán at Segovia, the little Mozárabe church of San

Baudel de Berlanga, and in the mosque called the Santo Cristo de la Luz at Toledo. At San Juan de Duero at Soria there is a cloister, originally roofed in wood, of intersecting horse-shoe arches, in design not unlike some to be seen at Ravello and Amalfi, where Eastern influences must also have been at work. In numberless side-chapels and sacristies, as the middle ages wear on, Moorish plaster work and tiles are used [PLATE 2, B], as in domestic architecture everywhere south of the Guadarrama, and also the elaborately fitted and joined *artesonado* wooden roofs and inlaid wooden doors which were the speciality of Mudejar carpenters. Thus, while the Alhambra was being built at Granada, in the Christian kingdoms Spanish taste was showing its fundamental agreement with Moorish ideas of the beautiful. Even after a tide of consciously anti-Moslem, Christian nationalism had set in when Spain was united under Ferdinand and Isabella, the same tendency persists under other forms, and to a great extent determines the uses to which Spain was to put the art of the Low Countries and of Italy.

The Peninsula, save for the granite bulwark protecting it from the Atlantic, running from Galicia through Portugal and striking a spur eastwards to the Guadarrama, is rich in easily quarried and worked limestone which hardens with exposure to the atmosphere, lasts well and takes on a golden or silvery surface. Except in the great alluvial valleys of the Ebro and the Guadalquivir, where it was so much cheaper to build in brick that Moorish architecture developed on the lines laid down by that material, with the corollary of plaster, the art of stone-cutting never appears to have suffered any long eclipse. Visigothic builders and Mozárabes practised it with no little distinction, and in each succeeding age it has given architecture in Spain a certain lordly character of its own, independent of style as usually defined, so that there is something in common between many a Romanesque and many a Baroque building. Possessing much stone, the Spaniards early took to carving it. The spirit of their pre-Romanesque was against human representation, but admitted plant and other forms; the French fashions from the late eleventh century on released an ardour for sculpture which was with difficulty cooled down for a brief generation by Cistercian influences only to flame up again afterwards. The models were French [PLATE 10, B], and French discipline was required to impose order upon the Spanish growth which when unpruned rapidly became so rank that it choked itself, but even in the most French of Spanish churches the sculptured decoration bears witness to the speed with which native apprentices learned the art, and the Spanish spirit in which they practised it, revelling, apparently, in an excess of the figure-sculpture at which for centuries Spaniards had not been allowed to try their hands at all. The carefully planned, consistent ensembles dear to the French, as respectful of the principle of unity as was ever any tragedy of the *grand siècle*, are broken up and confused in a manner that must have revolted French masters, as it offends their descendants of the present day. But, however displeasing to the most refined French taste, and quite seriously wrong as its general tendency must be admitted to be, Spanish mediæval sculpture has lively qualities that will continue to captivate lovers of the adventurous in art. And there is a great mass of it, crowded with iconographical matter, much of which has never been worked out.

CATALONIA.—Two decades of the twelfth century were over before Zaragoza was taken from the Moors and the Ebro valley once more became what the letters M Z A (Madrid-Zaragoza-Alicante) embroidered on the upholstery of railway carriages tell travellers that it is to-day : the main line of communication between the Castilian kingdoms and the east coast. For four hundred years the vigorous little maritime State that expanded from Charlemagne's Spanish marches into the independent county of Barcelona and, finally, into the kingdom of Aragon, had been cut off from intercourse with the rest of Christian Spain and had formed associations and habits of its own which were to keep it different from the Castilian lands throughout the middle ages and apparently for the rest of time.

Architecture in Catalonia was to some slight extent influenced by the Mozárabe tradition, which has left a couple of indifferent monuments in the principality, but the little early churches at Barcelona and Gerona owe their origin to influences moving westward from Lombardy, and Catalonia's main relations were with Southern France, with Italy and even, though here the bearing on architecture has been greatly exaggerated, with the Levant. The Eastern Pyrenean valleys north and south of the crests—for both sides are Catalan—abound in curious little Romanesque churches like those at St. Genès des Fontaines [PLATE 12, A] and Arles-sur-Tech, which have preserved very early sculpture of great interest. Although Catalan religious houses were placed under Cluny, there was no such invasion by French monks, builders and colonists in Catalonia, by that time an old-established community, as in the newly reconquered plains of the North-West. Apart from the Cistercian, which entered here as they did throughout Christian Spain, none of the influences successively brought to bear on Castile and León affected Catalonia. Few Burgundian builders came, or Poitevins or Auvergnats or Angevins or men from the Ile-de-France. Thus there is in Catalonia a unity throughout the varieties of style which is not to be found in the rest of Spain.

Perhaps the most characteristic feature of Catalan architecture is a raised lantern, carried on squinches, built usually over the crossing. It is to be found in San Nicolás at Gerona, San Pablo del Campo at Barcelona and Santa Maria at Tarrassa, to mention a few primitive examples; it reappears on a larger scale in the Cathedrals of Lérida and Tarragona [PLATE 11] and, in the fourteenth century, in the Cathedral of Barcelona itself. The general conception of the Catalan Romanesque church is that of a rather early Lombard type [PLATE 12, B]. Arcaded corbel tables and courses are the chief ornament, sculpture is more sparingly used than in France or in the Castilian dominions. The very elaborately sculptured doorway at Ripoll [PLATE 13, A] is Italian in disposition, though Catalan in its subject matter. Doorways are made to project a little from the façade. Bell towers are usually square, without enriched openings; a few early round towers still survive in he Pyrenean valleys. Several fine cloisters survive like that at San Cugat [PLATE 14, B], near Barcelona.

The thirteenth century produced little of note, but the fourteenth, a period of civil war and artistic decline in Castile, was one of great prosperity in Catalonia. Barcelona was the capital where the Catalan kings of Aragon ruled a Mediterranean empire, including Naples, Sicily and Sardinia, as well as part of Southern France, Valencia and the Balearic Islands. A grand type of church, appropriate to the climate and to the requirements of populous towns, owing something to models of Ile-de-France descent such as Narbonne, but thoroughly assimilated by Catalonia and built by Catalans, is represented by many examples, the most notable of which are the Cathedrals of Barcelona [PLATE 15, A], Palma de Mallorca [PLATE 14, A] and Gerona, and the church of Santa Maria del Mar at Barcelona. At Gerona there is a vaulted nave without aisles, 73 feet wide in the clear, of immense effect [PLATE 15, B], but the classical Catalan fourteenth-century church has nave and aisle vaults spring-ing from the same height and supported by internal buttresses provided by the walls separating the side chapels which open out of each bay. Cathe-drals have a chevet with a choir aisle on the Northern French plan, parish churches are ended eastward with three polygonal apses. The light comes from the great windows in the East end and, much less, from narrow ones in the side chapels, and is thus prevented from breaking garishly into the nave in the manner which Castilians found so offensive in Ile-de-France churches with great clerestories. There is sobriety in the detail within and without, propriety and unity. Barcelona Cathedral and Santa Maria del Mar make a strong impression of conscious purpose and achievement such as is conveyed by the work of few schools, particularly in Spain where there is often an obvious conflict between what the builders knew how to do and what the people wanted.

Barcelona, again unlike military and clerical Castile, had an active municipal, industrial and commercial life, monuments of which remain in the fourteenth-century Town and County Halls, the Exchange and the slightly later Cloth Hall. The Exchange, which is still used, with its three vast arcades formed by semi-circular arches carried on slender piers, is a proud civic building, and like much else in the Catalan capital bears witness to a resolute secular frame of mind, not irreligious necessarily but determined to keep up the lay end as against the clerical and particularly the monkish [PLATE 13, B]. The old part of the town has also preserved many mediæval houses with double or triple round-headed or cusped windows divided by slender shafts, much like those to be found in Sicily.

This curious province of Mediterranean civilisation fell on lean times after the union of Aragon and Castile and, particularly, the establishment of the Burgundian connection which transferred the centre of Spain's foreign policy from the Mediterranean to Northern Europe. At the same time, the newly-discovered wealth of America profited the ports not of Catalonia but of Andalusia. From the fifteenth century to the nineteenth, the principality produced no remarkable buildings.

WORLD-POWER ARCHITECTURE.—Civil wars brought the Castilian monarchy to a low ebb during the fourteenth and parts of the fifteenth centuries. In Toledo and Seville a semi-Moorish style of domestic architecture, characterised by the use of brick for building and plaster and coloured tiles in decoration, reproduced degenerating forms. In the cities of old Castile and León there was no need for new building; the reduced vitality of the period was unable so much as to finish what an earlier age had begun, let alone starting new enterprises.

Also, Spain perhaps had a surfeit of French art after some three centuries of feeding on it, especially as the Gothic of the Royal Domain of France, the official style of the age of St. Louis, was less well adapted to the Spanish climate and spoke less to the Spanish heart than did the Romanesque of Aquitaine. At any rate, it seems that during the long barren period which, in Castile, makes a gap between the middle ages and modern times, artistic links with France fell to pieces, and when in the fifteenth century Spain began to develop into a world power, she looked elsewhere than to France for architecture befitting her great-ness and found it in the Low Countries, whose material substance she was to use in her long attempt to wrest from France the leadership of Christendom. The Italian Renaissance had admirers in Spain from the outset, and finally, after the middle of the sixteenth century, ruled there without dispute, but by that time the monuments commemorating the House of Habsburg's bid for universal domination had been built.

Don Juan II, whose reign coincides with the first half of the fifteenth century, had a taste for Flemish painting and patronised Jan Van Eyck. At about the same time, northern architecture was introduced into Castile by Alfonso de Cartagena, Bishop of Burgos. This prelate's father, being a Jew, caused himself and his children to be baptized after reading Jeremiah xxxi, entered the Church, became Bishop of Burgos, and was succeeded in that dignity by his son, the most powerful churchman of his day, who traversed the Low Countries and the Rhineland on his way to the Council of Basle and brought back to Burgos an architect called Hans von Köln, who not only built the Cartuja de Miraflores [PLATE 10, A] in the new style but did what he could to correct the French cathedral of Burgos by adding the western towers, a huge lantern and other embellishments in his own manner.

After the union of Aragon and Castile and the end of the Moorish wars by the taking of Granada under Ferdinand and Isabella, the Catholic Kings as Spaniards call them, order was restored, wealth again became available for building, and the Spaniards were able to give full rein to the passion which late northern Gothic architecture, sculpture, painting and stained-glass aroused in them. Artists came from the Low Countries in increasing numbers, and when Philip the Handsome, son of the Emperor Maximilian, married Jane the Mad, who was to inherit Castile and Aragon, it looked as if differences of climate, race and custom were powerless to prevent the Spanish cities from being rebuilt after the fashion of those of the Burgundian inheritance. The gold and silver that came pouring in from the new world provided abundant means until Charles V and Philip II had found another use for them in fighting France and the Reformation. Flemish and Rhenish builders and craftsmen settled in Spain, the Köln family became Colonia, Jan Van der Eyken of Brussels became Juan de Egas, Waas was changed to Guas, Harfe to Arfe. No doubt much the same process of assimilation of foreign artists had gone on in Romanesque and early Gothic times; the difference lay in the manner in which Spain reacted. There was something in the Flemings' art that at once turned Spaniards into apt pupils, and a native generation of Siloes and Hontañons rapidly grew up, prepared to build as big and decorate as lavishly as their splendour-loving patrons could wish.

The New Cathedral of Salamanca, the Cathedrals of Segovia, Seville and Granada, the churches of San Gregorio [PLATE 16, B] and San Pablo at Valladolid, Santa Maria at Aranda de Duero, San Juan de los Reyes at Toledo and San Esteban at Salamanca may stand for the age. Their scale is huge in comparison with anything produced in Spain up to that time. In ground plan the New Cathedral of Salamanca, the most complete example of the style, is nearly square and consists of a nave and double aisles of great height, leaving little or no room for a clerestory, the light being regulated by a sparing allowance of windows [PLATE 17, B]. Here and elsewhere the vaults are built on the ogival principle disguised by complicated tracery. From without, the mass is like a huge block, inexpressive of structural system. Most of the walls are bare and little attention is paid to refinements of moulding and profile. But the wall in which the main door is placed is covered with a rank growth of sculpture: human figures, heraldic beasts, colossal escutcheons, trees, banners, inscriptions, gabions, cables and attributes like a petrified royal procession. In the houses of the great nobles there are monstrous aberrations such as the Court of the Palacio del Infantado at Guadalajara. Inside the churches, each altar is provided with a wooden, carved and painted retable in the Flemish taste, but often on a far larger scale and coarser than that taste would have tolerated.

While these enormous erections were being run up—and not infrequently, as in the case of Seville Cathedral, toppling over before they were finished, symbolically of the Spanish dream of universal lordship, a more chastened taste was being displayed by a few prelates who brought Italian works of art to Spain and encouraged Spanish architects to study in Italy. The Plateresque style represented by the façade of the University of Salamanca [PLATE 16, A] is refreshingly sane after the bombastic excesses just alluded to, and in the courtyards of the Colegio del Arzobispo and the cloister of Santo Domingo [PLATE 20, B] at Salamanca, the University at Alcalá de Henares, as in much of Berruguete's and Becerra's sculpture, there is a calm, distinguished bearing. The Plateresque, however, is rather a fashion in decoration than a style of architecture; it found expression in well-proportioned and tastefully enriched arcades and wall-surfaces, as in the Town Hall of Seville [PLATE 21, A], but did not attack structural problems. Vaults continued to be built on the ogival system, as witness the chapel of the Colegio del Arzobispo at Salamanca.

Spain's great building time was drawing to a close when the system of construction evolved by the Italian Renaissance came in, and in the hands of Juan Bautista de Toledo and Juan de Herrera created the Escorial [PLATE 17, A, and 18]. Here, at last, is a building which not merely records a phase of Spanish history, but expresses mid-sixteenth century Spain's outlook upon life. Spain had, at the cost of much blood and prosperity, attained a national unity which swept aside the picturesque diversity of religion, race, custom, law and administration left over by the middle ages. In the Escorial, built of granite from the hills upon which it stands, all ornament is foregone. The grand proportions of the palace, the enormous wealth lavished upon it, its disdain of detail, admirably express the temper of a generation that had made up its mind to sacrifice every interest that had captivated it in the past, every sentiment and every material advantage in order to save the world by the imposition of Tridentine orthodoxy. Herrera may be counted as the greatest Spanish architect; in him the country found a man who built as it felt. More of his work may be seen in the unfinished Cathedral of Valladolid, the Lonja at Seville and the Colegio del Patriarca at Valencia, but the Escorial was his life's task and left him little time for anything else, just as the crusade against indiscipline left Spaniards of that age little time or means for building. The Renaissance palace which Machuca began for Charles V at Granada remained an empty shell. Jaén Cathedral [PLATE 22, A] exhibits Spanish taste returning to ornament.

It is a misfortune that Spain should have been over-built and financially ruined during the Baroque period, for when Spaniards tried their hand at Baroque the results were often of the happiest. In the north, Churriguera's Plaza Mayor at Salamanca [PLATE 20, A], the seminary in the same town [PLATE 19], and the west front with towers which Novoa added to the Cathedral of Santiago de Compostela show what they could produce in the way of large composition. The Segovia and Toledo bridges at Madrid [PLATE 21, B] also deserve attention. At Valencia an entertaining local school appears to have been more generously patronized than its Castilian contemporaries, for it has left a number of delightful churches, and particularly steeples in which something of the general plan of the Moorish bell-tower survives amiably associated with the billowing forms of the seventeenth century. But Valencian Baroque is a passage out of a book the main action of which takes one to places in Sicily and to Lecce in Apulia. The French style introduced at La Granja in imitation of Versailles, after the House of Bourbon had mounted the throne, was little practised in Spain. Indeed, with the exception of the Italian Royal Palace at Madrid, hardly any building of note was undertaken during the eighteenth century, although all over the country earlier churches were defaced in the attempt to dress them up in a new fashion.

While the blazing Gothic of the Catholic Kings and the Italian fantasies of their ministers were setting the stage for Spain's great tragedy, their subjects went on building houses, many of them on a palatial scale, which owed much less to foreign influences and perpetuated an ancient Spanish tradition in which Christian and Moorish elements are inextricably mixed. Even to the present day the native strain still lives, and is here and there drawn upon in domestic architecture. As has always been the case with the Spaniards' own creations, there is no uniform style; each province has a tradition of its own, worked out and determined by climate, environment and custom. In Andalusia, the Moorish house with its central courtyard wainscoted with tiles, a type only differing in accessories from the Byzantine dwelling from which it derives, is likely to persist as long as the Andalusian sun continues to shine. At Zaragoza and elsewhere in Aragon, a style of brick architecture long continued to flourish, related on the one hand to the Moorish and on the other to the brick building of the Garonne valley [PLATE 22, B]. In New Castile and Estremadura, Mudéjar and late Gothic produced bizarre façades. Wherever there was limestone, that is to say, in most parts of Spain, effective use in a local manner was made of it, and where limestone was lacking, brick was made to serve such purposes as the material would admit. The Spanish towns have unexplored reserves of savoury domestic architecture, sprung of a strong stock that the chances of Spain's political history prevented from being pruned and strengthened into a national style capable of furnishing the great churches and palaces which Spain's impatient rulers have always called in strangers to build. Take both together, the native and the foreign, and the country can show as brave an array of architecture, in a climate which is particularly kind to man's creations of stone, as any in the world.

NOTE.—Since this essay was written, the frescoes have been removed from San Baudilio de Casillas de Berlanga. Some of them are said to be going to the Barcelona Museum. Others have left Spain, doubtless never to return. Thus, in the year of grace 1926, and apparently with the approval of the authorities, the one Mozárabe monument in which architecture and painting had weathered the storms of seven centuries together, has been irreparably mutilated.

At the same time, it is announced that the Spanish Government propose to devote large sums to the restoration of the Monastery of Poblet.

B—Mihráb of the Mosque, Cordova

A—Interior, San Juan de Baños de Cerrato

B—Interior, El Transito, Toledo

A—Interior, Santo Cristo de la Luz, Toledo

San Miguel de Linio, Oviedo

A—Interior, with iconostasis, Santa Cristina de Lena, Oviedo

B—Interior, Santa Maria de Naranco, Oviedo

A—San Miguel de Escalada

B—East end, San Vincente, Avila

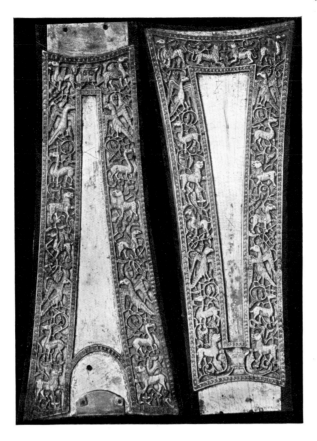

A—Arms of an ivory cross, 12th century. (Louvre)

B—Carvings from the ruins of Azzahra (Victoria and Albert Museum)

A—Castle of Medina del Campo

B—Apse of the Cathedral, Avila

B—Interior of the Capilla Mozirabe in the Old Cathedral, Salamanca

A—West porch, San Vincente, Avila

B—Interior, showing altar, of the Cathedral, Burgos

A—Interior of the Cathedral, Toledo

A—Cartuja de Miraflores, Burgos

B—Coroneria door, Burgos Cathedral

Exterior of the Cathedral, Tarragona

B—Façade of the Cathedral, Seo de Urgel

A—Doorway of S. Genés des Fontaines, Pyrénées Orientales

A—West porch, Ripoll, Province of Gerona

B—Courtyard of the Audience Chamber, Barcelona

A—The Cathedral, Palma de Mallorca

B—Romanesque cloisters of the monastery, San Cugat del Vallés

B—Interior of the Cathedral, Gerona

A—Main door of the Cathedral, Barcelona, from the Cloisters

B—Façade of San Gregorio, Valladolid

A—Façade of the University, Salamanca

A—General view of the Escorial

B—The New Cathedral, Salamanca

A—Interior of the Chapel of the Escorial

B—The Library of the Escorial

The Jesuit Seminary, Salamanca

A—The Plaza Mayor, Salamanca

B—The Cloisters, Santo Domingo, Salamanca

A—Façade of the Ayuntamiento, Seville

B—Puente de Toledo, Madrid

B—Apse of La Seo, Zaragoza

A—Jaén Cathedral

PAINTING.

I—Spanish Painting and the Spanish Temper. *By Sir Charles Holmes*

IT has become a commonplace that Spanish art in general resembles the country which produced it. Patches of luxuriance start up and die away amid vast expanses of sterile earth and stone. Sometimes these florid half-exotic growths occur with almost seasonal regularity.

For metalwork and wood-carving, for ceramics and for textiles, the demand and the supply have been more or less continuous. Some three centuries of magnificent building, may be held to establish a similar continuity for architecture. In the case of painting the sequence is far less complete. Church and State, especially the Church, were no less steady patrons for painting than they were for the applied arts and for architecture : but the result was not the same. Spanish fabrics, Spanish carving, Spanish metalwork and Spanish architecture, have a florid intricacy and a decorative splendour, which distinguish them immediately from other European products. Spanish painting too often lacks this national character, and the scanty relics of its early history are even more disconcerting from their unlikeness to each other than from their rarity.

In my private school-days there was a fashion for teaching the elements of history by means of a summary or synopsis. To master such a synopsis was then a dry and hateful task ; but when the task was once done the victim, or the victor, undeniably had a mental framework to which any more coloured and particular impression of historical events could be attached in its proper place. Limits of space have compelled my friend Mr. Kay to compress his knowledge of early Spanish painting into a few pages, but for many of us this enforced brevity will have the merit of those " Outlines of History " which I have mentioned. With the aid of the illustrations we may thereby gain a definite idea of the problems which beset every student of Spanish art, and of the lines on which its diverse products may be classified.

In Italy and the Netherlands, in France and in England, painting has been a more or less spontaneous fruit of the native temper. France may have made it a part of the great national organization : the Netherlands may have utilized it as a branch of commercial industry ; in England an interval of three centuries elapsed before its early blossoming was followed by consistent fruitfulness. But in Spain, with but few exceptions, painting appears as an artificial culture, an industry responding to specific demands, yet not generally carried on by the artist with any particular ambition or enthusiasm.

The rigorous conditions imposed by Spanish ecclesiastical patrons and the crushing etiquette of the Spanish court are usually held responsible for this want of spontaneity : with some truth in the former case, for the temper which prohibited the young artist from studying the nude, as contrary to public morals, was enough in itself to render any great school of figure-painting impossible. Yet neither the terrors of the Inquisition, nor the formalities which hedged round the court painter could, I think, have prevented creative genius from showing itself in Spain had the creative genius been there in force. And when we consider the origins of the race we can see good reasons why its activities should be more consistently successful with the applied arts than with the human figure.

I do not know who the indigenous Iberi and Celtiberi may have been, but the successive waves of invasion which have swept over the Peninsula must have considerably modified these primitive races, except perhaps in the mountains of the North and West. They remain, however, a definite and considerable factor in the modern Spanish peasant type. Before the Roman Conquest, Spain had been colonized and partly occupied by the Carthaginians. This potent Phœnician infiltration was the beginning of a long connexion with Africa and the East. The final conquest of the country by Rome under Augustus came at a time when the native population of Italy was declining. The colonization of Spain, like that of Britain, may thus have brought with it a relatively small proportion of pure Latin blood. Yet since men like Seneca, Lucan, Quintilian, Martial and Trajan were of Spanish birth, it is clear that many of the early settlers came of excellent stock.

Spain, however, has a way of exhausting her invaders, as she has exhausted her ancient forests and injured thereby both her climate and her soil. In the people which endured four hundred years later the passage of the Vandals and conquest by the Visigoths, little or nothing of the old Roman temper survived. The Visigoths contributed a fair-haired aristocracy and a fighting quality to succeeding generations, but their capacity for the arts appears to have been negligible. Then came occupation by the Arabs, introducing a further fighting strain, a fine sense of personal dignity, impatience of manual labour (except when performed by slaves), and a very definite taste in architecture and the applied arts. Only the people who had taken to the mountains, mostly of the indigenous races, escaped this new admixture. All the rest of Spain was affected. Intermarriage became common, so that the Spanish character, like the Spanish language, acquired in the course of seven hundred years distinct Moorish elements. When at last the Christians were able to make head against the infidel, this condition of things could not be changed by massacre or expulsion. The sternness of the conflict left a final mark upon the national temper. But for the fierce animosity towards the heretic which the Moorish wars had inculcated, we cannot conceive that Spain would have endured and encouraged her Inquisitors.

The effective artistic resultant of these different forces has been Realism. From Spanish Realism, from Ribera, Velazquez and Goya, the great French innovators, Courbet and Manet, drew their strength. So Spain laid the foundation upon which almost all subsequent painting of note has been content to build. It is not easy at first sight to understand why the country should have attained this remarkable prominence. The general achievement of Spain in painting had been far less consistent than that of most other parts of Europe; her racial record, as even our brief survey will indicate, does not seem to promise great things. A little inquiry into the nature of Realism will possibly supply the explanation.

The first instincts of primitive man towards the arts are to decorate something, or to represent something. From the former instinct come all the applied arts. From the latter springs the art of painting, modified as Society develops by conditions of climate, material and function, and, above all, by racial tendencies. In Greece, for example, ubiquitous marble, and the habit of watching the unclothed human figure in action, made sculpture the natural mode of expression; the fine genius of the race did the rest. Italy inherited this great tradition. Greco-Roman ideals coloured all her searchings after perfection of form during the Renaissance: they formed a part of the Eclectic creed: Caravaggio and the Naturalists could not altogether break away from them. In the Netherlands Realism was modified by pleasure in minute workmanship, a pleasure which led all but the greatest to over-polishing of the picture surface, and to a certain pettiness in style and conception. In England the Realist can seldom resist the call of Romance, the temptation to accentuate grace or charm; distractions which quickly beguile him into prettiness or anecdotage.

Spain, in virtue of the intermixture of races of which she is composed, has escaped any such disturbing bias. The church, it is true, kept a tight hand upon the painters whom it patronized: the court too, perhaps, gave the artist less freedom than he might have enjoyed elsewhere. But these external restraints, troublesome as they doubtless were, could never have the same blighting effect upon creative minds as a definite inherited tendency which, when conditions are not wholly favourable, may become a source of decay, the more inevitable because it is unsuspected. When the Spanish School sinks from time to time into ineptitude, it does so from sheer want of capacity, not as with other nations from the corruption of some specific racial virtue. Realism, in fact, seems to involve an absence of other factors in the perfect artistic equipment; an absence which, if judged quite impartially, must be reckoned as a limitation.

We have thus to take into very serious account the sequence of influences from without, which from time to time modified this somewhat indolent and negative racial temper. Catalonia, the first of the great divisions of the Peninsula to be subjected to these influences, presents us with a curiously complex problem. Direct contact by land with Provence made Latin and Romanesque infiltrations natural. Then Barcelona and Valencia were great Mediterranean powers and ports, into which flowed the commerce, not only of Italy and Byzantium, but of the Levant and the Near East. So the relics of Catalan painting may recall Ravenna and even Persia as well as Rome. Some of the most beautiful examples combine a Sienese grace of line, with an Oriental splendour of colour and pattern.

Netherlandish influence also came at first by the sea. John van Eyck visited Portugal. Nuño Gonzales, the great master of Lisbon, and Luis Dalmau at Valencia, both show an appreciation of the larger aspects of Netherlandish art which could hardly have been obtained except by such a journey as that which Dalmau actually made to Bruges. It was from Lisbon probably that the Flemish technique came to Morales in Estremadura, and perhaps to the Gallegos in Salamanca. The Gallegos are so thoroughly equipped with the Netherlandish manner and spirit as to suggest that one of them at least had made the northward journey. There were, of course, a number of imported masterpieces available for study, as the Escorial and the Prado still testify. A really surprising feature is to find among them so many fine works by that fantastic satirist Hieronymus Bosch—an alien, one might think, to the austere Spanish temper. Still more puzzling, to me at least, is the close resemblance between some of the ruder Spanish products of the fifteenth century and a group of pictures, generally representing scenes from the Passion, which are often classified as English. The gross types and rather stumpy proportions of the figures suggest the Low Countries as their native place. Can there have been some centre between the mouths of the Scheldt and the Ems, where these things were manufactured for export both to East Anglia and to the Spanish littoral?

So much has been written, and well written, upon the greater masters of Spain from the Cretan Greco to Goya, with whom all the national feeling pent up for two centuries seems suddenly to burst forth, that it is unnecessary to comment upon them here. And it must be confessed that search among the secondary painters does not yield more than occasional and accidental finds. If some rather striking picture arouses interest in a little known Spanish artist, acquaintance with the average of his work will usually justify his obscurity. Yet all through the sixteenth and seventeenth centuries, pictures appear which deserve to be remembered. At the time when Spain like the Netherlands was trying, with lamentable ill success, to graft Italian graces upon her native Realism, Alonso Sanchez Coello, following in the footsteps of Mor, painted some portraits which from every point of view are excellent. The elder Herrera, under whom Velazquez worked, is a perplexing figure. So clumsy and rustic is his earlier manner that it is difficult to associate with him the power shown in such pictures as the *S. Basil* of the Louvre, and *S. Gregory* in the Prado. Nor can Pacheco, the second and more kindly master of Velazquez, be regarded as only a dull pedant, when he could produce such a design as the *Embarcation of S. Pedro Nolasco* at Seville. In decorative breadth Pacheco here anticipates Juan Bautista Mayno, whose *Allegory of the Re-conquest of S. Salvador* is to-day the most striking feature in the Entrance Hall of the Prado. This is a picture which might well have inspired Puvis de Chavannes, so fully have the conditions of mural painting been realized, so thoroughly modern both in colour and simplification of form is the group in the left foreground. Mayno's repute in his own day was considerable. His extant works prove that the contemporary estimate was not unjust, and that his name might well be added to the slender list of Spanish artists whom everyone remembers. The far less accomplished Castillo y Saavedra now and then shows considerable power as a designer and colourist. Carreño is surely not so uniformly servile as Mr. Kay's summary might suggest? His best portraits, though they are not masterpieces, lack neither character nor force. Mateo Cerezo, studied Van Dyck to some purpose, attaining at times to a grace of gesture and a beauty of colour which deserve respect. Modern criticism seems inclined to place Antolinez very close to Cerezo. Such work of Antolinez as I have seen does not bear out the resemblance : he seems a man of altogether lighter temper, and more flimsy accomplishment.

Most of these seventeenth century paintings are of devotional subjects, often treated on a considerable scale and, like nearly all oil paintings of the period, rather dark in general tone. They may not therefore appeal to many collectors of to-day. But for those who delight in the gymnastics of critical study they provide unlimited exercise. Take, for example, a few pictures in our own National Collection. That striking decorative canvas termed *A Betrothal,* or more properly *The Morning Compliment* (1434), came to the Gallery as the work of Velazquez and bore his name for many years. Then the great Beruete, sifting the master's work, saw that this ascription was impossible and gave the picture to Luca Giordano. Others seem to have proffered the name of Francesco Maffei. At last, in 1920, an early portrait by Claudio Coello, of identical workmanship, appeared and settled the question. I wish some fortunate searcher could find an equally convincing document bearing upon our much debated *Dead Warrior* (741), by tradition associated still more closely with Velazquez. Of alternative Spanish names that of Zurbaran comes most naturally to mind, but the painting has a suave Italianate accomplishment which he did not possess. Will it ultimately turn out to be Italian, like two other " Spanish " pictures? *Christ disputing with the Doctors* (1676), long attributed to the younger Herrera, was shown by Señor

Salazar to be a typical specimen of Mattia Preti, " Il Calabrese." The noble *Dead Christ* (235), which so long did credit to the name of Ribera, had to be ceded, on technical grounds, to Ribera's most accomplished Neapolitan rival, Massimo Stanzioni. Spain on the other hand has gained one recruit. *Peasants warming themselves* (1444) for half a century bore the name of Honthorst, with occasional suggestions of other northern alternatives, until it was recognized as a typical work by José Martinez.

It is, however, upon the greater masters of the Spanish School that attention will always concentrate. Greco is but a marvellous adopted child, alien to Spain in intellectual temper as he was in race. With the others the national spirit shows itself clearly in various combinations. Realism, tinged with sternness, or even with cruelty, but made effective by the best technical science of the day, is well exhibited by Ribera. Realism, inspired this time by a peasant's rude honest faith in the church, and an occasional peep at the pleasures of the world, is the sustaining force in Zurbaran. With Velazquez the quiet dignity and chivalrous good breeding of the aristocrats of the race—Visigoth, Moor and Castilian alike—tempers this same Realism, till it loses its hardness, its roughness, its grim monotony, and becomes, for once, an impeccable artistic instrument. In Murillo we see the opposite side of the Spanish problem. He is a son of the soil, and of a soil so fertile that it assures a living even to the sluggard. So Murillo takes the line of least resistance, adopting without question the style which pleases his patrons, and indolent even when exercising his great natural bent for Realism.

Sixty years later Spanish art and Spain herself seemed to be dying of this contented inaction when Goya appeared, another son of the soil, and another Realist. Acquiescing at first in things as he found them he depicted the life of Spain, its pastimes and its perils, with a freshness of colour and a vivacity of observation which were wholly novel. Gradually the degradation of the Court and the tyranny of the Inquisition roused him to anger and revolt, feelings which the horrors of the French invasion stirred still more deeply. The earlier Spanish Realists had painted from the life. Goya's Realism was not thus limited. So vivid was his memory that he was able to conduct from his easel and his etching table an incessant guerilla warfare against the follies and the cruelties which he had witnessed, and with so much artistic vigour and variety that the tradition of the new century was shaped, in a large measure, by his example. The lithographs of Daumier are a connecting link. But while Europe has borrowed and utilized Spanish Realism, she has still to combine it either with the superb refinement of Velazquez, or with the immense variety of invention which Goya possessed. If in view of its previous manifestations Spanish painting as a whole appears just a trifle static and monotonous, the thought of Goya's immense and audacious energy is enough to redeem the national credit.

II—A Chronology of Spanish Painting. *By H. Isherwood Kay*

ROMANIC PERIOD.—The earliest painting of which visible record remains in the Peninsula is the standardized Romanic art of Western Europe, which was devoted to the service of the Christian church. Even during the Moslem occupation—a territorial, not a religious conquest—this art was generally practised in Spain until, in the eleventh and twelfth centuries, fanatical Moslem puritans swept in from Africa to persecute the Christians and destroy their abominated churches. Thus the relics appertain to the Southern Pyrenees and Asturias, where the free Christians held their ground.

The remnants are wooden reliquaries, altar-frontals, retablos (retables), and apse decorations. The most ancient panel, a frail and blackened altar-frontal of the ninth century, exemplifies the plan of decoration which was traditional until the early fourteenth century. This was an oblong surface divided into a large central compartment and two rows of laterally disposed niches or squares. In early panels, *Christ in Majesty*, or the *Mother of God*, enthroned in a mandorla, occupied the central, and saints or apostles the side divisions; in later work, saints of local origin were placed in the centre, with legendary scenes right and left [see PLATE 2].

In the eleventh, twelfth, and thirteenth centuries Christian Europe, stimulated by tempting Papal indulgences, and by the prospect of fabulous loot, combined to drive out Islam. To foster the crusade Cluny monks, welcomed by the reigning princes, built monasteries in the wake of the retreating Moslems in León, Old Castile, and Navarre, where they established famous seats of learning, as at San Millar de la Cogalla in Old Castile. Cistercians from Narbonne settled in 1150 at Poblet, near Tarragona, when the Moors retreated beyond the Ebro, and founded a mighty monastery—now desolate—peopled with scribes and illuminators. Lay specialists, artists by inheritance, appeared in the early thirteenth century.

Of the easily portable relics many of the most remarkable and well-preserved are in private collections, sometimes difficult of access. For the student, however, the chief hunting grounds will be the Museums of Barcelona (the Museo de la Ciudadela, the Museo de Santa Agueda, and the Museo Diocesano), and the Episcopal Museum at Vich, forty miles north from Barcelona, into which have been gathered representative examples. In respect of apse decorations the Barcelona City Museum (Museo de la Ciudadela) is unique. There may now be examined, under favourable conditions, and with the assistance of an admirable catalogue, the most important Romanic mural decorations extant in Spain. These until recently adorned the interiors of ten widely separated Romanesque churches, situated in half-forgotten, and almost inaccessible mountain villages. They were removed from the ancient walls by Italian specialists, and transported to Barcelona, where with zealous care, but with no attempt at restoration, they were reaffixed to new walls, and apses shaped to receive them. The majority are of twelfth century manufacture. The oldest, which come from Pedret, are related to eleventh-century frescoes in S. Clemente, Rome. In reproductions, many of these decorations would pass for mosaics. In the same way, one or two privately owned altar-frontals which preserve in great measure their original surface, have the appearance of enamel. In the case of frontals, at least, this quality of illusion was expressly sought. A few monasteries became rich enough to afford costly retablos of enamel upon metal, which, in the twelfth century particularly, were imported in considerable numbers. Executed in low relief in silver or gold, gem studded, they were the wonder and envy of their age. Few have escaped the melting pot. The poorer foundations had to be content with the substitutes which now almost alone survive. These are constructed on panel, either in carved stucco in high relief, gilded to resemble solid gold, or in gesso in low relief, cunningly painted and gilded to resemble translucent enamel and gold [see PLATE 2, A and B]. So far as is known mosaic was never introduced by the Christians in Spain, who could afford only fresco imitations of the great Italian and Byzantine mosaics [see PLATE 1, A], which were probably supplied in the first instance by Lombard immigrants. The painters adhered closely in style, design, and colour to their appointed models, whose vitreous reds, acid blue-greens, maroons, purples, and gold, they reproduced with astonishing skill. Roman tradition lived long, but as French influence grew a strong infusion of Gothic grace, and joy in life, produced such delicate fantasies as the story of St. Michael in St. Miguel Barluenga in Old Aragon, which is in reality a series of hunt scenes peopled by contemporary crusaders, priests, and peasants. West of the Pyrenees, where ran the great pilgrim road to Santiago de Compostela (known in Spain as the " French Highway "), the most important surviving decorations of the Romanesque period are the vault paintings in S. Isidoro at León (*c.* 1200), which are Franco-Byzantine in style [PLATE 1, B]. Catalonia had a " water-gate " to Italy at Genoa, and enjoyed commercial privileges in the Levant, and there a Byzantine current flowed in during the thirteenth century and submerged the Gothic.

The earliest altars were simply boxes, painted on three sides [PLATE 3, A]. Interest became concentrated upon the front surface, and at length the detachable frontal, in all its varieties of material, structure, and colour, was evolved. Presumably, two end pieces went with every frontal; few exist. Frontals were superseded by retablos. At the back of the altar was a low wooden rail to support the Crucifix. Some time in the twelfth century this rail developed into a predella, later into a small retablo—the Crucifix then coming in front. Early in the fourteenth century fully developed retablos, with two central and numerous side compartments, appeared. Transition pieces are very rare, and an attempt has been made to reproduce one [PLATE 3, B], which is on gesso on panel, now terribly battered and blackened. The background was once of silver. It is Romanic in composition, Gothic in treatment, and was painted in Aragon.

The Christians finally drove the Moslems from Barcelona in 984. Old Castile was recovered in the eleventh, and Aragon, with French aid, in the twelfth century. Valencia was freed in 1238, and Seville in 1248; Granada held out until 1492. Painting spread approximately in the same sequence, following upon the erection of new churches, which the Reconquistadores founded whenever they made an advance.

The Moslems, whose faith forbade the portrayal of divine personages, sometimes employed Christian artists to decorate their palaces with hunt or battle scenes, but painting as an art had no place in their advanced civilization. They left no mark on Spanish painting as we now see it, except here and there to furnish a Moorish cast of countenance, or lend an air of Arab breeding, to the art of Valencia and Seville. Mussulman decoration, used lavishly in architecture, frequently appears in the frames of altar-frontals in beautiful running relief, and is sometimes visible in the stamped gold backgrounds, notably in a twelfth century altar-frontal at Vich, in which St. Vincent Martyr, silhouetted against the diapered ground, sits beneath an incised Arab arcade.

CATALONIA.—Spanish primitives are a new study. The Catalans form the most important group, and only they have been well explored. Catalonia was embraced in Greater Aragon, but this meant only an extended field for her craftsmen, who executed commissions in, or for, every town in the realm. The princes were Catalans, and lived at Barcelona. In the thirteenth century the Kingdom of Aragon embraced Roussillon and Montpellier in France, and the Balearic Isles, Sardinia and Sicily in the Mediterranean. In the same period Catalan became the vulgar tongue from Alicante in the south to Perpignan in the north, and in the Balearic Isles. The capital made great use of her early deliverance from the Infidel. She built and manned vast merchant fleets, imposed her Maritime Code upon the Mediterranean, and ranked with Venice and Bruges in the Middle Ages as one of the wealthiest commercial cities in Christendom. Through her ubiquitous agents she developed a lucrative Eastern traffic in such articles as silks, richly patterned carpets, and manuscripts. In the thirteenth century the Florentines organized a regular sailing service to Catalonia, with ports of call at Majorca, Barcelona, and Valencia. With these facts in mind it will be easy to understand why the art of the capital, Barcelona, should be so frequently in touch with, and responsive to, that of Italy and, in the later fifteenth century, France.

In 1257 King James I of Aragon appointed four members of the Guild of Armourers and Painters to the newly-constituted Council of One Hundred of Barcelona. This is the earliest evidence of painters operating as recognized city craftsmen in Spain. In 1450 a distinct painters' guild was authorized. Then, the officers gave notice that "from this time forth," no young painter of images, retablos, curtains ("serges"—such as bed hangings painted with the *Adoration of the Kings*, or the *Judgment of Paris*) banners, pennons, gonfalons, screens, might open a shop until examined and approved by the guild councillors. Having regard to the indiscriminate labelling of all panels found in the South of France as "French School," it is worth noting that the painters of Rousillon—which is now, of course, part of France—were affiliated to the guild at Barcelona.

Probably the latest altar-piece produced under the Old Dispensation is the retablo of Alfonso and Eleanor of Castile [PLATE 3, C]. It is ascribed to Bernat de Pou, a painter of Barcelona, whom Alfonso, son of King James II, carried off to his castle at Balaguer in 1314. Constructed in the ancient manner, with two small scenes on each side of a large rectangle, it preserves the traditional monumental contours in the silhouette of the two saints in the centre; but the types and temper are new. The rustic, cumbersome figures, the blue eyes, and homely, genial faces, the large heads, one of them red haired and yellow bearded, have a surprising local—one dare say Catalan—air. The colour is brilliant; carmine, rose, vermilion, greens, and yellows predominate. This panel dates from about 1340. Its native promise was not fulfilled. A few years later the King's household painter and book illustrator, Ferrer Bassa [1] (active 1315-1348), painted on the walls of the convent of Pedralbes at Barcelona a series of Passion scenes taken direct from Italy. The convent, still occupied, preserves its seclusion, and nothing certain was known about the decorations until Señor Sanpere managed to see and have them photographed in 1911. Ferrer Bassa was not a creative artist, but he was virile, observant, and a skilled crafts-

[1] Between 1333-39 Ferrer Bassa illustrated a codex, the *Usatges de Barcelona i Costums de Catalunya* for the kings Alfonso IV and Pedro IV. Throughout the XIV and XV centuries miniaturists were so employed by the kings.

man, and he possessed in a high degree a faculty which is peculiarly Spanish. He and, to quote one later instance, Fernando Gallego, had a capacity for assimilation, a power of identifying themselves artistically, in form and spirit, with foreign personalities, which is uncanny. The Catalan's work is an astonishing compound of the types and pictorial designs created by Giotto, Simone Martini, and the Lorenzetti. His charming *Annunciation* is Sienese; in Passion scenes [PLATE 4, A] he adopts Giotto's vigorous forms and dramatic grouping. There is no documentary evidence to show that Ferrer Bassa ever left Spain. Yet it is impossible to believe that he had not seen the original art which he re-arranged so dextrously. He had few imitators in mural decoration. With Gothic architecture mural painting fell into disuse, and the vast, imposing retablos, which are such a prominent feature in Spanish churches, came into fashion. These are huge, gilded polyptychs in Gothic frames, four, five, and six stories high, divided into numerous panelled compartments. The backgrounds are of gold, minutely diapered, or engraved with leaf patterns. The apex is always a *Calvary*. Until the fifteenth century, flowered dresses painted in transparent tempera, modelling without shadows, and a child-like candour of expression are characteristic. The leaders of the school were the brothers Jaume and Pere Serra (active 1361-1399), Lorenzo Saragossa (active 1365-1402), and Luis Borrassá (active 1380-1424), with whom Sienese influence predominates. Their *Annunciation*, *Madonna of Humility*, and their *Crucifixion*, with mounted lancers silhouetted against the gold ground, are typically Italian. The Catalans, like the French, were in direct touch with Italy. Avignon was on one radius, Barcelona on another. Borrassá [see PLATE 6, A] used to be regarded as the head and fount of the Catalan School, but fresh documents have revealed the earlier men and claimed for them their works. One or two fragments at Vich have been tentatively ascribed to Ferrer Bassa himself: they do not count for a great deal. The Serra brothers are well represented [see PLATES 4, B, and 5]. Saragossa is not certainly identified.[2]

Much of the work that has survived is anonymous, although names abound. Signatures are unknown, and it is difficult to connect painters with paintings. The contracts are Byzantine in their severity, and fidelity to custom; they order every detail, and sometimes include an outline sketch showing the plan of the compartments, with a Saint's name, as " Jerome," scribbled in each, for the painter's guidance.

OLD ARAGON.—For about one hundred years nearly every altar-piece commissioned in Greater Aragon was of Catalan manufacture. Towards 1400 this monopoly ceased. Native, yet nameless work appeared in Old Aragon, and a school grew up in Valencia, where Lorenzo Saragossa settled in 1377. The early Aragonese, founded perhaps in the first instance upon Ferrer Bassa, whose work done for the King in Zaragoza has vanished, are said to have followed their compatriot Lorenzo Saragossa. Their surviving work is, however, too like indifferent Serra school work, too Catalan in type, to be of use in identifying Lorenzo himself.

VALENCIA.—The Edinburgh National Gallery has a remarkable picture of *St. Michael*, in yellow and black armour and a green and gold cloak, killing the dragon. This panel [PLATE 7, A] is typical of a small group of works, of

---

[2] The position among the leaders is not yet clear. Three or four Madonnas, very similar in type and handling, are attributed to Pere Serra upon apparently conclusive documentary evidence. Upon less decisive documentary evidence there is assigned to Lorenzo Saragossa, however, a Madonna (from Torruella de Montgri) which, though more genial in spirit and asymmetrical in type, is so nearly akin to those ascribed to Serra as to suggest that the authorship of the whole group may have to be reconsidered.

unknown authorship, painted in Valencia between 1400 and 1450. They were supposedly inspired by Florentine work executed in Valencia about 1400 by Gherardo Starnina. But the colour schemes, the pale faces and auburn hair of the saints stamp them racially as Spanish. In one or two instances rocks, figures, and weapons are woven into rhythmic linear designs that recall the Chinese. They are not the work of one hand, but they are, probably, from one workshop. These panels had no descendants. Alfonso V of Aragon, who lived mostly in Valencia, favoured Netherlandish art, therein following his grandfather, John I, who towards 1400 had introduced Netherlandish tapestry makers into Catalonia. The Valencians assert that in 1427 John van Eyck, with an embassy, touched at Barcelona and Valencia. This belief is contested. It is well known, however, that van Eyck spent several months in Spain during 1428. Soon after, a school of van Eyckian oil painters appeared in Lisbon. From Valencia the King sent in 1431 one of his household painters, Luis Dalmau (active 1428-1460) to Bruges. After his return, Dalmau settled in Barcelona, and there, in 1445, painted for the city councillors his one known work (now the show-piece of the Barcelona Museum) [PLATE 6, B]. It is an attempt, by a talented craftsman, at painting a van Eyck altar-piece on the scale of life; but in tempera, not in oil. In place of the usual gold ground for which he had contracted, he had the audacity to paint, beyond the Gothic architecture, a Flemish landscape and sky; a unique breach of faith and tradition. His influence is not directly traceable; but in his time, links with Flanders and Burgundy multiply, and the Sienese tradition fades out. He did not introduce an oil technique. Valencians usually, and Catalans always painted in tempera; outsiders using oil in their midst had no imitators.

Fourteenth and fifteenth-century Catalan altar-pieces are very similar in arrangement, but the later group is far more barbaric in appearance, and the types are more naturalistic and native. In those days colour was used very boldly. Everything was painted, sculpture, architecture, leather work, arms, and accoutrements, no matter what the material. The art patrons were chiefly city brotherhoods, wealthy and arrogant, who demanded that their chosen legend should be, not only dramatically and realistically presented, but gorgeously staged. Costumes were to be of gold brocade, of crimson, vermilion, and ultramarine. Halos and all accessories were to be in relief, and gilded; backgrounds had to be gold, deeply engraved. These retablos took from one to ten years to construct, and contracts frequently settled who should inherit a commission in the event of death.

Retablos are scarce outside Spain. The National Gallery has none. But in this country it is not usual to draw blank entirely, and students will find a superb retablo, complete and well preserved, in the East Hall of the Victoria and Albert Museum. The unknown author has illustrated seventeen scenes from the *Legend of Saint George*, including, just above the centre, the Battle of Alcoraz, at which the warrior Saint assisted to rout the Moor. This battle piece is a brilliant adaptation of a favourite theme of a miniaturist, the " Maître aux Boqueteaux," who worked for Charles V and Charles VI of France.[3] Burgundian influence prevails in the various martyrdoms at the sides.

After Dalmau, the chief masters of the fifteenth century were Jacomard (Jaime Baço, *c.* 1410-1461); Jaime Huguet (active 1448-1487); Jaime Vergos

---

[3] Although, particularly in view of Starnina's activities in Valencia, Italian versions of this ancient theme (such as Spinello's fresco of 1391-2 in the Campo Santo at Pisa) are not to be disregarded, French miniatures seem to afford the closest parallels to this delightful rendering. But the motif did not originate with the " Maître aux Boqueteaux," who is mentioned here only because he was active and influential not long before the Valencian retablo was produced.

the Younger (1459-1503), and his sons Pablo (*d*. 1495), and Rafael (*d*. 1503 ?) ; Master Alfonso (-1473-), and Bartolomé Bermejo (active 1474-1495). Jacomard [PLATE 8, A], who was of French extraction, was court painter at Valencia with Dalmau. Between 1440 and 1451 he worked in Naples and Rome for Alfonso V, and founded a Neapolitan-Catalan School. After his return to Valencia he became the most influential painter in Aragon. Though in Italy he painted in oil, perhaps in imitation of the King's two pictures by van Eyck, he did not adopt that medium. Burgundian, even more than Flemish art, enriched his style : in view of which it is worth noting that Fouquet, who owed much to the miniaturists of the Dukes of Berri, was active in Rome during Jacomard's Italian sojourn. Jacomard painted a notable series of saints and bishops, magnificently attired, framed in niches of classical architecture, as in current Italian practice. Bermejo, with a harder brilliance, painted at least one picture worthy of their tradition, namely, Sto. Domingo de Silos [FRONTISPIECE]. Huguet and the Vergos are the most representative Catalan artists. Huguet, though resident in Barcelona, is the true successor to Jacomard, and the leader of the next generation. The influence exerted by his altar-piece of SS. Abdon and Sennen [PLATE 9, A] in S. Pedro de Tarrassa, Barcelona, spread even to Valencia. The Vergos family worked with, and in succession to him upon the same altar-pieces, as for example, upon the now dismembered retablo of Sarria (Barcelona Museum). The Catalans are serious, realistic, dramatic. Their martyrdoms, typical of the age, are rendered with a verisimilitude and dramatic sincerity rarely excelled. They were saved from the grisly minutiæ, the theatricality of the worst Flemings by their ignorance of anatomy, and by their simplicity. Their compositions are well grouped tableaux, perhaps taken direct from the religious theatre. When they let themselves go they are capital decorators, but they do not run to great design. Work so arresting and individual in design, spirit, and colour as the *Angels comforting St. Vincent in Prison* [PLATE 10, B], ascribed to Jaime Vergos II, is exceptional. Gold was their bane : embossed gilding was carried to its furthest pitch by Pablo Vergos [PLATE 10, A], whose faces at times seem to fuse with the gold ground. The tendency of the Vergos was to perpetuate Huguet's type [PLATE 9, A and B] of pensive, elegantly clad saint, and lean soldier, tall and lank. They did not paint much from life. Portraiture for its own sake did not interest the school ; even donors were rarely introduced. As early as Borrassá discontented patrons demanded that faces should be " well differentiated one from another," but without apparent success. Pablo Vergos more particularly made all his characters in one image.

Huguet, by exporting altar-pieces to Sardinia, founded there a school in all respects Catalan. A beautiful and richly decorative *Madonna Enthroned*, painted in Sardinia, now hangs in the Birmingham Art Gallery, strangely out of place in a room filled with English nineteenth-century portraits.

Nothing is known of Alfonso except one damaged work, the *Martyrdom of San Medin* [PLATE 11], in the Barcelona Museum. The realism and cold ferocity of the martyrdom are Spanish ; but Alfonso, who used a landscape background and did not gild, was probably not a Catalan. His tempera has the richness, subtlety, and force of oil. His formidable spectators, with their heads in silhouette against the sky, suggest contact with Hugo van der Goes. His mastery of the nude would seem to involve prolonged study in some traditional school of drawing, which may have been that of Roger van der Weyden. Bermejo (also called " Rubeus " and " Cárdenas ") was a Cordovan, employed successively in Daroca (1474), Zaragoza (1477), and Barcelona (by 1490). Cordovans seem to have been specially subject to Flemish influence. Bermejo, who used both oil and tempera, was the most individual and accomplished Spanish follower of the Van Eycks, not excepting the Valencian Jacomard, from whom, probably, he derived some of his culture. His work in Old Aragon [see FRONTISPIECE] is at least in the style of Jacomard, and his *St. Michael killing the Dragon*, in the Wernher collection, actually came out of a Valencian church. The *St. Michael* is specially interesting. He stands poised upon the dragon, his right arm raised, his sword falling to the left shoulder. This was a favourite design in Catalonia for about one hundred years. The pose was traditional and roused many a dull artist to momentary vivacity. Historically, the relations of the Catalans with the school of Avignon are obscure, but there is frequent evidence of contact in the late fifteenth century. Possibly Bermejo, whose wanderings are scantily recorded, acted as a go-between. At all events we find in Barcelona Cathedral, painted by Bermejo in 1490, a free rendering, which is Flemish in quality, of the Louvre *Pietà* from Villeneuve-lès-Avignon.

The Catalan School virtually ended with Gabriel Guardia (-1501-), whose subjects and types were imported from Southern France. Seville was invested with a monopoly of the new American trade in 1493. Barcelona fell upon bad days, and her school of artists dwindled away. In the later fifteenth century two Aragonese, Martin Bernat (active *c.* 1466-1496 ?) and Miguel Ximenez (active 1466-1505 ?), worked in partnership in Zaragoza, where, in the provincial museum, their work may be seen. They were disciples of Bermejo, whom Bernat actually assisted in and after 1477. Formerly attributed to Bernat, the superb retablo of St. Martin [PLATE 8, B] at Daroca is now ascribed to Bermejo himself. Though stiff in execution, the figures in design are lordly enough.

Whereas in Barcelona retablos of the established pattern held the field until after 1500, they went out of fashion in Valencia after the death of Jacomard. A fire destroyed many paintings in the cathedral, and to replace them the archbishop, a Borgia, imported Umbrian paintings, and also two second-rate Renaissance artists, who with their sons enjoyed a great vogue between 1472 and 1520. Jacomard's follower, Master Rodrigo de Osona (active 1464-1512), a capable but undistinguished artist, succumbed to their influence and transmitted his hybrid style to his son, " Lo Fils de Mestre Rodrigo " (active 1505-1513), who, however, in his signed *Adoration* in the National Gallery, revived for once a more native hardness, and strength of tone and colour. Tempera and gold grounds gave place to oil and Italianate landscapes, and a new iconography began. The Rodrigos were the last of the mediæval painters.

CASTILE.—The two chief Christian kingdoms of mediæval Spain were differently organized internally. Greater Aragon had done with crusades two hundred years before the Kings and Bishops of Castile drove out the Moor. Castile was vexed by a turbulent nobility, solely educated for war; she had no equivalent of the class of wealthy, democratic merchants on the Mediterranean. Patronage was confined to the Church and King. The nobles employed artists only to stage tournaments, and to paint arms and banners. Consequently, pictures are scarce, though many painters are known by name. In 1262 Antón Sanchez of Segovia signed the decorations in the old Cathedral of Salamanca. Alfonso and Rodrigo Estevan worked in the cathedrals of Burgos and Valladolid for Sancho IV in 1290-3-4. These were wall painters: few panel paintings were produced outside Catalonia, almost none outside Greater Aragon, before the fifteenth century. Foreigners appear early. A Frenchman,

Master Nicolas Frances, painted the retablo mayor in León Cathedral before 1434, and remained in the Chapter's employ till his death in 1468. His numerous wall paintings have nearly all disappeared, but five large and eighteen small portions of his altar-piece remain. They are painted in tempera upon gold, in the style of the Sienese and Florentines of the Trecento. Master Nicolas took genre motives from the sculptures on the cathedral—which is French built, and fellow to Rheims—and on one occasion he carved and painted a wooden figure for a tournament at León. He designed stained glass for the windows, and illuminated a Cantoral for the choir in the style of the Très Riches Heures. Perhaps he hailed from the Ile de France. Dello, another Florentine, painted a huge fresco of the *Last Judgment* above a ring of fifty-five small panels in Salamanca Cathedral in 1445, and his brother Samson was active in Castile until at least 1465. These men had no successors. Trade linked Castile to the Netherlands, whence she imported many altar-pieces, particularly from Bruges; John van Eyck's visit in 1428 having opened the way. The earliest work of certain date executed in Castile clearly showing Flemish influence is an altar-piece commissioned for the hospital of Buitrago in 1455 under the will of the Marquis Santillano, who named the painter, Jorge Inglés. Except for a stray resemblance to Nicolas Frances, Jorge's work is very northern in character. If he was English, as his name suggests, we may hope that research will one day reveal the fact, and so to some extent establish a link between the early Flemings and William Baker of Eton, whose grace and spirit are so English.

The first native group, centering upon Salamanca, gathered round Fernando and Francisco Gallego (1440-5-1507 ?), perhaps father and son, able and sincere artists who were steeped in the work of Roger van der Weyden, Campin, and Dirk Bouts. Their best efforts have almost the air of being composite productions of the three Flemings, with Bouts in control. Like the Catalan, Ferrer Bassa, they assimilated completely a foreign art congenial to their temper [see PLATE 12, A]. The retablo of Ciudad Rodrigo, one of the largest ever constructed, came out of their circle. Its twenty-six panels in the Cook Collection illustrate the Creation and Life of Christ. In the *Last Judgment*, ascribed to Fernando Gallego, the slender Christ and his retinue are very Boutsian; the little nudes below doomed to hell seem to be derived from Roger and Memlinc. The elder Gallego has much of Memlinc's refinement; his assistants have an aggressive geniality, a hard, fierce realism, and melodrama which is less engaging but more spontaneous and truly Spanish.

Native work in Castile had no settled character until the national destinies were decided by the accession of the Hapsburgs. Before the Gallegos had finished their labours Granada had fallen and the heads of the Church were at home again in Toledo, which became the new art centre. There the first painter of note was Pedro Berruguete, a native of Paredes de Nava, who worked in Toledo Cathedral from 1483 to 1495, and in Avila from 1499 to 1504. His Toledan wall paintings have vanished, his remaining work is divided between Avila and Madrid. He is Spanish in his use of gold grounds and rich brocades, which he combines with a Flemish oil technique acquired perhaps from the Gallegos; but his models are Italian. Both in Toledo and Avila he worked with a Frenchman, Juan de Borgoña, whose style is a strange compound of the Milanese, Melozzo da Forli, Signorelli, and the Venetians. Borgoña is suave. Berruguete is rugged, and recalls Domenico Ghirlandaio and Carpaccio so vividly that first-hand acquaintance with their work seems probable. Later painters in Toledo are Flemish-Italian in style, and too insignificant to dwell on. The future of painting in Castile rested with the Hapsburgs, the first of whom, the Emperor Charles V, lived much abroad.

ANDALUSIA.—Seville was the headquarters of art in the south, but though a painters' guild was established there in 1280, the extant painting dates only from the fifteenth century. The earliest work, Sienese in style, such as the *Virgen de los Remedios* in the cathedral, might well have come from Catalonia or Valencia. So, too, the ruined altar-piece, *Santa Maria de Gracia*, signed "Juan Sanchez de Castra," which is in tempera with embossed gilding. The name Sanchez was common to a group of painters active in Cordova and Seville towards 1500, two of whom, Antonio and Diego, signed a *Road to Calvary* [PLATE 12, B], which is now in the Fitzwilliam Museum. This oil painting, in part gilded, is Flemish in inspiration and somewhat repellent, but it is notably Spanish in its vigour and dramatic temper. Italian influence vanished with Pedro de Cordova, whose signed and dated (1475) *Annunciation* in the great Mosque, though executed according to tradition, in tempera with gilded gesso, is almost wholly Van Eyckian. The school of Cordova is an enigma : its origin, its composition are unknown. Bermejo, who wandered about Greater Aragon, and perhaps into France, began here. Juan Nuñez, an indifferent oil painter in the Flemish manner active in Seville, evidently came in contact with Bermejo. The mysterious Alfonso at Barcelona has been called Cordovan. Though historical evidence is lacking it is surmised that these Cordovans, real and supposed, should be linked with an equally unaccountable artist, Nuño Gonzales of Lisbon (active 1450-1471), whose work is in technique and spirit akin to, and worthy of, Hugo van der Goes. The Sanchez family of painters may even have originated in Lisbon, for the name is Portuguese.

Columbus and the Conquistadores unexpectedly made Seville a wealthy trading centre, upon which a group of Italianate-Flemish artists converged. These were led by Alejo Fernandez, a Cordovan of perhaps German ancestry, whose prosperous career in Seville (1508-1543) prepared a welcome for mid-sixteenth century Spaniards trained in Italian bottegas. Alejo's soft and pretty Madonnas, part Teutonic, part Italian, were very popular. The best known is the *Virgen de los Conquistadores* in the Seville Alcazar, which would be interesting indeed if, in place of the rather Germanic donors kneeling in the clouds, the artist had been able to depict some of that immortal, desperate company of whom the picture is a memorial. After Fernandez, Pedro de Campaña of Brussels, a vigorous disciple of Raphael, Michelangelo and Signorelli, wielded most influence. He worked in Seville and Cordova from 1537 to 1562. The change from tempera and gold and primitive vigour of expression to oil and chiaroscuro and an educated style was fairly rapid. At first it involved decadence.

SERVITUDE TO ITALY.—In the fifteenth century not all the Catalan artists could sign their names. A new era opened with the establishment of printing presses at Valencia in 1474, at Barcelona in 1478, and at Seville in 1477. Many years elapsed before the grim censorship of the sixteenth and later centuries was instituted. In the interval, foreign philosophic and scientific literature threatened to obtain too free circulation. But that danger was averted—thought was stifled—and perhaps in consequence the ecclesiastical functions of painting were exercised in Spain during three more centuries with a naturalness rare elsewhere.

The final Spanish conquest of Naples in 1504, and the appointment of a viceroy, quickened intercourse with Italy. In Valencia the Italians introduced by Rodrigo Borgia (the profligate Pope Alexander VI) inspired two Spaniards, Ferrando Yañez (active 1506-1531 ?) and Ferrando de los Llanos (active 1506-1525) to study in Italy, whence they returned full-fledged Italianizers, dominated by Leonardo. They were imitated by Juan de Joanes (Vicente Juan Masip, 1505-7 ?-1579) a pious, decadent artist, who is redeemed by his portraiture, which is based upon Bronzino and Primaticcio. He left a large following which ran to seed. An Andalusian, Luis de Vargas (*c.* 1502-1568) spent twenty-eight years in Italy studying Raphael and Correggio, and returned to Seville to edify and instruct his less travelled brethren. There was an exponent of chiaroscuro even in Estremadura, where Luis de Morales (*c.* 1509-1586) painted devotional pictures. His intense religious fervour and ascetic zeal now and then invest with nobility his too delicate, consumptive personages, whom, however, he more often burdens with a fatal excess of melancholy. Besides the Italians, he seems to have studied Roger van der Weyden and Quinten Massys.

ESCORIAL.—The extent of the influence wielded by third-rate Italians, followers of Pontormo and Sarto, whom Philip II imported to decorate the vast walls and innumerable altars of the Escorial, has probably been overstated. J. F. Navarrete ("El Mudo"—the deaf, 1526-1579), the chief Spanish artist employed among them, was already a disciple of the Bolognese and changed his style only to imitate, with indifferent success, the King's Titians.

What is called the "Golden Age" of art and literature in Spain lasted from about 1550 to 1650. In painting it began with Ribalta and ended with Velazquez. It was a period of political and commercial decline and slow impoverishment, so that, except at Seville, artists became more and more dependent upon, and attracted to, the Court, particularly in the seventeenth century. Automatically, painting fell into two main divisions, religious art and portraiture. The cleavage was not strict, but the religious artists, though they painted donors well, rarely indulged in portraiture for its own sake. The portrait painters, no doubt recognizing their inaptitude, seldom attempted devotional works.

RIBALTA.—Decay was arrested, and religious art regained vitality when Francisco Ribalta (1551 or 5-1628) settled in Valencia, where he painted Dominican friars, Passion scenes [PLATE 13, A], and saints in ecstasy for the college of the Patriarch, and for the monasteries. Ribalta's inspiration is Italian; his sombre religious temper, and naturalistic bent, are Spanish.

RIBERA.—Ribalta is eclipsed by his celebrated pupil Jusepe de Ribera (1589-1652), a similarly inspired, but far more accomplished artist, who developed his exceptional talents by giving himself, despite poverty, a thorough schooling in Italy. In so far as all his work was done abroad, Ribera is not of the Spanish School; but because he is one of the most considerable artists of whom Spain can boast, and was an influence there in his own day, he cannot be ignored. His work was sent to Spain by the Spanish viceroys in Naples, where for nearly forty years he enjoyed—or rather, by intrigue usurped—the patronage of the Court and of the local churches. His favourite models were Neapolitan beggars, chosen for their bearded heads, great frames, and scarred bodies. Enveloped in fantastic shadows, and painted with morbid zest and searching realism, they figure as emaciated anchorites, or as saints in numerous sinister martyrdoms, sometimes tragic, sometimes revolting. The restraint and nobility of the *Holy Trinity* [PLATE 13, B] in the Prado are exceptional.

Ribalta's naturalism and chiaroscuro were a useful introduction to Caravaggio's savage realism and daring tricks of lighting, which Ribera, a superb draughtsman, a bold designer (qualities rare in a Spaniard) and a born dramatist, exploited with zest and great skill. A typical instance, and a characteristic early work is the celebrated martyrdom of *St. Bartholomew* (1630), in the Prado, in which the massive forms of the chief actors are placed so near the front, and are so strongly lit and realistically modelled, that they affect the spectator with the almost physical impact of a " close up " in the cinema theatre. Draperies of brown, black, and olive green, with a patch of bright red, and a blue sky with a diagonal white cloud, compose Ribera's usual colour scheme. His trick of leaving his favourite hot red ground almost untouched in the contours and shadows of the flesh is here especially noticeable in the faces, hands, feet, and bony knees of the men. Venetian in origin, this practice, carried to excess, degrades the work of a host of seventeenth-century painters, particularly in Seville and Granada.

Ribera's early study of Titian and Correggio seemed to modify his treatment of feminine subjects, as for example, in the *Ecstasy of the Magdalen* of 1626 (Madrid Academy) and the *Immaculate Conception* (1635) at Salamanca. In the *Immaculate Conception* the Virgin floats before a warm yellow haze, from which cherubs dimly emerge. Below are putti, taken, like the cherubs, from Correggio, but naturalistically modelled in Ribera's usual style, over a hot ground which tells strongly in the contours, and gives a dissipated look to the rather beaky noses. This picture was celebrated. The tall Virgin is one of the many so freely repeated by that inveterate plagiarist Alonso Cano; whilst the hazy, yellow sky may well have inspired Murillo's second manner. Under the influence of Massimo Stanzioni (whom nevertheless he persecuted malignantly) Ribera developed in mid-career a cooler tonality and—for a time only— an Italian sauvity of modelling. As he also studied closely Stanzioni's colour, and as both used analogous types, Ribera during this phase bears a remarkable superficial resemblance to Stanzioni.

The *St. Paul Hermit* (1649) in the Prado [PLATE 14, A] represents to perfection his last phase. The handling is extraordinarily thin and smooth, the figure is modelled to a hair; yet the touch is light, the flesh tones are cool, and the effect is atmospheric.

In Seville the native temper slowly asserted itself. The city was again a centre of culture; this time Christian. First, the national spirit stirred the rising poets and dramatists, and animated the sculptors who, despite their servitude to Italy, had never quite lost their pungent, racial flavour, or wholly relinquished their traditional polychrome incrustation (" estofado "), vivid and realistic. The painters were slow to find themselves. Juan de las Roelas (1558 or 60-1625) and Francisco de Herrera the Elder (*c.* 1576-1656) were at the mercy of too many influences, and made little headway. Roelas probably saw Venice. After 1606 he painted in Olivares and Seville a series of compositions based on Tintoretto, Bassano and Correggio, which are heavy and dull, but unique in Spain for their reminiscences of Giorgione. Roelas is mainly Italianate, but his uncouth executioners and naturalistic detail [see PLATE 15, A] are Spanish. Roelas influenced Herrera, a violent personality who challenged notice with his hard, blunt naturalism—which Zurbaran, at least, appreciated [see PLATE 15, B]—and with heretical experiments in impressionism which earned criticism resembling Ruskin's abuse of Whistler. Roelas' productions are not great art, but they lead up to Zurbaran and Velazquez. It was the turn of the century. These youths, moved by the spirit which Caravaggio had raised, and which was now permeating Europe, and brought up no doubt upon the new popular literature which had revealed Spain to the Spaniards with full-blooded humour and grim love of fact, now concentrated upon naturalism. Their interest in their surroundings was further induced by a circumstance peculiar to Spain. Death might relax the iron rule of Philip II, but not that of his ally the Inquisition. Down to the eighteenth century the nude was banned. The author of a " pintura deshonesta " was liable to excommunication and exile—his client's treatment was determined by social considerations. Even the royal Titians, such as the *Danaë*, had to be enjoyed in a " galeria reservada," underground. The portrayal of *Adam and Eve*, or the *Last Judgment*, presented great difficulties. St. Sebastian in Spanish art is rarely martyred : in the fifteenth century he sometimes appears as an Arab archer, highly bred and richly clad. Instead of the nude, therefore, students were set to study foreign prints, to draw statuary and, in particular, to paint " bodegones " (kitchen scenes, or plain still-lifes). The art-policeman in Seville was Francisco Pacheco (1564-1654), whose work, apart from an unexpectedly witty portrait in Sir Herbert Cook's collection [PLATE 17, A], is empty and laboured. In his academy he imposed the accepted rules, and taught the etiquette of religious painting which he recites, mingled with valuable biography, in his curious, prolix book, the *Arte de la Pintura*.

ZURBARAN.—Velazquez was nourished in Seville ; but, as his destiny led him straight into the King's household, he must be considered with the School of Madrid. Francisco Zurbaran (1598-1664) was trained by an obscure painter of images, P. D. de Villanueva. A study of Ribalta in Valencia fixed his religious sympathies, and his interest in chiaroscuro. Returning to Seville he became influenced by Herrera, whom he worked alongside during 1629 upon the well-known *Bonaventura* cycle, which is now scattered about Europe. After 1630 he struck out for himself in novel style. Such inventions as the *Carthusian Refectory with St. Hugo* in the Seville Museum are Zurbaran's own. Their unconventionality and native inspiration are as refreshing as, in Seville, they are rare. Zurbaran's life work was the portrayal of a whole generation of monks, of various orders, in different parts of Spain ; he combined keen, uncompromising portraiture with religious painting. The actors in his scenes from monkish legends are not ideal types, but the cloistered brethren who employed him. Zurbaran is rare in England, but it would be difficult to point to a finer example of his sombre, religious power than the *Franciscan* (after 1650) in the National Gallery, a single praying figure which is the epitome of his monastic style. His more elaborate compositions, which are frequently to be found in their original places, are mainly allegories of patron saints, such as the sumptuous *Apotheosis of St. Thomas Aquinas* (1631) in the Seville Museum. They include also a few official portraits of conspicuous dignity and integrity, like that of Gonzalo de Illescas, Bishop of Cordova (1639) [PLATE 16, A], in which chiaroscuro is employed with great flexibility to emphasize the importance of the sitter, and to give force, depth, and unity to the large design. This, one of a much extolled, but unequal series of thirteen canvases, is in the remote monastery of Guadalupe, in Estremadura. The side lighting is typical. It grew probably out of Zurbaran's studio acquaintance with painted sculpture. Towards 1630 he painted four versions of Christ on the Cross, one of which has the relief and texture of smoothly carved and painted wood. At the end of his career he imitated the work of his junior Murillo in its most sentimental aspects.

MURILLO.—Bartolomé Esteban Murillo (1618-1682) was a pupil of Juan del Castillo (1584-1640), an Italianate artist ; but he acquired his technical facility, and learned how to combine it with a show of rich harmonious colour, from a study of Titian, Rubens, and Ribera during his early visit to Madrid. Rubens taught him to paint his own graceful townswomen rather than classical types.　His Andalusian Madonnas were enthusiastically received, and he fell a victim of his own popularity.　The citizens of Seville, who call their fertile plain " La Tierra de María Santísima," in the early sixteenth century forced the Pope to issue a decree forbidding preachers to question the doctrine of the Immaculate Conception ; thenceforward this subject was in great demand. Murillo produced at least twenty versions [see PLATE 14, B], and no one became so popular as he, " the painter of Conceptions."　He was adroit and obliging, but without religious fire and spiritual insight, and even his easy, picturesque formulas grew stale by repetition.　He took a keen interest in the street life of Seville, which he treated at first as pure genre, and in later years freely introduced in religious work.　Murillo's three styles are labelled respectively " cold," " warm," and " vaporous."　The cold style (" estilo frio ") is marked by leaden shadows and cold, dull lights, as in the Prado *Annunciation*, and as a rule by laboured, naturalistic modelling.　His two years in Castile (1643-1645) produced the warm style, and its attendant realism and chiaroscuro.　The widely scattered Fianciscan series (*c.* 1646), and the Louvre *Madonna of the Rosary* (before 1650), with warm brown shadows, and deep, warm, red and blue draperies, are the best known examples of this phase.　Slowly Murillo's modelling softened, his clear outlines grew vague, his lighting became nebulous.　A warm, yellow glow suffused first the shadows, then the half-tones, and at last the whole picture, including the flesh tones.　Transition pieces, such as the *Dream of a Patrician* (1656) in the Prado, in which the smouldering reds and blues are as yet scarcely sullied, are as near as Murillo ever got to the sumptuous harmonies and decorative splendour of his Venetian exemplars.　The vaporous style came fully into being in the long-vaunted series of canvases painted for the Caridad Church in Seville in 1671.　Colour and form are muffled in a grey yellow haze ; even the flesh tones are gilded.　One of the series, *St. Elizabeth healing the Sick* (Prado), otherwise typical, is noteworthy for the realistic treatment of the cripples and lepers who fill the foreground, and for a return to smooth outlines.　One or two virtually domestic scenes followed, simple and dignified in spirit and composition, firmly and smoothly drawn, such as the Prado *St. Anne teaching the Virgin*.　These were exceptional, and the *Holy Family* in the National Gallery, painted towards the end of Murillo's life, shows that the " estilo vaporoso " persisted to the last.

CANO.—His prolific contemporary Alonso Cano (1601-1667) was a brilliant sculptor, with no originality to spare for painting.　Throughout life, in the medium of oil, he devoted his astonishing sleight of hand to a sauve, eclectic rendering of motives taken from the religious works of Titian, Van Dyck, Ribera, Correggio, and Guido Reni.　In 1651 he was appointed canon in Granada, where he worked in the cathedral till his death.　The seven huge *Scenes from the Life of the Virgin*, which at a great height ring the Capilla Mayor at Granada, are his most sustained effort.　They are elegant, imposing, and cosmopolitan ; Cano's art had no nationality.　His assistants and imitators composed the school of Granada.

CASTILLO.—A minor artist undeserving total obscurity is Antonio del Castillo y Saavedra (1616-1668), a student of Tintoretto who had at least a nodding acquaintance with Elsheimer.　His scriptural compositions are usually farm scenes with several figures, designed and seen in excellent relation to settings of grey upland landscape.　Low in tone, composed in cool blues, browns and blacks, with a silvery note in the sky, his studies are very freshly observed. The school of Seville came to an end with D. Juan de Valdes Leal (1622-1690), a would-be tragic artist, whose gruesome extravaganzas, designed as moral curbs, provoked even Murillo's amusement. Ambitious, prolific, but unoriginal, his Spanish, Italian, French, and Flemish exemplars are too numerous to find mention here. His meretricious technique is a prominent example of the slip-shod facility produced in Andalusia by the persistent misuse of hot red grounds, which whenever possible were left untouched in the shadows, and covered with a smear of grey or blue in the half-tones.

The Hapsburgs were the most painted monarchs in Europe. After Charles V, who reserved himself for Titian, every king had his own portrait painter in close personal attendance. Philip II established the custom by importing Antonio Mor from Flanders. Mor established a tradition which lasted, with dwindling force, until Velazquez took service with Philip IV. Following Mor's precipitate departure from Spain, his pupil, Alonso Sánchez Coello (c. 1531-1588) became Philip's Painter-in-ordinary, and " well beloved son." Coello's pupil, Juan Pantoja de la Cruz (c. 1549-1608), served Philip II and Philip III. Bartolomé González (1564-1627), a follower of Coello and Pantoja, painted for Philip III and for a few years, for the young Philip IV.

SANCHEZ COELLO.—Coello, who worked under Mor in Flanders, is sometimes difficult to distinguish from his master, whose grave temper, and sober, scrupulous technique he assimilated fully. Indeed, at his best, Coello is capable of a delicacy, and a faint smiling mockery, which are absent in Mor, and, as in the Dublin portrait [PLATE 18, A], of sudden flashes of brilliance. Many first-rate portraits which pass for Mor may be by Coello, who is barely represented outside Madrid. Venetian influence is visible in his late portraits, which are more solid in handling. Set to paint altar-pieces for the Escorial towards the end of his life, he fell automatically into line with his fellows, in empty imitation of the Italian mannerists.

PANTOJA.—Until recent years, one or two early Pantoja's passed for late Coello's. Usually, however, Pantoja's touch is heavy, his modelling wooden, his temper lethargic. Moreover, in painting court dress, jewelled and intricate, he frequently used a solid, horny impasto in marked contrast with Coello's Flemish brushwork. On the other hand, his accomplished, liquid handling should be noticed in one or two surviving specimens of copies after Mor, a large number of which he was charged to execute for the king. He surpassed himself in one or two portraits of Philip II in old age, which arrest us by their literal, cold presentment of the wasted physique, and nervous mentality of the king [PLATE 18, B].

EL GRECO.—In sixteenth-century Toledo the sculptors and carvers were deservedly pre-eminent until the arrival of that great painter, El Greco (Domenico Theotocopoulos, c. 1545-1614). Born a Greek at Candia, the Venetian headquarters in Crete, he migrated early to Venice. He was in Rome in 1570, and about 1575 finally settled in Toledo. El Greco was at heart a Byzantine. We do not know when he left Crete, and whether he ever attached himself to a Venetian bottega in Candia, or, later, to the colony of Cretan ikon painters in Venice. Julio Clovio described him as a pupil of Titian, but El Greco's known early work indicates that his Western teachers were actually Bassano, Tintoretto, and Veronese. In Venice he imitated Bassano with remarkable success. But he never forgot that he was a Greek. In Toledo his technique remained Venetian, and the influence of Tintoretto persisted in his audacious figure designs; but racial characteristics asserted themselves. One of his first commissions in Toledo, the famous *Expolio* in the cathedral, is a Byzantine composition.   Some of the heads recall Bassano, others Jerome Bosch, who was very popular in Spain, and some are portraits of Spaniards.

El Greco was a masterly portrait painter [see PLATE 19].   He depicted with rare insight and authority the personal charm, pride and temper of the Toledan aristocracy, notably in his series of single heads [see PLATE 21, B], the greater part of which is now in the Prado.   His acclaimed masterpiece, the *Burial of Count Orgaz* (guarded like the Crown Jewels by an iron screen), has always been justly famous for the row of portraits which form the lower half of the composition.   Individual and aloof, every personage has that air of breeding which El Greco, like Van Dyck, never failed to impart.

El Greco probably hoped to establish himself at the Escorial, but his trial piece, *St. Maurice and the Theban Legion*, failed.   Students may remember seeing the picture at Burlington House in 1920-21.   The daring design, indifference to academic drawing, and the, perhaps, intolerably vivid colour, were too much for the conservative king, who exiled the altar-piece to the Escorial Chapter Room—where, in an excellent light, it now hangs.

Visionary and creative, El Greco sought to symbolize his emotion by colour and design.   He based his whole design upon his figures, and used backgrounds of tossing, flame-like clouds which echoed his forms, emphasized their wild gestures, and consummated their rhythmic, upward flow [PLATE 20, B].   His ardour sometimes resulted in strange distortions of form, but the gaunt, heroic Baptist in the Prado *Baptism* [PLATE 20, A] sufficiently vindicates his means. He could express emotion plainly enough, as in two or three renderings of the *Adoration of the Shepherds*, wherein the Babe is lost in his own radiance, as with Rembrandt fifty years later.   His colour is the complement of his form; cold, sharp greens and blues, ashy whites, carmines, and vivid lemon yellows predominate.

Study of his development is complicated by his habit of repeating favourite compositions at long intervals of time, and by his unconsciously reverting, in some instances, to earlier standards of proportion.   His Spanish work falls roughly into three periods.   The *Expolio*, with its finely proportioned figures, is typical of the first (1575-1584).   The " exaggerations " of El Greco are at once foreshadowed in the lengthened heads, in the schematized folds and planes of the drapery, and in experiments in cold colour.   The emotional flash in the eyes, and the sensitive, spread fingers of Christ, are permanent characteristics. The *Baptism* [PLATE 20, A] comes about midway in the second epoch.   A variant of the same subject in the Hospital of St. Juan Bautista at Toledo, dating between 1609-1614, well illustrates the last phase.   The heads are tiny, the figures unnaturally elongated, and a strange rippling movement runs through the limbs.   Something of the older sculptural quality remains, but form is apt to be sacrificed to movement.

Almost the only authentic work by El Greco's son, Jorge Manuel (1578-1631) is a signed replica of the *Expolio*.   El Greco's disciples were Luis Tristan (1586-1640) and Fray Juan Bautista Mayno (1569 ?-1649), who in their religious works caught his mannerisms rather than his spirit. Tristan's colour is marred by a misuse of hot undertones. He overloads his compositions, and fills his drapery with crinkly, stringy folds.   His portraiture is obviously inspired by El Greco, but his dry thin technique is far from that master's liquid brushwork.   Mayno's colour is apt to be over bright and hard.   His heads recall El Greco, but his forms are smooth and naturalistic. He became drawing master to Philip IV, for whom he painted large historical pieces : one, the *Allegory of the Recovery of San Salvador* [PLATE 22, A] is surprisingly atmospheric and spacious, largely composed, and simple in spirit. The foreground figures are drawn with uncommon ease and delicacy ; the wounded man, whose pale flesh, in colour and texture, is most naturally rendered, is particularly fine. Contemporary versifiers asserted that Mayno drew with diamond pencils ; probably, however, he found the methods of Velazquez more efficacious.[4]

VELAZQUEZ.—The idleness and incapacity of Gonzalez and his fellows were forcibly described by Rubens in 1603. They were superseded by Velazquez (1599-1660), who became painter to Philip IV in 1623. Through him, the king is known to us perhaps better than any other monarch.

Velazquez cannot be fully comprehended outside Madrid. English private collections contain the best of the bodegones, and the National Gallery and Wallace Collection share works comparable with anything of the kind in Spain, but all the larger canvases, such as the *Breda* and *Las Meninas*, are in the Prado.

Velazquez lived in Seville until 1623, thenceforward in Madrid. The three landmarks in his career are his arrival at Court, and his two voyages to Italy (August, 1629, to early 1631, and January, 1649, to June, 1651). Placed early with Herrera the Elder, Velazquez passed at the age of fourteen into Pacheco's cultured household, a strange fish in that tank of learning and piety. There he painted Sir Otto Beit's *Servant Girl* (c. 1617), Sir Herbert Cook's *Woman frying Eggs* (c. 1620), the National Gallery *Christ in the House of Martha* (c. 1620 ?), and the *Water Carrier* (c. 1620) at Apsley House. These bodegones are exercises in elaborate composition and in hard, exact, sculptural modelling, solidly built up almost in monochrome over a hot ground. In every case the light falls sharply from the left. One with them is the Prado *Adoration* (1619), an ambitious composition in the Bassano manner, low in tone, and with a thick, rather oily surface [PLATE 23]. Apart from problems of design, form is of first importance in this herculean effort. The personages are black haired, olive skinned Sevillians, studied from life, and drawn with iron precision. A fold of white and green drapery emerging sharply out of dense green shadow, and certain touches of rose, afford the only relief in the scheme of olive brown and green. The same olive tone and oily surface are found in the earliest known portrait proper, a *Head of a Man* (Prado), in which the features, as though they were cut with a knife, are like carved teak. A resemblance to Herrera about 1620 may indicate only a like aim ; the real formative agent was Caravaggio, whose influence touched even Roelas.

A full-length portrait of the *Infant Don Carlos* (Prado), of about 1626, is typical of the first period in Madrid. It is higher in tone, the thinly painted background is grey, and although hot underpaint gives a wine tinge to the shadows and half-tones, the general effect is cool. The face is modelled in practically two planes, pale broad lights, and narrow, green brown shadows, and drawn with clean, strong outlines [PLATE 24, B]. The flesh is pale and a trifle dry. In this phase the ideal silhouette is the chief object, and the cause of frequent pentimenti.

Just before Velazquez' first Italian journey the king paid him one hundred silver ducats for *Los Borrachos* (Prado), the last and greatest of the bodegones. The wrinkled brown hands and heads of the topers are rendered with Hals-like

[4] The exact date of Mayno's picture is not yet known, but the available evidence points to its having been painted about 1634. It is one of a series, uniform in size and shape, which numerous artists (Carducho, Castelo and Velazquez, for example), were commissioned to execute about 1634 for the newly built Buen Retiro.

force and freedom. The nude Bacchus, on the other hand, is modelled firmly and roundly in a thin, subtly broken impasto, creamy and soft, with a faint violet tint in the half-tones, which in a flash seems to anticipate certain portraits of the 'thirties.

Each of the Italian voyages is a landmark, betokening a long stride forward. During the first, Velazquez copied Tintoretto from whom, probably, he gained the fresh insight into figure composition which is apparent in *Joseph's Coat* (Escorial) and *Vulcan's Forge* (Prado). The main interest in these Italian exercises, however, is atmosphere, depth, and volume. *Joseph's Coat* is painted smoothly and thinly on coarse canvas with loaded high lights. The softly modelled atmospheric figures stand out like sculpture. The *Vulcan* is more even and solid in handling. After these Roman works (which Velazquez sold to Philip in Madrid) and inspired this time by Guido Reni, may be placed *Christ at the Column* (National Gallery), in colour the most silvery and beautiful of the three.

This atmospheric modelling developed slowly in official portraiture. In the second Madrid period it was first tried out in the lovely and subtle portrait (of the artist's wife ?) called " a Sybil " (Prado), in which the canvas shows clearly through the thin, fused brushwork. The delicate shadows are worked into a grey-green paste on a broken ground of thinnest grey and brown. The lights are in a soft, broken impasto of faint rose ; a clot of rose pink on the nostril is almost the only touch of solid pigment. After this, in feminine portraits, the impasto becomes so thin and melting that brushwork is difficult to detect. A similar technique is used for the head in the incomparable equestrian portrait of the boy prince, Baltasar Carlos (Prado, No. 1180), in grace and spirit the finest of Velazquez' studies of children.

Impressionism, devised to surmount the difficulties of costume painting, appears without apparent warning in the " Silver Philip " (1631-2) in the National Gallery. The undertone of Philip's dress was first brushed in ; the embroideries were then rendered by curling flakes of colour, sharp yet perfectly gradated, applied over this broad foundation. This form of brushwork, which gave such animation to ceremonial portraiture, never hardened into a formula. Constantly adjusted, it was an admirable instrument for those investigations into light and atmosphere which culminated in *Las Hilanderas* and *Las Meninas*.

It is not easy to settle Velazquez' chronology. He met new problems with novel devices, so that on occasion he seems to be in advance of his general line of progress ; *Los Borrachos* is a case in point. In the main, during the second Madrid period his brushwork grew steadily more liquid, sweeping and transparent, and his colour rose in pitch from silvery grey and brown to red and blue, with notes of carmine and violet which suggest that a study of El Greco assisted the transformation. The change began in the series of equestrian and hunting pieces, including the *Surrender of Breda* and the National Gallery *Boar Hunt*, painted between about 1634 and 1640. These involved the study of landscape, out of which arose the recognition of daylight, whose mysteries Velazquez explored during the rest of his life.

The most brilliant equestrian piece is the above-mentioned Baltasar Carlos (*c.* 1635). The boy is an enchanting figure. He wears dark blue velvet, yellow sleeves and boots, a black hat, and a rose scarf with floating gold tassels, and rides against a background of white and blue clouds. The landscape below, composed of cool green plain, and tree-dotted slopes, backed by the white-capped Guadarramas, is in the same brilliant key; nothing could be more spacious and airy, more fresh and true.

Velazquez seemed to find extra scope in treating the court dwarfs and buffoons, such as *El Primo* (1644), *El Niño de Vallecas* and *Calabacillas* (all in the Prado), whom he observed with rare understanding and detachment, and depicted with great force and freedom. The head of *El Primo* [PLATE 25, A] is literally smacked in, plane by plane, in broad, liquid strokes over a thick warm ground. In the *Calabacillas*, on the other hand, an equal force of modelling, and the most subtle play of light and air are obtained by means of a supple, creamy impasto, which anticipates by some years the handling of *Las Meninas*. These studies directly prepared for the famous portrait of Pope Innocent X which Velazquez, with devastating candour and mastery, painted in Rome during his second Italian journey.

The supreme masterpieces fall into the last decade, in which Velazquez gathers up and weaves together the many threads of his art. He studies light and fluid air in conjunction with portraiture and three-dimensional design, as in *Las Meninas;* his *Rokeby Venus* (1657 ?) is a consummate rendering of form; but, in these last years, as though Italy had deeply stirred his emotions, he lays final emphasis on colour. In the *Innocent X*, for example, white and purple-red are employed with great audacity and effect. The undamaged central part of *Las Hilanderas* (1657?) in the Prado, which is a painting of light and air drenched in colour from sunlit tapestry and dresses, is a radiant mass of rose, orange, apricot, blue-green and lemon yellow. In the portrait of the Infanta Margarita, with which he wound up about 1660, all possible colour has been extracted from the red, rose-pink and flashing silver dress (the head [PLATE 25, B] is incomplete). The *Rokeby Venus*, it is worth noting, is unique not only in Velazquez but in Spanish art before Goya, as a study of the female nude.

It would be difficult to over-estimate the range and quality of his last works, or to exaggerate the power and subtlety of Velazquez' technique. The handling is extraordinarily felicitous. It varies from the indescribable refinement of the *Old Philip* (*c.* 1655) in the National Gallery, to the fierce, loose, impressionistic modelling of the female dwarf in *Las Meninas* (1656). Though executed with incredible dispatch, there is nothing irrelevant or unconsidered in these final designs. They are the work of one of the greatest picture-makers, as well as one of the profoundest interpreters who ever lived.[5]

MAZO.—Velazquez did not crown a century of conscious effort, nor did he establish a tradition. The truths he made known were forgotten, so that thirty years after his death no trace of his influence on living art remained. Juan Bautisto Mazo (1612-?1667), his son-in-law and assistant, who succeeded him in the office of King's painter, and Juan Carreño de Miranda (1614-1685), who succeeded Mazo, were elderly hacks, content with routine by the time they were promoted. Mazo was noted for his skill as a copyist of Velazquez, Titian, Tintoretto and Veronese. His independent work is uncertain in drawing and faulty in proportion. Flaccid hands with fingers that fuse into red underpaint in the shadows, and too-small feet and ankles, particularly in the case of children, are his more obvious defects. In portraiture his impasto is thick and even, without accent; the emphatic, liquid touches of Velazquez escape his brush. His landscapes have mostly darkened. He had a pleasant sense of open air,

[5] It is worth noting that Velazquez' library contained Leonardo da Vinci's *Trattato della Pittura*, published for the first time at Paris in 1651 (See *La Libreria de Velazquez* by Sánchez Cantón, 1915).

but atmosphere with Mazo means usually blurred outlines and weak modelling, not, as with Velazquez, added depth and fullness. The National Gallery *Mariana of Austria* (1666), and the *Infanta Doña Margarita* in the Prado [PLATE 26, A] are typical of Mazo's work after the death of Velazquez.

CARRENO.—Carreño was a religious painter influenced by Van Dyck and Titian. He took to portraiture, modelled himself upon Velazquez, and was appointed to Court. He is best known for his numerous presentments of Charles II and the Queen Mother, Doña Mariana of Austria, which are all much alike in composition, tone and colour. The backgrounds of shadowy brown and black curtains, mirrors and pictures are a weak imitation of Velazquez' *Meninas* and *Mariana of Austria* (c. 1653). His portrait of Doña Mariana at Munich [PLATE 26, B], firmly drawn and consistently executed, commemorates a moment of exceptional diligence.

SCHOOL OF MADRID.—The school of Madrid proper existed alongside, and independent of Velazquez, and outlived him. It was chiefly concerned with historical, allegorical and religious painting, in which it followed the great Venetians, Rubens and Van Dyck. It made no original contribution to art, and did not add greatly to our entertainment. As in the rest of Europe, the number of painters active in this epoch was large. The majority need not detain us. The outstanding figures have already been made familiar to English readers through such informative monographs as Beruete's *School of Madrid*. Antonio Pereda (1608-1678), a religious and historical painter who followed Ribera and Titian, and Mateo Cerezo (1635-85), a pupil of Carreño and a faithful, somewhat effeminate student of Van Dyck and Titian, were able draughtsmen and good colourists. The school ended with Claudio Coello (1642-1693), a painter of large religious compositions, which he borrowed from the Italian eclectics, and overloaded with naturalistic detail in the style of Rubens' followers. His chief work is an official ceremonial picture, the *Sagrada Forma*, in the Sacristy of the Escorial. He was supplanted by Luca Giordano in 1692, and died almost immediately.

From the Middle Ages to the nineteenth century the development of painting in Spain was conditioned to an unusual extent by historical factors. For instance, Spanish political activities in Italy from the thirteenth century onwards and alliance with the House of Burgundy, led to repercussions in the sphere of art. Coello was the last of the Hapsburg painters. With the Bourbons (Philip V, 1700) came Houasse, Ranc, the Van Loos, Mengs, and, in 1762, Tiepolo, who died in Madrid after decorating the royal palace.

GOYA.—Under this incubus the national art seemed to be sapped of race and vitality, when, without warning, came Goya (1746-1828), painter and etcher, portraitist and satirist. He studied firstly under José Luzán y Martinez (1710-1785), who derived from Giordano, secondly under Francisco Bayeu y Subias (1734-1795), a scholar of Martinez and Mengs, and visited Italy between 1769-1771. He became "pintor de Cámara" in 1789, and first painter to Charles IV in 1799, shortly after completing his etched *Caprichos*. During the reign of the interloper Joseph Bonaparte (1808-14) he produced most of his etched *Disasters of War*. Following his reinstatement at Court by Ferdinand VII he painted comparatively few portraits, but he etched the *Tauromáquia* (c. 1815) and the *Proverbs* (1815-19?). He retired to Bordeaux in 1824, and died there. His output was large and varied. Besides etching, he painted three or four hundred portraits —some in miniature—decorated churches, and for fifteen years (from 1776) produced designs for the royal tapestry factory. With Bayeu, between 1772 and 1783 he executed ceiling frescoes in the style of Giordano and Tiepolo in the Pilar Cathedral and churches of Zaragoza. About 1798 he painted in tempera the better-known decorations in S. Antonio de Florida—the little church in Madrid which it is proposed to turn into a Goya memorial. These later white and gold and orange-red designs are more obviously influenced by Tiepolo.

The etchings are mainly devoted to social and political satire. More dramatic and strange, even sinister in conception are a series of designs which Goya painted late in life upon the walls of his own house. Transferred to canvas these "visiones fantasticas" are now in the Prado [PLATES 28 and 29]. Their qualities of design and rhythm, their breadth of handling and sculptural projection are no less remarkable than their mingling of pathos, mystery and supernatural terror. Low in tone, they are composed in silvery blacks, browns and greys, with notes of red. They powerfully influenced both Manet and Daumier, whom they exceed in imaginative grasp and surpass in technique.

Goya began regular portraiture comparatively late in life. He grounded his style upon that of Mengs, who was obviously the model for the elaborate portrait of the *Conde de Floridablanca* (privately owned in Madrid), signed in 1783. Goya began to find himself in his so-called "grey" (or more precisely grey-green) portraits, of which a characteristic early specimen is the *Osuna Family* (1787), in the Prado. The children, with soft, pale faces, are like flat dolls in vaporous grey and green frocks. The Duchess is in the same vaporous grey which, tinged with green, pervades the whole picture. In the treatment of her transparent dress there is a foretaste of that affinity with Gainsborough which is so frequently noticeable in feminine portraits from about 1795 to 1815. The Prado *Francisco Bayeu* (1796) and *La Tirana* (1798) in the Madrid Academy are mature examples of the "grey" phase. Most typical is the *Bayeu*, with the silvery dress tones relieved against a cold grey-green background, and with its thin, liquid brushwork. The watery pinks, and the shot effect in the grey lights are not uncommon. The marble reds, bronze greys and gold of *La Tirana* prepare us for the shimmering cream and gold, the black, crimson and blue of the *Family of Charles IV* (1800), with which Goya opened his great middle period. His fiendish eye for character had full play in the corrupt court and capital of Charles IV. The spell of royalty did not bind him, and the royal portraits themselves are conspicuous examples of his mordant humour. Strong colour, free and forcible brushwork, and towards the end a heavy impasto with thick touches of black in the eyes and shadows, characterize male portraits of this epoch, such as the Prado bust of the actor *Maiquez* (1807). The National Gallery *Isabel Cobos de Porcel* (1806) is a fairly typical female portrait. Many portraits of Goya's middle years recall English masters, such as Reynolds and Gainsborough. The likeness, which is not accidental, is confined to composition and pose. Beruete attributes this to Goya's acquaintance with English engravings. The Prado *General Urrutia* (1798) and a recent bequest to the Prado, *Doña Tomasa Palafox, Marquesa de Villafranca* (1804), notably recall English portraiture.

The bust of *José Munárriz* (1818) in the Madrid Academy, and Sir Otto Beit's *Doña Maria Martinez de Puga* (1824) are typical late works. After the sieges and famine of the invasion Goya's temper grew sober and his colour sombre. In his old age he frequently painted with a palette knife. His last portraits are experiments in impressionism. Their vibrating strokes of pure colour helped to set in train fifty years later the impressionist movement in France, and it is surely not fanciful to see in Goya's latest phase the germs of Cézanne.

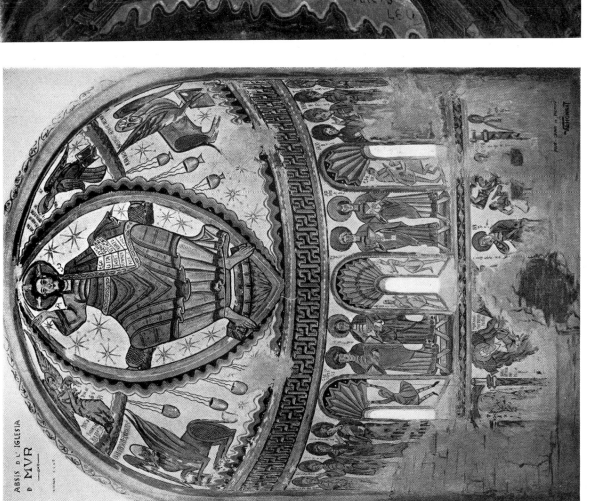

A—*The Ascension of Christ.* Fresco from the Church of Sta. Maria de Mur; 12th century. (Boston Museum of Fine Arts)

B—*The Ascension of Christ.* Vault painting of about 1200. (S. Isidoro, León)

A—*Saviour enthroned with twelve Apostles.* Altar frontal; stucco, gilded and painted; 12th century. From Ginestarre de Cardós. (Barcelona Museum)

B—*Madonna and Child with Saints.* Altar frontal; stucco gilded and painted; 12th century. From the Leridan Pyrenées. (Barcelona Museum)

A—Altar from Encamp, Andorra; 12th century. Gesso. (Barcelona Museum)

B—*St. Peter Martyr.* Retable from Aragon; early 14th century. (Barcelona Museum)

C—Retable of Alfonso and Eleanor of Castile, Counts of Urgell, by Bernat de Pou (?) Catalan School, early 14th century. From the Cathedral of Huesca. (Private Collection, Barcelona)

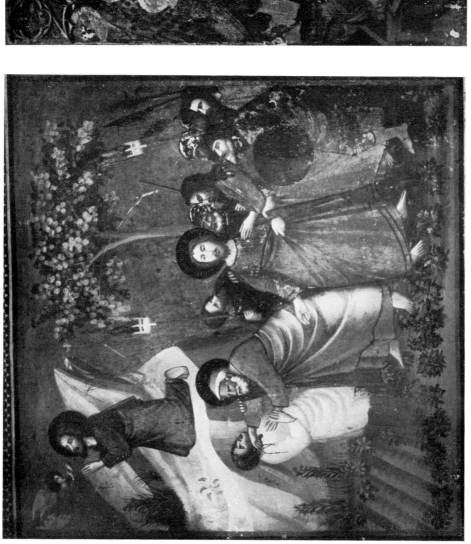

B—*The Resurrection*, by Jaume Serra, 1361. (Saragossa Museum)

A—*The Agony* and *Betrayal in the Garden*, by Ferrer Bassa, 1346. (Convent of Pedralbes, Barcelona)

Retable of Sigena, ascribed to the brothers Serra. (Barcelona Museum)

B—Retable of the Councillors, by Luis Dalmau, 1445. (Barcelona Museum)

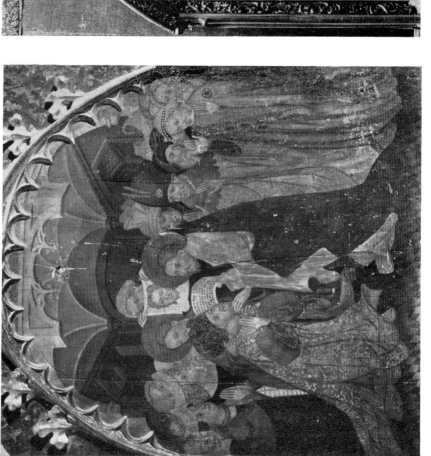

A—*The healing of King Abgar*; retable of Sta. Clara, by Luis Borrassá, 1415. (Episcopal Museum, Vich)

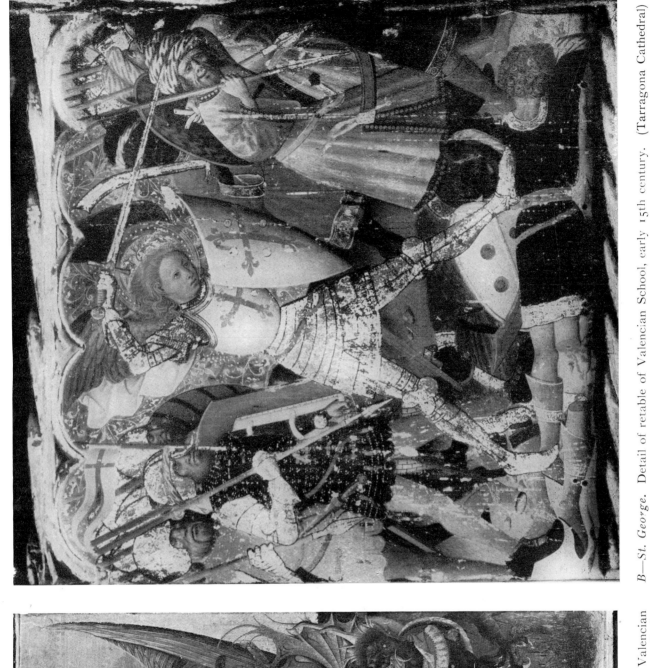

A—St. George and the Dragon. Valencian School, early 15th century. Panel, 73¾ by 36⅛ ins. (National Gallery, Edinburgh)

B—St. George. Detail of retable of Valencian School, early 15th century. (Tarragona Cathedral)

B—Retable of St. Martin, attributed to Bermejo (and collaborators?); before 1474. (Sta. Maria, Daroca)

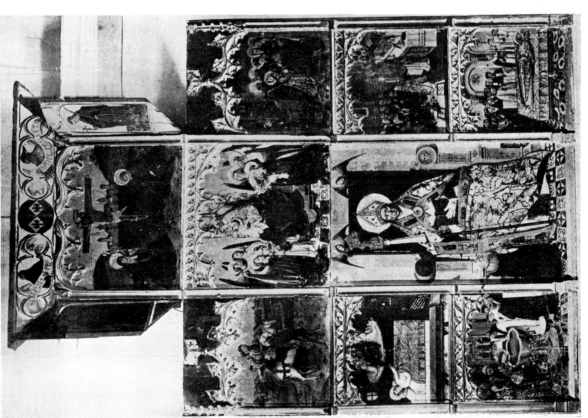

A—Retable of St. Martin, by Jacomard. (St. Martin's Church, Segorbe)

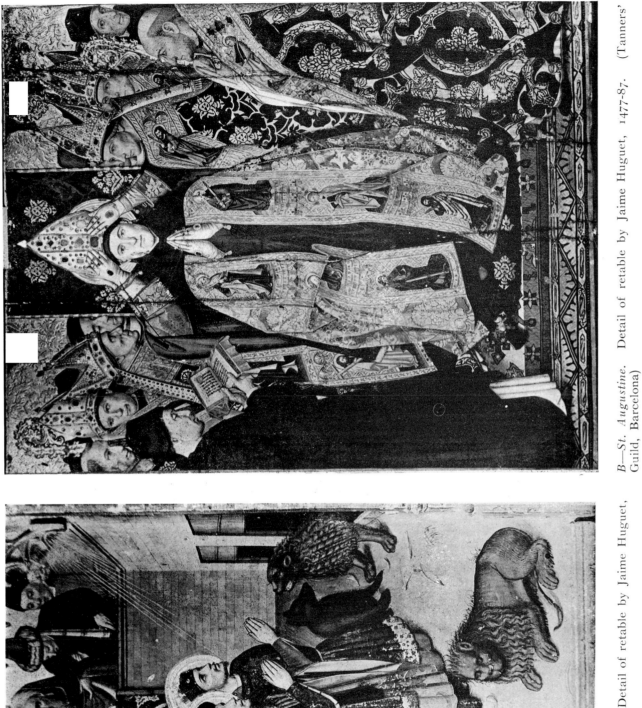

B—*St. Augustine.* Detail of retable by Jaime Huguet, 1477-87. (Tanners' Guild, Barcelona)

A—SS. *Abdon and Sennen.* Detail of retable by Jaime Huguet, 1460. (S. Pedro, Tarrassa)

C—The Legend of St. Michael. Aragonese School; 15th century. (Barcelona Museum)

B—Angels comforting St. Vincent, by Jaime Vergós II (?) Retable from St. Vincent, Sarriá. (Barcelona Museum)

A—A Prophet, by Pablo Vergós. Gesso. (Barcelona Museum)

Martyrdom of St. Medin, by Alfonso, 1473. (Barcelona Museum)

A —The Triumph of the Christian Religion, by Fernando **Gallego**. Panel, 66½ by 52 in. (Prado)

B—The Road to Calvary, by Antonio and Diego Sanchez. Panel, 39 by 50½ in. (Fitzwilliam Museum, Cambridge)

B—*The Holy Trinity*, by Ribera.   Canvas, 7 ft. 5 in. by 6 ft. (Prado)

A—*Christ bearing the Cross*, by Francisco Ribalta, 1612.   Canvas, 84 by 43½ in.   (National Gallery)

B—*The Immaculate Conception* (called *la Grande*), by Murillo. Canvas, 14 ft. 4 in. by 9 ft. 6 in. (Seville Museum)

A—*St. Paul Hermit*, by Ribera, 1649. Canvas, 56 in. square. (Prado).

B—St. Bonaventure as a child presented to St. Francis, by Herrera the Elder

A—The Martyrdom of St. Andrew, by J. de las Roelas. 17 ft. by 11 ft. 4 in. (Seville Museum)

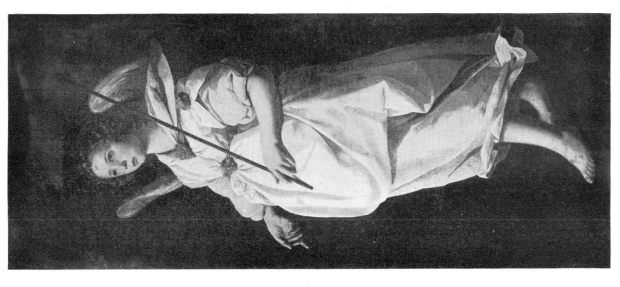

B—*The Angel Gabriel*, by Zurbaran. Canvas, 57 by 24 in. (Montpellier Museum)

A—*Gonzalo de Illecas, Bishop of Cordova*, by Zurbaran, 1639. Canvas. (Guadaloupe)

B—*Portrait of a Lady*, by Alonzo Sanchez Coello. Panel, 26½ by 22 in.
(Prado)

A—*A Knight of Santiago*, by Pacheco, 1626. Canvas, 22½ by 18¼ in.
(Sir Herbert Cook, Bart.)

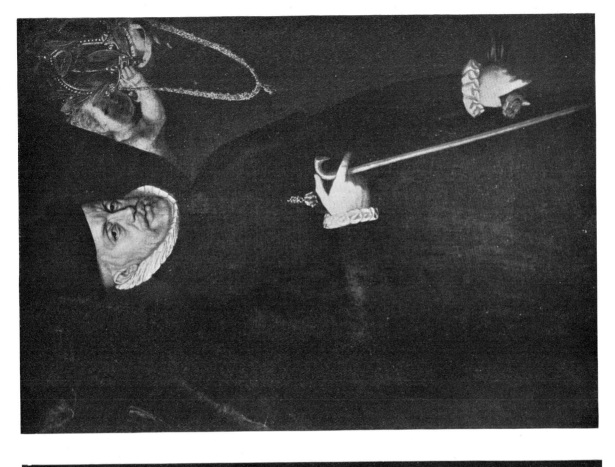

B—*Philip II of Spain*, by Pantoja de la Cruz. Canvas, 47 by 35½ in. (Ehrich Galleries, New York)

A—*Portrait of a Young Man*, by Alonzo Sanchez Coello.   Canvas, 42 by 31 in. (National Gallery of Ireland, Dublin)

The Inquisitor General Don Fernando Niño de Guevara, by El Greco, 1596-1600. Canvas, 48 by 42½ in. (Havemeyer Collection, New York)

A—Baptism of Christ, by El Greco, 1595-1600?
Canvas, 11 ft. 6 in. by 4 ft. 9 in. (Prado)

B—The Assumption of the Virgin, by El Greco, 1608-13.
Canvas, 10 ft. 7 in. by 5 ft. 6 in. (S. Vincente, Toledo)

B—*Portrait of a Man*, by El Greco. Canvas, 25¼ by 21¼ in. (Prado)

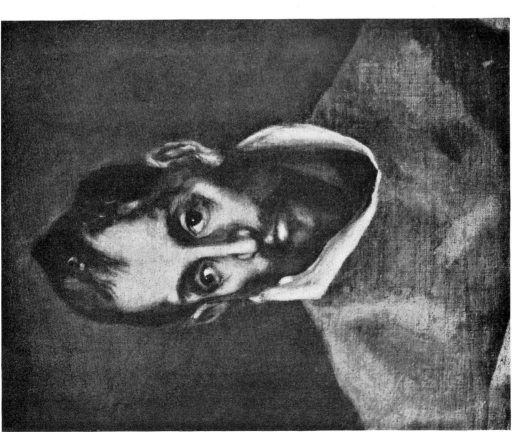

A—*St. Bartholomew*, by El Greco, 1600-4 (?). Canvas, 18⅞ in. by 15 3/16 in. (Mr. J. Goudstikker)

A—Allegory of the Recovery of San Salvador (detail), by Mayno. Canvas. (Prado)

B—In the Garden of the Villa Medici, Rome, by Velazquez, 1650-1. Canvas. 19 by 16½ in. (Prado)

Adoration of the Kings, by Velazquez, 1619. Canvas, 6 ft. 8 in. by 4 ft. 1¼ in. (Prado)

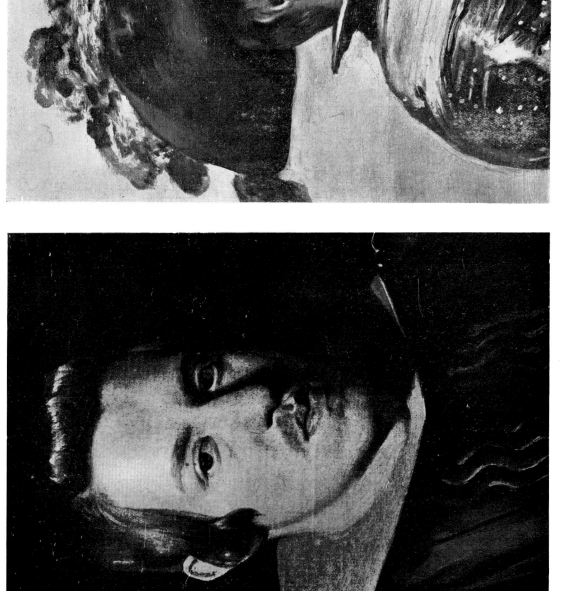

B—*Philip IV*, by Velazquez. *c.* 1636. Detail of equestrian portrait. (Prado)

A—The *Infante Don Carlos*, by Velazquez. *c.* 1626. Detail. (Prado)

A—The Dwarf " El Primo," by Velazquez, 1644. Detail. (Prado)

B—The Infanta Doña Margarita, by Velazquez, *c.* 1660. Detail. (Prado)

B—The Queen Mother Doña Mariana of Austria, by Carreño.   Canvas, 72 by 52 in.   (Alte Pinakothek, Munich)

A—The Infanta Doña Margarita, by J. B. del Mazo.   Canvas, 6 ft. 11 in. by 4 ft. 6 in.   (Prado)

Doña Maria Teresa Apodaca de Sesma, by Goya; *c.* 1787. Canvas, 50½ by 38 in. (Messrs. Lewis and Simmons)

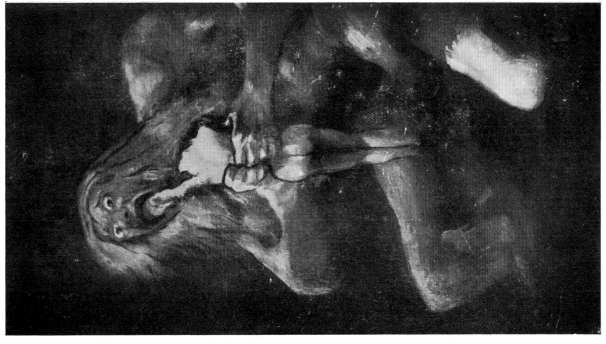

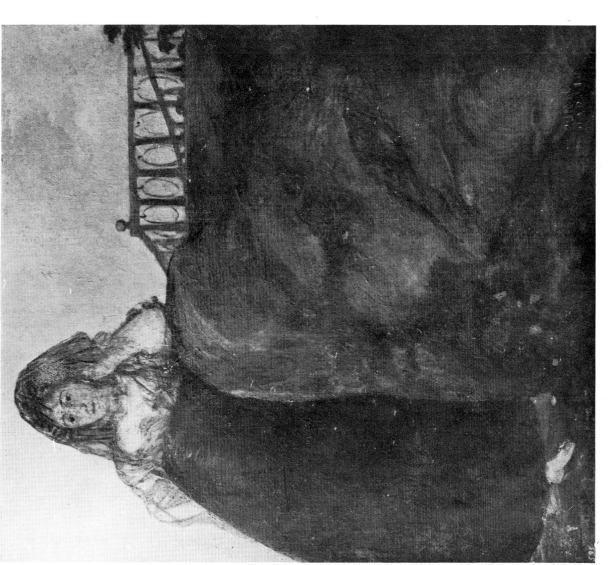

A—*Manola*, by Goya; after 1815. 58 by 52 in.   B—*Saturn devouring his Sons*, by Goya; after 1815. 57½ by 32¾ in.

Wall paintings in oil, transferred to canvas; removed from Goya's dining-room. (Prado)

A—*Vision of S. Isidro's Fair*, by Goya; after 1815. 4 ft. 7 in. by 14 ft. 4½ in.

B—*Fantastic Vision*, by Goya; after 1815. 4 ft. 0½ in. by 8 ft. 9 in.
Wall paintings in oil, transferred to canvas; removed from Goya's dining-room. (Prado)

SCULPTURE. *By Geoffrey Webb*

THE importance given in the following account of Spanish Sculpture to works of the Romanesque and early Gothic periods, before the art could be said to have developed any distinctively national characteristics, may seem to call for some apology. But in the opinion of the writer, the scarcity of books upon this subject and its almost complete neglect in England—there is only one book on Spanish Sculpture published in London—justify him in making æsthetic importance his first consideration. To do this, it has often been necessary to interpret the word Spanish in little more than a geographical sense. For it cannot be maintained that these early works have anything of the characteristic Spanish religiosity of the fifteenth century and post-Renaissance carvings, with their wealth of sensational detail calculated to stir the emotions of the devout. Some critics have claimed another quality as Spanish, an inherent feeling for formal relations, which persists in many works of even the most extravagantly devotional periods; and this quality, common to almost all European work of the Romanesque period, may perhaps be traced in its especially Spanish manifestation in some of the twelfth and thirteenth-century tombs. But it would be dishonest not to acknowledge at the outset that the best periods of sculpture in Spain, or at any rate those most æsthetically sympathetic to us, are in some ways the least characteristically Spanish.

There exist in Spain a number of sculptures of pre-Roman date, of which the bust known as *The Lady of Elche* now in the Louvre is the most famous. Allied to this work and cut in the same limestone, though of a much less elaborate and sophisticated technique, are the figurines from Cerro de Los Santos now in the Archæological Museum at Madrid. These monuments have aroused great interest, and many suggestions as to Greek and Phœnician influences have been made. They remain, however, a comparatively isolated phenomenon.

THE VISIGOTHIC PERIOD.—The real precursor of the Spanish art of the Mediæval period is that strongly Byzantinesque culture which seems to have flourished in Spain and immediately to the north of the Pyrenees in the Dark Ages. In Spain this culture is generally called Visigothic. We have plenty of evidence of the intimate relations of the Spanish Church in the period preceding the Moorish invasions with the Eastern Empire, and to these Byzantinizing influences must be added a certain amount of commerce via Barcelona and Cartagena, and direct contact in the period following the reconquest of Southern Spain by Justinian's generals. Even after the Moorish conquests this culture would seem to have persisted on both sides of the Pyrenees until it merged gradually with that Catalonian-Languedoc " civilization " discussed below. The monuments that survive from it belong more properly to the history of architecture than sculpture, and are so treated in this book. Mention must be made, however, of the low relief figures at San Miguel de Linio, though these have been assigned by some authorities to a date as late as the twelfth century.

THE ROMANESQUE PERIOD.—At the beginnings of considerable sculpture in Spain, in the Romanesque era, it is necessary to distinguish the two cultural regions into which South Western Europe was divided, rather than to confuse the issues by adopting relatively modern national units and speaking of Spain and France as we now understand them. These regions are the Plateau and the north-west, including Aragon, León, Asturias, and Galicia and, later, Castile on the one hand, and Catalonia-Languedoc, including a good part of Southern France as far as the Rhône on the east and almost to the Dordogne to the north on the other. The former region, arid and inhospitable, essentially

47

non-commercial, its politics and society dominated by the continual warfare with the Moors, is in the strongest contrast with the lush Mediterranean commercial culture of Catalonia-Languedoc, where wealthy seaport towns, as Barcelona and Montpellier, fellows with Pisa and Genoa in the trade with the Levant, and a feudal nobility, with their fingers in every pie of the Crusading movement, were open to every influence of Byzantium Italy and the East. This Catalonian-Languedoc culture, of which Troubadour poetry is the literary product and the Albigensian Heresy the theological, produced in the visual arts the Romanesque sculpture of Toulouse, Moissac and so many " Spanish " churches. In the region of the Plateau, in the north-west of which, if anywhere, the Visigothic tradition may have lingered, the influence of this school is paramount in sculpture, though other influences are claimed here and there, and may be examined as they occur.

The history of sculpture in Mediæval Spain is so largely a matter of disentangling these influences that some attention must be given to the vehicles by which they passed. In the Romanesque period, before the emergence of the Gothic of the Ile-de-France as a dominating style in the later thirteenth century, the various regional schools seem to have interacted upon each other mainly by the circulation of works of the minor arts, such as ivories, illuminated manuscripts, and metalwork. For example, the all-important Byzantine influence was transmitted largely by the traffic in such objects, especially ivories. Indeed, the importance of these minor arts can hardly be exaggerated in this connexion, to quote a recent authority : " Books from the East, especially sacred books, were regarded as authorities ; sacred designs were not made up at will, but were handed forward as traditions." As to the question of the movement of the actual artists themselves, this is difficult to treat shortly. Undoubtedly society in the Middle Ages was much less static than has often been supposed : among the factors making for movement must be accounted the patronage of the great " international " figures of the Church, and the influence of the example of magnificence set by the great monastic centres, such as Cluny—the sculptures of the twelfth century at Malmesbury, Wiltshire, for instance, are of purely Burgundian character, and so unlike any other work in England as to suggest the actual presence of foreign artists. It has been suggested that craftsmen from comparatively free municipalities, such as the Italian towns, and to these must be added the French communes on the Royal territory at a later date, were at greater liberty to travel than those attached to the great monastic establishments. This must have been true in the main, but should be modified to some extent by considerations as to the nature of such organizations as those of Cluny and Cîteaux. In Spain the influence of the great Pilgrimage Road to Santiago de Compostela is a special factor to be added to these other more general considerations.

Returning to the Minor Arts, the importance of Byzantine ivories has already been emphasized, and mention of the Rhineland of the " Othonian Renaissance," a strongly Byzantinesque movement, must not be omitted as a source both of metalwork and ivories. Certain notable objects must be noticed individually as the ivory Crucifix of León and the Crucifixes of the Cid preserved at Salamanca, all very Byzantine in style. One authority attributes the excellence of the León ivory and those of San Millan de Cogalla to Moorish influence. The same authority sees German influence in an ivory Arca, also at San Millan, and in the more famous Arca Santa at Oviedo (*c.* 1075). Among the treasures from the monastery of Santo Domingo de Silos, near Burgos, are several small caskets of ivory of Spanish Moslem origin, one of which belonged to the Caliph Abd-er-Rahman III in the early tenth century, while another bears a representation of a Mussulman; with these must be taken the casket made for Almagueira, son of Abd-er-Rahman III, now in the Louvre. These Spanish Moslem ivories reinforced the influence of direct importations from the Eastern Empire and contributed towards the marked Byzantine character of the art of the Catalonia-Languedoc region—though it would be hard to explain the domed churches which are a feature of this part (Toro and Zamora are Spanish examples[1]) without supposing some more direct influences than those of the minor arts. The sculptures of Moissac are agreed to have been influenced by this Spanish Moslem ivory work, as well as the related work at Santo Domingo de Silos. The importance of the cloister sculptures of the latter church [PLATE 1, A and C] has been emphasized by Mr. Kingsley Porter as one of the earliest works of the first rank. He dates them in the last third of the eleventh century, and suggests a direct relation with Monte Cassino comparable with that of Cluny with the same fountain head. This would lend the Santo Domingo sculptures an importance relative to the whole south-western school which continental authorities show no signs of admitting. The capitals in this cloister must also be noted.

To the first half of the twelfth century belong the earlier works at Santiago de Compostela, i.e., the Puerta de Platerias (*c.* 1140), and possibly some work at San Isidoro de León. The Santiago sculptures bear distinct resemblance to those of Saint Sernin de Toulouse. The portico of Ripoll [PLATE 1, B] seems also of the twelfth century, albeit the building was begun as early as 1017. But the most famous monument of the period is the Puerta de Gloria at Santiago, signed and dated 1168 to 1188, as the work of the master Matteo. This popular '' masterpiece '' is the darling of antiquarians, not only by reason of its date and signature, but for the remarkable realistic and dramatic qualities of the individual figures, in which it seems to foreshadow what were to be the most persistent, if not the most admirable, characteristics of later Spanish sculpture. Its derivatives, the *Apostles* of the Camera Santa at Oviedo [PLATE 2] share these qualities to some extent, and are acclaimed by certain authorities as the best examples of true '' Spanish '' work of this period extant. The Oviedo figures have the advantage over their prototypes at Santiago in several respects, notably in architectural disposition. Santiago was the goal of the great Pilgrimage (the importance of which in the history of the art of this time has recently attracted the attention it deserves), and was in consequence enormously rich. The Puerta de Gloria is a typical piece of Cluniac expensiveness comparable with the adornment of some of the Burgundian Churches and against which the Puritan Saint Bernard was shortly to lead the Cistertian reaction. This blemish—'' expensiveness ''—is, of course, most apparent in the ensemble of the Gloria, but the individual figures also fall below the æsthetic standard set by contemporary work elsewhere. We may contrast with them the figures from the south door of San Vincente d'Avila [PLATES 3, A and B] dating from the turn of the century (1200). A variety of influences has been suggested for these outstanding works—more especially the *Annunciation* group —as Burgundy and Poitou (Mayer and Enlart) and Burgundy and Matteo (Porter), and an almost equal diversity of opinion is found in regard to the western door of the same church. The two capitals from Santa Maria de

[1] A most interesting essay on the specially Oriental tendencies of these Douro Valley buildings is contained in '' Art Studies by Members of the Universities of Harvard and Princeton,'' 1926. Among other questions discussed is the curious problem of the canopy of the Templars' Tomb at Zamora (see below and Plate 5, A).

Alabanza, now in the Fogg Museum, U.S.A. [PLATE 4] are dated 1185. They would seem to have affinities with the contemporary work at Santiago, but are more satisfactory as being less " slick."[2]

The knight's tomb in the Templars' Church of the Magdalena at Zamora [PLATES 5, A and B] is another work of the first rank. M. Enlart suggests associations with various Burgundian church details as regards some parts of the architecture of the tomb. There is a castellated and arcaded canopy, markedly Byzantine in character, supported on short fluted columns straight and twisted. Altogether the effect is strangely exotic, suggesting as a whole if any one region, South Italian or Sicilian eclecticism translated into the plainer Spanish materials.[3] Opinions are united, however, in praising the result, and M. Dieulafoy is at one with Mr. Fry's " everywhere there was a choice of proportion in the different elements and of relief in the carvings which indicated some greatly daring and original genius."

In the cloister chapels of the old cathedral of Salamanca are a series of tombs dating from the twelfth and thirteenth centuries of great merit, in a distinctively local tradition described as lacking the elegance of contemporary French work, but of a massive and sombre power. Some of these Salamanca tombs retain their original painting, and M. Dieulafoy cites their yellow, black and white with touches of red and green—the gold has probably disappeared—as showing the range of colouring of the period. An earlier range of colours is given by the frescoes at León, red-brown, yellow ochre, indigo, black and white. The present colouring of the Puerta de Gloria is of the seventeenth century, according to the same authority.

To treat of polychromy here with special reference to wooden figure sculpture may, perhaps, give a wrong impression. Painting of sculpture, both wood and stone, was almost universal in the Middle Ages, but it is impossible, partly owing to the nature of the surfaces, not to associate the practice in a special sense with the wooden figures and groups. M. Dieulafoy, in his great book " La Statuaire Polychrome en Espagne," has traced the whole history of this subject at length, and explained the processes involved and the division of labour between the carvers and painters, which latter in the later Middle Ages were subdivided into several different crafts, as Encarnadores or flesh painters, Estofadores and Doradores, stuff painters and gilders. It is in the work of these painting crafts that the Moorish influence is most clearly to be traced; indeed it is the Spanish preoccupation with surface texture, which is directly attributable to Moorish influences, which has gone far towards making polychrome sculpture seem peculiarly their art. Apropos of this oriental influence on the surface treatment of polychrome figures, we may here take out of due order the observations of M. Dieulafoy on the colour treatment of the *Entombment* group of Perpignan, a Catalan work of the fourteenth century:

> " Il ne s'agit plus de ces tons plats ou de ces larges parties dorées que l'on remarque sur les sculptures du Musée de Léon ou sur les tombeaux de la vielle cathédral de Salamanque; . . . les fonds des étoffes sont constituées par de fines rayures où l'or alterne avec l'ochre jaune, le brun rouge ou l'indigo."

He goes on to compare this with the Persian decoration of the Mihrab of the Mosque of Cordova, and concludes:

---

[2] The inscriptions on the Capitals has been read as follows: On the Majesty Capital—Petrus Caro Prior/ (f) ecit ista eclesia et domus et claustra et omnia que a b e fudat (is? omnia quæ videte ab eorum fundamentis) (Era MCXXIII i.e., A.D., 1185). On the Maries Capital—Isto arco feci Rodericus Gustiutus (?) Vir valde bonus /Milite orate pro ilo; and on the sepulchre itself—Simile sepulcro DN Quado. For these readings I am indebted to Professor Tremlow, of Liverpool, and Professor Porter.

[3] This suggestion is made merely as a descriptive comparison.—G. W.

" Il se pourrait qu'au nombre des emprunts si multiples et si variés faits par les Espagnols à leurs voisins Musulmanes, il convienne de ranger cette manière d'utiliser l'or dans la decoration, comme il faut y mettre les damas sompteux, qui de la Perse où ils etaient tissés, se répandirent sur l'Europe et dont les polychromistes reproduisirent les dispositions et les couleurs."

It must be remarked that such Persian textiles could find their way to Catalonia direct by the Barcelona trade with the Levant, at the height of its prosperity in the fourteenth century.

Of the early polychrome figures illustrated here, the noble seated Virgin [PLATE 6, A], possibly as early as the latter end of the twelfth century is of unknown origin, but the Byzantinesque treatment of the drapery has suggested Catalonia. The *Deposition* group from San Joan de las Abadesas [PLATE 7, A] is another remarkable example of the Catalonian Romanesque; it makes an interesting comparison with the similar group from San Andres Cuellar in the very heart of the Plateau region [PLATE 6, B]. One important point with regard to these early painted sculptures should be stressed here. The continuity of ecclesiastical tradition in Spain has envolved fairly frequent refurbishing and occasional added embellishment of early figures, especially such as have achieved any reputation for sanctity [see PLATE 7, B and C].

FIRST GOTHIC PERIOD.—The tombs, such as those at Salamanca mentioned above, the Zamora tomb (Porter dates this in the thirteenth century) and its companion in San Vincente d'Avila with others as the later tomb of a bishop at Tuy[4] (*c.* 1300) [PLATE 8, A] and that of Martin, first Bishop of León, in the cathedral of that city, form an almost continuous series showing the Spanish Romanesque tradition unbroken to the fourteenth century. And here may be cited the sarcophagus of St. Eulalia at Barcelona, said to show Pisan influences and dating from 1327. The new influence of the North French Gothic School first made itself felt in architecture, by the agency of the Cistercians, enemies of all decoration, and in consequence there is little sign of it in sculpture until the thirteenth century was well advanced, when it was the fully matured Gothic style that was introduced. From this period onwards the works of foreign artists are often better documented in Spain than in the countries of their origin.

It is a feature of the Spanish Gothic sculpture that it is, by a North French standard, very up to date. Mayer compares the work at Burgos of about 1275 in this respect with the far more provincial character of contemporary sculpture at Nüremburg and Bamberg; and Professor Lethaby sees resemblance in the Apostle door of the same church to Amiens and Rheims. Again the late thirteenth-century sculptures at León, according to Mayer by a group of young artists allied stylistically to the masters of Bourges, are acclaimed (especially the Righteous in the Resurrection Tympanum) by French authorities as one of the masterpieces of French sculpture. The nine of the Apostles on the façade at Tarragona, which were carved by a Catalan master, Bartolomé, in 1287, are similarly abreast of the movement. This work was completed a hundred years later by another Catalan, Jaime de Castayls. The work of such Spanish followers of French masters spread over Castile in the course of the fourteenth century, for example, Vittoria and the North Porch of the cathedral of Toledo, and Navarre, where Pamplona can show an almost complete series covering all phases of fourteenth-century work [PLATE 8, B]. As examples of

4 It is interesting to note the coincidence that at or about the date of this tomb with its archaic character flourished Luke, Bishop of Tuy who, between 1260 and 80, wrote a tract against the Albigenses and expressed in it strong but reactionary views on art. (See Coulton *Social Life in Britain,* pp. 474-5.) The Bishop especially condemns the new fangled practice of portraying our Lord on the cross with crossed feet. Does this shed any light on the date of the San Joan *Deposition* group (PLATE 7, A).

true Spanish work of the earlier Gothic period Mayer gives the great doors of Sasamon bei Burgos and Burgo de Osma, and to these, as an example of full fourteenth-century work, may be added the *Entombment* group of Perpignan. As to polychromy, a series of figures in the cloister of Pamplona show two tints added to the range of the Salamanca tombs, a clear blue and a wine red.

SECOND GOTHIC PERIOD.—Up to the beginning of the fifteenth century the interest of Spanish sculpture has been divided between architectural, or façade sculpture, and church furniture, such as tombs and the more rarely surviving wood polychrome figures and groups. The distinction may be compared with that between fresco and easel painting. From now on we shall be increasingly preoccupied with the church furniture, to which category two new classes of objects must be added, the Retable or Altar Screen and the new fashioned elaborate Choir Stalls. The churches have embarked on that career of accumulation of " bric-a-brac of all ages which a Spanish church collects, as a caddis worm does pebbles." Two generalizations may be exploited here by way of explanation of this change in the direction of sculpture. Of these the first is the general change in the relation of the church and the layman which becomes patent in the later fourteenth and the fifteenth centuries. The layman *vis-à-vis* the church has an increased importance, the church must lay herself out to cater for him, and his gifts to the church are of a more personal character. Hence the vogue of chantries and side chapels and church furniture generally, which is, of course, not confined to Spain. It is in this characteristic of the importance of the individual that the fifteenth century is one with the Renaissance age that succeeded it, quite irrespective of any revival of interest in the antique or any influence from Italy. The change accompanies the growing commercial wealth of this period, and in Spain, Barcelona and Valencia were enjoying an unparalleled prosperity in the fifteenth century ; it is worth remarking in this connexion that Catalonia is noted as possessing the most numerous, as well as the earliest, and some of the richest examples of the characteristic late Gothic Spanish Retables. The second suggestion is, that as Spanish architecture absorbed the foreign styles the well-known national tendency to reduce decoration to a mere enrichment of surface began to drive the best sculptors into the interiors of the churches, there to carve groups and scenes illustrating Bible stories and lives of the Saints. This characteristic tendency of Spanish art has been noted above, and its usual attribution to Moorish influence mentioned. Again it may be noted that Catalonia is acknowledged to have been more receptive of these influences than the other Spanish Kingdoms. Similar commercial prosperity and preponderant Moorish influence was to be found in fifteenth-century Seville, where the Andalusian School, so celebrated later, originated in a late Gothic " bric-a-brac " sculpture of the most extravagant type. The High Altar of Seville, designed by Dancart in 1483, and executed by his pupils Marco and Bernardo Ortega, still shows, in spite of sixteenth-century modifications, the characteristic Spanish qualities raised to their highest power, in its Moorish treatment of the Gothic decorative motifs and its expensive architectural irrelevance.

These Retables or Altar Screens are not, of course, exclusively Spanish, but in Spain they enjoyed a popularity and were constructed on a scale, and with a magnificence, that seem to make them peculiarly her own. The Retable is said to have developed from the small portable carved Diptych or Triptych passing through a stage when a larger variant was used by priests as a kind of camp-altar for ministering to the armies in the field. They are, therefore, it

is added, intimately bound up with the most cherished religio-military traditions
of Spain. The earliest Retables, as that of St. Feliu at Gerona still shows,
retained structural reminiscences of the Triptych form in the division into a
centre piece and two wings and in other details.

The use of the expression " bric-a-brac " as above must not be taken as
any indication of size. The great Retables of Tarragona, the Capilla Mayor,
and the Seo at Zaragoza are enormous, many of the complex reliefs being life-
size, as that of the centre panel at the Seo [PLATE 9, A]. The Tarragona
and Seo screens are of alabaster richly coloured and gilded. It was at
this time that the subdivision of polychrome crafts was made (see above
p. 50), and the whole industry most carefully regulated under the Catholic
kings. The works of the fifteenth century are all very well documented
and the various craftsmen's names recorded, and there follow in natural course
from this a great many nice points of attribution which it will be impossible to
enter into here. The reader will find them all set forth in M. Dieulafoy's great
book. In respect of authorship, the Tarragona and Zaragoza screens may be
taken together. The first is the work of Pedro Juan de Valogona, a Catalan,
assisted by Guilermo de la Monta ; Pedro Juan worked on the screen from 1426-
36, when his assistant carried on the work to completion. The second screen
was finished in part in 1447 and completed after an interval in 1480 ; it was also
begun by a Catalan of the name of Pedro Juan. These two artists are identified
by some authorities, but Dieulafoy will not allow this, stating that the work of
Pedro Juan at Tarragona was cut short in 1436 by his death, and adding that
the particulars in respect of this screen are very precise. Mayer, who clings to
the identification, attributes the centre relief at Zaragoza [PLATE 9, A] to a
German master (Meister Hans aus Schwabische-Gmund). I have gone into
greater detail in respect of these two important screens than will be possible
in succeeding cases, in order to show the more defined issues that arise with
these fifteenth-century works.

At Toledo there are two early Retables of about 1420, which were coloured
by a painter called Juan Alfon ; and there is a more important work, dating
from the latter end of the century, by Sancho de Zamora, Juan de Segovia and
Pedro Gumiel, whose names go to show that Catalonia had by no means a
monopoly in the execution of Retables. In the same chapel are tombs ordered
in 1489 by a sculptor, Pablo Ortiz, whose name should not be omitted. The
Retable itself is claimed as showing signs of the new Flemish influence, of which
Toledo was one of the most important centres. The list of masters employed
on the external sculpture of the cathedral clearly shows the incoming of the
Flemings. At the opening of the century we find such names as Ruiz Martinez
and Diaz, and in 1425 these are replaced by a staff under the direction of
Alonso Gomez, but between 1459 and 1466 the names appear of Guas (Was)
and the brothers Egas (Hantje van der Eycken), of whom the most eminent was
Annequin Egas, afterwards raised to the position of architect to the Chapter.
This Flemish invasion was doubtless furthered by the Royal inter-marriages,
which brought first Portugal and then Spain into touch with Burgundy and the
Low Countries ; but it should be noted that already in the fourteenth century
Flemish sculptors had invaded France, and Huy, Valenciennes, Cambrai, Liège,
etc., appear as the places of origin of sculptors at work on French buildings of
the period. The school of Burgundy also rose to prominence in the latter part
of the fourteenth century, to which time belong the celebrated tombs of Jean
Sans Peur and Philip le Hardi by Claus Sluter, now at Dijon. Burgundian

sculptors are found alongside the Flemish and German masters in Spain towards the end of the fifteenth century.   The earliest Flemish master to visit Spain was the painter Jan van Eyck in 1428 ; the sculptors began to appear a little later, as we have seen at Toledo.   But from the middle of the century onwards they increase in numbers rapidly and are found at Burgos—notably a family from Cologne—Valencia and Seville, and the surname Aleman is continually appearing in the documents.   Among the works either by Flemings or most strongly influenced by them, the Retable from the Convent of San Francisco now in the Museum of Valladolid must be mentioned.   It is quite un-Spanish in character, its sensational realism appears quite devoid of any redeeming formal merits, and its Gothic decorative part entirely lacking the " Arabesque " quality so marked in the High Altar we have noticed at Seville.   These unamiable qualities of Flemish fifteenth-century work reinforced already existing tendencies in the Spanish masters and found a ready following among them, though in justice it must be said that the distinction suggested above is generally valid.   Of purely Spanish sculptors of the end of the fifteenth century the most important is Gil de Siloe.   His great works are the Retable of the Cartuja de Miraflores at Burgos and the Sepulchros de los Reyes in the same church, with which is included the wall tomb of the Prince Alonso.   A similar wall tomb, only less sumptuous than Prince Alonso's, is now in the Burgos Museum ; it commemorates Juan de Padilla, a Royal favourite, and is attributed by Dieulafoy to Gil de Siloe.   Two tombs at South Kensington are also attributed to him [PLATE 10, A].   Gil de Siloe is strongly influenced by the Flemish fashion and his nationality has even been called in question, but it is admitted that his work shows the characteristic Spanish quality in the use of ornament.   A certain heaviness in his work, remarked by Dieulafoy in comparing him with his immediate predecessors, might also be taken as confirming his nationality.

FIRST RENAISSANCE.—In the last years of the fifteenth century the first signs of the coming Italian influence may be detected.   The work of Damian Forment of Valencia carries us well into the sixteenth century, but it is convenient to treat of him there, as his assured works shows the persistence of the flamboyant Gothic manner, at any rate in the architectural part, even in the face of direct contact with Italy.   The subdivision of labour on the great Retables among artists of different crafts may help to explain this trait as easily as hieratic conservatism ; it may well be that such a man as Damian Forment could not get subordinates for the architectural parts of his Retables who were able to work in any other but the inherited Gothic tradition.   Forment's native place Valencia was at this time in great prosperity and its relations with Italy particularly close.   The influence of Boccaccio and Petrarch on Valencian men of letters has been remarked before his day, and it need only be mentioned here that it was from the Valencia district that the Borgia family derived. Forment himself served an apprenticeship in Italy, it was long said as a pupil of Donatello ; but the established date of his return to Spain, 1509, most probably still a young man, almost finally disposes of this theory.   Immediately on his return he was commissioned to design the Retable of the Pilar at Zaragoza, which he completed eleven years later.   It is to this period of his return that M. Dieulafoy attributes the tomb of the Marquis Vasquez d'Arco at Siguenza [PLATE 10, B], which he gives to Forment in spite of certain difficulties as to dates.   Three more Retables are known to be the work of this master, those of San Pablo at Zaragoza, Huesca and Veluta d'Ebro, of which that of Huesca is perhaps the most notable and the most Italianate.   Forment died about the year 1535, and from the size of the fortune he left it is to be surmised that much of the anonymous work in his manner must be attributed directly to him.

Contemporary with Damian Forment were a number of sculptors working at Seville, representing both the dominating influences that ultimately went to form the post-Renaissance and Baroque-Spanish styles. Of these the most important is Pedro Millan, a pupil of Nufro Sanchez, the colleague of Dancart mentioned above. He appears first in 1505, and from that date onwards there survive a number of his works, of which the most famous is the Virgen del Pilar. He shows a strongly marked Flemish influence, which persisted in Seville longer than elsewhere in Spain, in spite of the importation of both artists and finished works from Italy. Of the Italians at Seville one of the earliest was Miguel, the Florentine, who was employed on the woodwork of the cathedral early in the last third of the fifteenth century, and continued to work for the Chapter until well into the sixteenth, when he was succeeded by his son. Another Italian early in Seville was Francisco Niculoso Pisano, by whom there is an altar signed and dated 1503. And lastly there is Pietro Torrigiano, well known in England, who came to Seville by way of Granada and settled there, dying in 1522. Only one authentic work of his remains, the St. Jerome in the Museum of Seville. It is this piece which Goya described as the " best piece of modern sculpture there is in Spain." Of the importation of finished works from Italy, Vasari mentions several by Luca della Robbia and a large bronze bas relief by Antonio Palladio.

Of the three great Italianizing sculptors of the early sixteenth century, Philip Borgona, Alonso Berruguete and Bartolomé Ordonez, it will be convenient to take Philip Borgona first, for, as far as we know, he never left Spain, and the full Italian influence did not come upon him until his career was well advanced. Philip Vigarni, his real name, came of a Burgundian family settled at Burgos, where he had already achieved a considerable reputation before he was chosen to design and supervise the Great Retable of the Cathedral of Toledo just before the turn of the century. This work, the largest of the Spanish Retables, he undertook with a large staff of collaborators, and had it completed in the fullest flamboyant Gothic style by 1505. Not long after he executed the bas reliefs of the Trassagrario (reverse of the High Altar) at Burgos. In these, though still Gothic in the main, the Italian influence has made a distinct appearance. By the date of the Retable of the Royal Chapel at Granada, undertaken 1520, the Italianizing process is almost complete ; already there seems a touch of the Michael Angelesque in some of the figures, which anticipates the collaboration with Berruguete on the Choir Stalls of Toledo to be completed in 1543. This late date has been given as that of the death of Philip Borgona, but M. Dieulafoy evidently does not accept this, as he is inclined to assign the Retable of the Chapel of the Condestable to him at a later date.

HIGH RENAISSANCE.—With the names of Michael Angelo and Berruguete we are brought to one of the most remarkable and influential figures in the history of Spanish sculpture. Alonso Berruguete was born about 1480, the son of a painter ; on his father's death he went to Italy and there he came under the influence of Michael Angelo. His return from Italy was in 1520 and in the same year Charles V appointed him Royal Sculptor and Painter, an exceedingly influential position. Berruguete's works are spread over the length and breadth of Spain, and it would seem as if fate had marked him out to set the standard and fashion for all Spanish sculpture after him. The earliest works of the first importance are those undertaken from the Monastery of San Benito Real at

Valladolid (1526), of which fragments are now in the museum there [PLATE 11, A]. The Choir Stalls from the same church also in the museum are now said to be the work of another sculptor, Andres de Najera (1520), but some of the fragments illustrated are extremely like Berruguete's work and the long standing attribution to him is readily understandable. Of his other works the Toledo Choir Stalls have already been mentioned, and to them must be added the tombs of Juan de Rojas and his wife at Valencia and that of Archbishop Tavera, the friend of Greco, at Toledo as examples of his work in stone.

Berruguete's exaggerated Michael Angelesque style was to be the determining influence on Spanish sculpture from this time onward. A variety of reasons for this suggest themselves. In the first place the violent emotional and dramatic possibilities of the Michael Angelesque manner appealed to the Spanish temperament, as the sensational realism of the Flemings had done in the century before, and lent itself readily to the " impressive " illustrational requirements of the churchmen of the day, while at the same time it was of the most unimpeachable Italian Renaissance " chic." Secondly, in the words of Mr. Fry, " The Spanish Altar builders seized with avidity on the poses of Michael Angelo's figures as the readiest language for emphatic gesture and florid ornamentation combined. It was a wonderfully useful formula ; these declamatory poses suggest an easy striking rhythm for the opulent gilt and coloured draperies, and the saliencies are strong enough to hold amidst the elaborate Barockery of the architectural setting." If the word " Barockery " is taken to mean as much the accumulation of fifteenth-century carving as the later Renaissance work which it more strictly implies, this suggestion will go far to explain the immediate success of Berruguete's style as its persistence. As to Berruguete himself, few critics, I think, would quarrel with the dictum of the same writer, " Berruguete seemed to me always highly competent, always effective, and little else."

A little aside from the main current of the Spanish Renaissance in the purity of his Italianiate style was Bartolomé Ordonez, the Catalan sculptor of the Royal Tombs at Granada. These are the tombs of Ferdinand and Isabella and of Philip the Handsome and Juana la Loca, and with them must be taken that of Don Juan in the Church of St. Thomas at Avila. These tombs have been assigned to Domenico Alessandro, the Florentine, who designed that of the Cardinal Ximenes in the Cathedral of Alcalá de Henares. But Domenico Alessandro, who may have been the master of Ordonez, is said to have died in 1520, in which year Ordonez was sent to Italy to cut the Ximenes tomb from his design, whereas the Granada tombs were not executed until two years later. I have not seen any attempt to surmount this difficulty in the way of the Domenic Alessandro attribution. The entire question of the extent of Ordonez's work is very confused, and it has been suggested that very many stylistically similar and contemporary works at present anonymous are indeed by him. He died in 1540. With Damian Forment he represents another Italian style which could not endure against the especially favourable qualities of the Berruguete School.

The multitude of sculptors whose works are surviving and documented in Spain from the mid-sixteenth century onwards is so vast that no attempt can be made to deal with them individually ; a few of the names only can be mentioned and the main tendencies distinguished. For the study of this period Valladolid is the centre and the museum there is crowded with examples of almost every master of importance, many of whom were natives, or more or less permanent residents of the town. The two main tendencies of the period are the pure Renaissance Italian and the more Spanish over realistic over dramatic, which seems to look back to the Flemish art of the preceding century, had that not become by this time so thoroughly bone of the bone and flesh of the Spanish flesh. The persistence and continued development of the technique of poly-chromy throughout this period is perhaps the most striking evidence of how deep-rooted were these characteristics in the Spanish national taste.

The first of the contemporaries of Berruguete to be discussed here must be Gaspar Becerra, born in 1520 and died 1571. A third part of his working life seems to have been passed in Italy, and only the last twenty-one years in Spain. His style is the inevitable Michael Angelesque, exceedingly accomplished, but rather more Italian, and with little or none of the peculiar devotional quality which characterises his more important contemporaries. Becerra's most cele-brated work is perhaps his *St. Jerome* at Burgos [PLATE 11, B]. There were, of course, other purely Renaissance artists at work throughout the sixteenth cen-tury, many of them Italians by birth as well as training; of such were the Leoni family, one of whom, Pompeo Leoni, was the author of the Charles V and Philip II groups in bronze at the Escorial. In Juan Juni (1507-77) and Tordesillas, whose work is often confused with that of Juni [PLATES 12, and 13, C], we find the real Spanish use of the Berruguete formulas. Juan Juni is more thorough going than Berruguete in his exaggeration of gesture, and with this carries realism in detail of the pathetic-sensational order as far as any fifteenth-century Fleming. There is indeed a question whether he was not of Burgundian origin, and it is almost certain that he never went to Italy. The celebrated *Entombment* at Segovia [PLATE 12, B] well illustrates his characteristics. The polychromy is brilliant and much gold is used; the figure groups have completely freed them-selves from the arrangement in compartments which the Plateresque Altar builders took over from their Gothic predecessors and have become self-contain-ing compositions. In spite of his exaggeration, or rather perhaps because of it, Juan Juni appears a more considerable artist than either Berruguete or Becerra, less glib and having made the " Michael Angelism " more really his own. Men-tion must also be made, before turning to the seventeenth-century schools, of the sculpture attributed to El Greco, the two figures of *Isaiah* and *St. Simeon* in the Church of The Holy Charity at Illesas, near Toledo, and the bas relief at the base of the marble fronton of his *Casting lots for Christ's garments* in the sacristy of the Cathedral at Toledo [PLATE 13, A].

BAROQUE.—The Michael Angelesque of Berruguete very soon became a " stylization " in the hands of his followers, with the exception perhaps of Becerra, who had been in Italy long enough to have lost any inherent national tendency that way, and whose work suffers in comparison with that of such men as Juan Juni for the lack of it. In Gregorio Hernández (1570-1636), a Galician, settled at Valladolid, there is a reaction towards naturalism. Hernández is still [PLATE 13, B] in the High Renaissance convention, but there is more than a foretaste of the peculiar but unsympathetic seventeenth-century quality.[5] It seems as if Hernández and his successors had broken through the last barriers of formalism in abandoning the extreme Michael Angelesque convention, only to let in the purest illustrationalism; no doubt this is unjust, and here and there among the mass produced " painted morals," seminary pietists and saccharine sweet Immaculatas works of formal merit may still be found; there are, indeed,

---

[5] In the works of Hernández the art of polychromy reaches its last phase. Juan Juni and his contemporaries had still retained a certain formal quality in the magnificence of their gilt draperies, but with the seventeenth century this disappears and nothing pleases but the purest naturalism. There are extant instructions from Hernández to his polychromist minutely detailing the complexions of his figures with regard to their age, sex and character.

throughout traces of formalism in this art of the Counter Reformation, tendencies that were never lost until the days of the mechanical dolls with eyes and mouths that really move, real hair and real dresses, and little glass bead drop tears wherein, in spite of the claims of historical continuity and the fascination of such oddities in the history of taste, Spanish sculpture may be allowed to cease.

Hernández founded a school at Valladolid which was in time transplanted by the Rios family to Madrid, where it lasted until the middle of the eighteenth century. The chief of these late Madrid school artists is Luis Salvador Carmona, in whom the direct line of descent from Hernández is still distinguishable. He died in 1767. Contemporary with Hernández and holding a very similar position as a link between the High Renaissance and the Baroque sculptors was Juan Martinez Montañés, the greatest figure of the Sevillan school [PLATE 14]. The origins of this school in the late fifteenth and early sixteenth centuries have already been noticed. In the mid-sixteenth century there seem to have been no outstanding figures, though the Capitan Cepada of Cordova (Montañés' native place also) should be mentioned as of the same tradition as Juan Juni. The other Sevillan sculptors of his time were more strongly Italianizing and in a more up-to-date manner than the Northern masters. Montañés is first heard of in Seville in 1582 and died there in 1649 in extreme old age, but working to the last. During this long career he was immensely productive, and an extraordinary number of his works survive, especially in Seville. Like Hernández, Montañés still retained much of the High Renaissance formal tradition, but even more than the former, he looks forward to the immediately ensuing generations; it must be admitted, however, that the " painted morals " of Montañés are of a weightier, less flighty, Baroque piety than those of his successors. Montañés founded a thriving school both in Seville and later, through a disciple, at Granada. Of the Sevillan followers the chief were Alonso Mena, Luis Ortiz and Alonso Martinez, and later, Roldan, who has the distinction of having begotten the only woman Spanish sculptor, Roldana, a most successful novelty. This talented lady married a Royal Chamberlain, was a great success both social and artistic in Madrid, and was appointed Sculptor to the Chamber in 1695. In Granada Alonso Cano (1601-67) founded a school deriving from that of his master Montañés. Cano was another romantic and successful character. Great difficulty is experienced in distinguishing his work from that of his pupils, Josef de Mora and Pedro de Mena, the more so by reason of his habit of working on his pupils' pieces either to finish them or when some difficulty had arisen. There is, in consequence, no little confusion as to the extent of his work at Granada.

C—*The Gift of the Holy Ghost at Pentecost.* Late 11th century. (Cloisters, S. Domingo de Silos)

B—*St. Peter.* 12th century. (Portico of Monastery of Ripoll)

A—*Entombment.* Late 11th century. (Cloisters, S. Domingo de Silos)

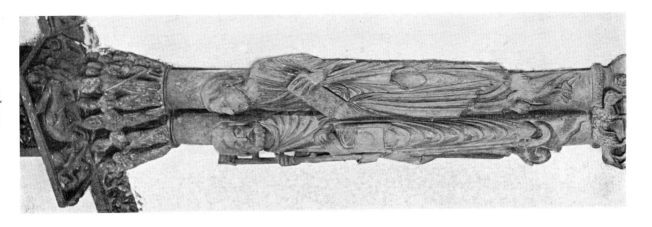

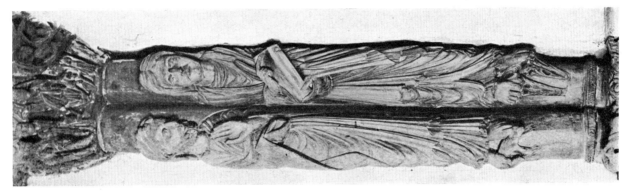

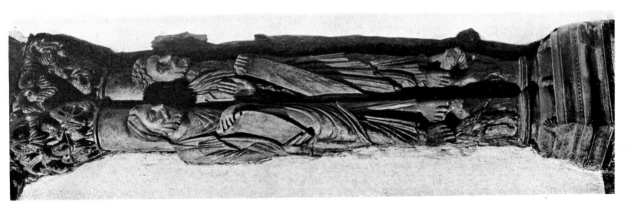

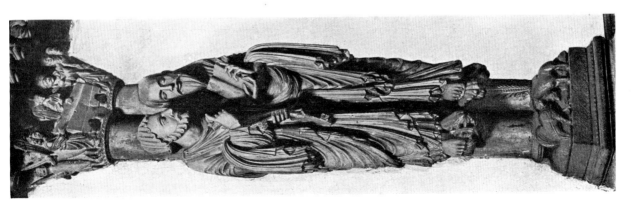

Apostles; late 12th century. Stone. (Camara Santa, Oviedo Cathedral)

B—*Queen of Sheba.* About 1200. (South Porch of S. Vincente, Avila)

A—*Annunciation.* About 1200. (South Porch of S. Vincente, Avila)

A—

B—

A—The *Majesty* capital; B—*The Marys at the Sepulchre*. Capitals, dated 1185,
from Sta. Maria de Alabanza, Palencia; 30⅜ in. by 31⅛ in. (Fogg Art Museum,
Cambridge, Mass.)

Tomb, early 13th century (?), from the Church of the Magdalena, Zamora. A—Interior of Tomb; B—Detail of *The Soul Caught up to Paradise*

B—*The Virgin and St. John Mourning.* Figures from a Crucifixion group; early 13th century. (S. Andres, Cuellar)

A—Wooden polychrome figure, Catalonian (?) Late 12th or early 13th century. Height, 25½ ins. Two views. (Messrs. Durlacher Bros.)

A—Deposition group (St. Joan de las Abadesas). Wood, 13th century

B—Crucifixion. Wood. Polychrome. (Cuellar)   *C*—Detail of *Crucifixion*

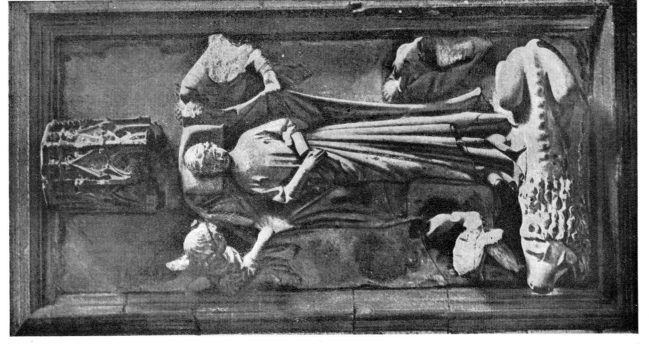

B—Tomb of Infanta Doña Blanca.   About 1400.
(Cathedral of Pamplona)

A—Tomb of a Bishop.   About 1300.   (Cathedral of Tuy)

B—*Pietà.* Wood; 15th century. (Sta. Maria de Nieva, Segovia)

A—*The Adoration of the Kings.* Alabaster, life size; *c.* 1447. Detail of a retable. (La Seo, Zaragoza)

A—Detail, attributed to Gil de Siloe, from the tomb of Don Rodrigo de Cerdanas in the Church of S. Pedro, Ocaña. (Victoria and Albert Museum)

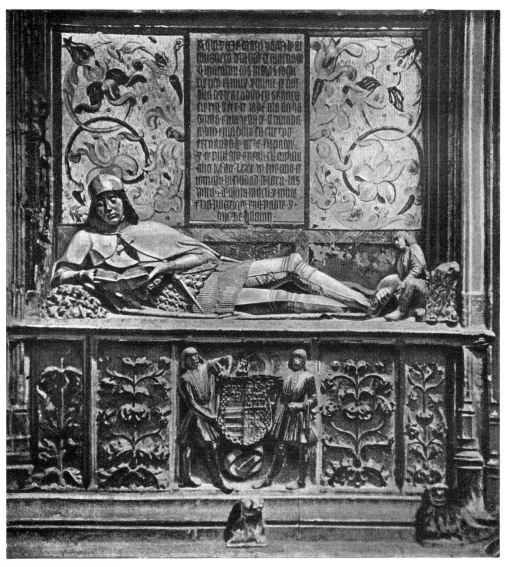

B—Tomb of the Marquess Vasquez d'Arce, attributed to Damian Forment. (Cathedral of Siguenza)

B—*St. Jerome*, by Gaspar Becerra. (Chapel of the Condestable, Burgos)

A—Fragments attributed to Berruguete. (Valladolid Museum)

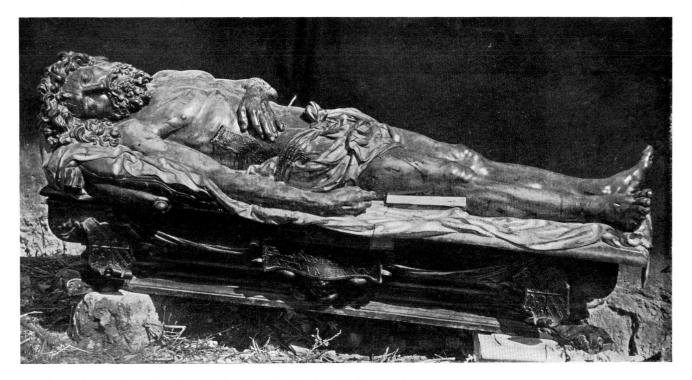

A—Christ in the Tomb, by Juan Juni. Wood. (Valladolid Museum)

B—The Entombment, by Juan Juni. (Cathedral of Segovia)

A—Sculptured ornament from fronton of *The Casting of Lots for Christ's Garments.* by Greco. (Sacristy of the Cathedral of Toledo)

B—*Baptism of Christ,* by Gregorio Hernandez, 1570-1636. (Valladolid Museum)

C—*St. Bernard,* by Gasper de Tordesilas, *fl.* 1562. (Valladolid Museum)

A—*Head of a Woman,* attributed to Montañes. (Victoria and Albert Museum)

B—*St. Francis Xavier.* School of Seville. Late 17th century. (Victoria and Albert Museum)

C—*St. Dominic de Guzman penitent,* by Montañes. Wood. (Seville Museum)

D—*St. Bruno,* by Montañes. Wood. (Seville Museum)

TEXTILES. *By A. F. Kendrick*

FOR various reasons, some of which are obvious, and none of which can suitably be discussed here, textile-patterns are very susceptible to the vicissitudes of political history. It is necessary to bear this in mind when studying the textiles of Spain, for the history of the country in mediæval times was one of continual change. Even when approached by way of historical events and documentary records the problem of identifying the textiles of Spain is peculiarly difficult, leaving ample scope for divergent views. All are agreed that the weavers in Spain have a claim to a larger share of responsibility for the fine silken fabrics in our great collections than has been conceded to them hitherto : but once the task of identification is seriously taken in hand, their obvious diversity seems to baffle all attempts at drawing the boundary-line. The place of the peninsula on the map rendered it even more liable than Constantinople or Sicily, for example, to become a battle-ground for opposing nationalities and religions. Every seafarer sailing out of the Mediterranean had to pass by the coast of Spain, and for those who journeyed by land the peninsula formed a most convenient means of access to the continent of Europe from the shores of Africa. Even the distant Arabs realized this. The rigours of the mountain regions of Asia Minor would have been disastrous to the sons of the desert, and instead of choosing that route they made their great assault on the mainland of Europe at the very farthest point from their native home. They were by no means the first invaders to descend upon Spain from the coast of Africa, but what effect previous incursions may have had upon the textile-productions of the peninsula we do not know, for no fabrics woven in Spain before the Muhammadan invasion can now be identified.

HISPANO-MORESQUE.—As the Arabs carried their arms through Egypt and along the Barbary coast recruits were enlisted on the way, and it must have been a mixed company of warriors that landed upon the shores of Spain in the year 711. Within the space of seven years all resistance was put down except among the mountains in the north-west, and the victorious armies passed on into France. The natural resources of Spain were considerable, and luxury soon gained a footing at the courts of the invaders.

It is usual to designate the textile art of Spain under the Muhammadans as Hispano-Moresque, and the term is not altogether inappropriate. Comings and goings between Spain and Morocco must have been incessant, and Moorish and Berber dynasties held sway from the latter part of the eleventh century until the middle of the thirteenth. But it should not be inferred that the weavers were necessarily either Spaniards or Moors. Until the middle of the eighth century the Arab rulers were lieutenants of the Umaiyad khalifs of Damascus, and after that dynasty was replaced by the Abbasids, and the khalifate was transferred to Baghdad, the Umaiyades of Spain became independent Emirs and ultimately khalifs of Cordova. The art of Damascus under the first Arab khalifs cannot have been other than a medley of various elements, and whether the Arab art of Spain was in direct line of descent from Damascus or not, there can be no doubt that it was composite likewise. How far the textiles woven in Spain were at first distinguishable from others produced elsewhere in the Muhammadan world is a question to which no final answer can be given at present. The contingent problem of the degree in which the early settlers were dependent upon other parts of the Muhammadan world for the richer sorts of textiles likewise awaits a solution. But it is certain that a

59

prosperous textile industry soon arose under the Umaiyades of Spain. Its seat was Andalusia, the southernmost province. Within little more than a century of the conquest such progress had been made that the fame of Spanish textiles had spread beyond the limits of the country. The papal inventories of the ninth century refer to Spanish stuffs in a context which shows that they were not of an inferior kind. To assume that all were Spanish that were called so may be hazardous, but the attributions would never have been made had not the fame of Spain for the manufacture of such stuffs already reached the papal court.

Records show that by the tenth century the culture of the silkworm, as well as the weaving of silk, was well established in the country. In the latter part of the following century there is a very illuminating statement to the effect that an Arab Emir of Palermo sent some Spanish stuffs as a gift to the Norman conqueror, Robert Guiscard.[1] This speaks well for the achievement of the weavers of Spain, for the industry in the Emir's own territory was already growing, and the story seems to indicate that the Spanish stuffs were superior to them.

Almeria, the capital of Andalusia, was the principal centre of the industry under the Arabs. Its woven silks are mentioned by Râzî, the Spanish-Arab historian of Spain early in the tenth century. They are again referred to, in 1154, together with those of Lisbon by Otto of Freising. Other chroniclers follow. Ibn-Saïd includes the silks of Malaga and Murcia with those of Almeria. Ibn-el-Khatib speaks with emphasis of the textile-industry of Almeria. He claims that its various silk weavings rendered it superior to all other cities of the world. The purple of Almeria is elsewhere coupled with that of Alexandria and of the Saracens. In the thirteenth century the silken stuffs of Almeria, Malaga, and Murcia are referred to by the chronicler, Ash-Shakandi, of Cordova. In the middle of that century Granada also was widely famed for its silk stuffs, which (a contemporary writer says) were preferred to those of Syria. Zaragoza in the north had by then gained repute as a silk-weaving centre.[2]

Such statements of the chroniclers and compilers of inventories serve to show that the industry was well in being by the century after the Muhammadan conquest, and that its progress from that time onwards was uninterrupted; but they throw little light on the characteristics which distinguished the early weavings of Spain from those of other Muhammadan lands. In passing from these records to the identification of the stuffs themselves our practical difficulties begin.

Spain possesses one of the most remarkable of all the earlier Muhammadan woven fabrics now in existence, bearing its own witness as to when, and for whom, it was made. But was it brought from Egypt, or Syria? There are some who are disposed to think that it must have been; yet there is a good deal to be said on the other side. This fabric, measuring about 110 cm. long by 39 cm. wide, is known as the " veil of Hishâm " [PLATE 1, A]. It was found in a casket under the altar of the church of San Esteban de Gormaz in the province of Soria, where it is supposed to have been deposited as a war-trophy; it is now in the possession of the Royal Academy of History at Madrid. The material is a thin gauze, of a pale reddish colour, with an inwrought band of tapestry-weaving in coloured silks, chiefly dark and light blue and pale red,

[1] See Francisque-Michel, " Recherches sur le Commerce des Etoffes," Paris, 1852. Vol. I, p. 77.

[2] Most of these records are quoted by Francisque-Michel, whose work is an inexhaustible mine of information on the subject of mediæval weaving in its documentary aspect. See also Juan F. Riaño, " Spanish Arts," London, 1879, pp. 250 foll.

and gold thread. This narrow band runs horizontally across the fabric. It is formed of three stripes. The middle one contains a row of compartments, roughly octagonal in shape and probably intended for circles, enclosing human busts, animals, and birds. Above and below this central stripe runs an Arabic inscription invoking the blessing of God and happiness for the Khalif Imam Abdullah Hishâm, the favoured of God and prince of believers. Hishâm II, to whom this inscription refers, was khalif of Cordova from A.D. 976 to 1013. This delicate fabric calls to mind those found in Egypt bearing the names of Fâtimid rulers. Indeed, it closely resembles them in texture and in the disposition of the ornament. The stuff inscribed with the names of El Hâkim, Fâtimid khalif of Egypt from A.D. 996 to 1021 (a contemporary of Hishâm II) resembles it more closely than any other known textile.[3] Does this resemblance involve a common origin? In regard to that question, it is as well to remember that we cannot be quite certain that El Hâkim's stuff was woven in Egypt, though evidence decidedly points that way. Hither Asia has also to be thought of, but Hither Asian craftsmen probably followed the Arab conquerors into Egypt, and for all we know Egyptian, or even Asiatic, weavers may have found their way to Spain. The more the early Muhammadan art is studied, the more complex is the problem seen to be. Hishâm's veil and the Fâtimid weavings of Egypt may owe their similarity to a common source beyond the limits of both countries. Two notable features of the veil may be referred to. They do not clinch the argument in favour of any nationality, it is true, but yet they are by no means negligible. One is the introduction of human figures. The busts, which alternate with the forms of animals and birds, have no place in Fâtimid art. The other has to do with the inscriptions. These run above and below the band of ornament, as in the weavings of Egypt, but the tops of the letters point towards the central band. In the Fâtimid stuffs either the bases of the letters are nearest to the band, or both inscriptions are the same way up. No violation of historical probability is involved in the attribution of Hishâm's veil to the weavers of Spain, especially if it be conceded that weavers from Egypt, or Hither Asia, may have settled there.

Perhaps a less convincing case is to be made out for another stuff which Spanish historians claim as the product of their own country. This silk weaving has a pattern of elephants in circular compartments [PLATE 1, B]. It was found in a church in the Pyrenees, on the borders of Catalonia and Aragon, and it is now divided between the museums of Barcelona and Berlin. Perhaps the only feature this fabric has in common with the veil of Hishâm is that the pattern is Eastern in origin; but it has none of the salient features of Muhammadan art. Spain was large enough, and its population diversified enough to have harboured two very different traditions among its weavers. Muhammadan and Christian were continually in conflict, and the tide of reconquest soon began to flow. As cities and provinces passed from the one side to the other, each found it convenient to suffer differences of race and religion among the population. The Arab himself was inclined to be tolerant; though matters changed for the worse at a later time under the Berber dynasties from North Africa. A Christian *Mozarabe* art was developed under the Muhammadans, and an Arab *Mudéjar* art survived in Christian territories.

This silk fabric with a pattern of elephants merits careful examination. The pattern, especially the floral ornamentation intervening between the circles,

[3] See Victoria and Albert Museum, " Catalogue of Muhammadan Textiles of the Mediæval Period," 1924, No. 857.

obviously has Persian leanings, but Persian motives travelled far. The elephant does not resemble that on the (admittedly) Persian silk fabric of the tenth century recently discovered at Saint-Josse-sur-Mer, Pas de Calais, and now in the Louvre, any more closely than it resembles the elephant on the Byzantine silk shroud of Charlemagne at Aix-la-Chapelle.[4] It has more in common with the elephants on the Cordovan ivory caskets than with either. In one such carving the elephants are represented within circles of guilloche pattern, as in this silk fabric.[5] These ivories show the influence of textile-ornament very clearly. On account of their mobility and relative richness textiles have always been agents in the spread of decorative forms. In this instance the silk fabric is probably a century earlier than the ivories. The colours of the stuff are chiefly red and yellow; while it will be remembered that these are the dominant colours in Spanish stuffs, it will not be thought advisable to lay too much stress upon any argument of origin based upon this circumstance. Colours may be copied as easily as patterns. It is possible that this silk fabric may be actually of Eastern manufacture. Should that be the case it would have been imported from some part of Hither Asia where the Sassanian tradition of pre-Moslem times still lingered. It can be shown that another silk fabric with a pattern of elephants which found its way into Spain in mediæval times was woven at Baghdad.[6]

By the twelfth century, at latest, the distinctive tendencies of Spanish silk weaving begin to show themselves more clearly. They are exemplified in a well-known stuff in the Cathedral of Salamanca [PLATE 1, C]. In this stuff the circles enclose pairs of eagles. The star-forms with radiating foliations, in the spaces intervening between the circles, are a feature to be noticed. Such forms are to be found with nothing more than minor changes, in most of the stuffs of this group. The pattern is in red and olive-green silk and gold thread on an ivory-white ground—a scheme of colour which recurs again and again. There is a Kufic inscription on the breast of the bird, and Kufic characters fill the out-lining circles. The brocade was used to protect a document of the period of Fernando II, King of León (1158-1188), in the cathedral archives of Salamanca.[7]

A chasuble in the Church of Saint Quiriace at Provins (Seine-et-Marne) has a pattern very closely similar. It is associated by tradition with St. Edmund, Archbishop of Canterbury, who died in France in the year 1241 [PLATE 3, A].

The group to which these stuffs belong is so well defined that specimens with no established pedigree may easily be identified in public collections. One, in the Berlin Museum, has pairs of deer in the circles, and the same sequence of Kufic characters on the outlining bands as the example at Salamanca.[8] Another piece, in the Episcopal Museum at Vich, has pairs of lions in the circles, and eight-pointed stars filling the intervening spaces. There are two specimens in the Victoria and Albert Museum. Both obviously belong to the group, although the rows of circles are replaced by lozenges. The first [PLATE

---

[4] See Victoria and Albert Museum, " Catalogue of Early Mediæval Fabrics," pp. 14, 21.

[5] See Nos. 10-1866 and 368-1880 in the Victoria and Albert Museum ; both of the latter half of the tenth century. An elephant is represented in the apse of the church of San Baudilio, province of Soria (Marcel Dieulafoy, " Art in Spain and Portugal," London, 1913, fig. 137).

[6] Illustrated in THE BURLINGTON MAGAZINE, XLIX, 1926, p. 267.

[7] Pedro Mg. de Artiñano, " Cat. de la Exp. de Tejidos," Madrid, 1917, Pl. 6 ; O. von Falke, "Seidenweberei," fig. 190 ; G. Migeon, " Manuel d'Art musulman," II, fig. 337. The inscriptions on most of these stuffs appear to be merely formulas.

[8] J. Lessing, " Gewebesammlung," Pl. 44 ; O. von Falke, " Seidenweberei," fig. 191.

4, A] shows pairs of wingless griffins and pairs of peacocks in alternate horizontal rows. The Kufic inscriptions on the outlining bands have been interpreted as signifying " Perfect blessing and victory." The horizontal band in gold which runs across the fabric regardless of the pattern has the word " Arrahman " (the Merciful) repeated in Kufic characters in black silk. In the other example, the lozenges enclose alternately two wingless griffins and two interlaced quatre-foils.[9] It has no inscriptions.

The treasury of Sens Cathedral contains an example belonging to the group, known as the " Suaire de Saint Léon " [PLATE 3, B]. It will be seen that the circles contain pairs of lions. The introduction of interlaced quatrefoils to enclose the circles is unusual in this group of stuffs. Their use here strengthens the claim to a Spanish origin, to be made presently, for Mr. Kelekian's red and green brocade [PLATE 5, A], and indirectly for the similar stuff with parrots in circles in the Victoria and Albert Museum [PLATE 5, B].

The calligraphic style of all these patterns is a feature which merits careful attention. The weaver has taken great pains to reproduce the slender lines introduced by the designer solely to remove any hardness in the contours and serving no representational purpose. Such elaborations, which come easily to the pen, involve extremely skilful manipulation by the weaver. The same characteristic is found in the most delicate mediæval silk weavings of the Near East, but it was retained and developed by the Spanish weavers in such a degree as to be typical of their work.

Three very remarkable Spanish brocades are in the Episcopal Museum at Vich in Catalonia. Two have their patterns disposed in circular compart-ments. The outlining patterns of these circles (rows of small discs within double bands) will be recognized as recurring often in Spanish textiles. In one of the stuffs at Vich [PLATE 4, B] a man in a long robe grasps a lion round the throat with each arm. This subject must be traceable to some Eastern story of heroic prowess, though it is quite likely that the duplication of the lion has no place in the original story; the tendency to repetition with the object of balancing the pattern is sometimes a little misleading in textiles. The rows of animals (griffins and winged lions) confronted in pairs which accentuate the outlining bands will be noticed; they have their place in later Spanish textile patterns. It will be seen that the radiated designs of the intervening spaces are an elaborated version of those appearing in the chasuble at Provins and the " suaire " at Sens [PLATES 3, A, and 3, B].

In the second piece at Vich [PLATE 4, D] human-headed griffins or sphinxes are attacked by diminutive lions; there are pairs of peacocks in the intervening spaces.[10] Both the " lion-strangler " and the " sphinx " stuff are to be attri-buted to the twelfth century. The colours are red and green silk, with gold thread, on an ivory-white ground. Tradition records that they were worn by Saint Bernard Calvó, Bishop of Vich from 1233 to 1243.

In the third fabric at Vich [PLATE 4, C] the pairs of composite winged mon-sters will be seen to have one head between them, while the peacocks in the alternate rows share a single tail in pairs. The colours are black and white on a red ground. This stuff is not so exclusively Spanish in feeling as the two just mentioned, and the possibility of an origin in some other part of the Muham-madan world may be admitted, though Spain has the best claim.

---

[9] Victoria and Albert Museum, " Catalogue of Muhammadan Textiles of the Mediæval Period," 1924. Plate XVIII, No. 990.

[10] The Coopers' Union, New York, possesses a fragment of this stuff.

The fine textile with a pair of peacocks reproduced on PLATE 2 provides an argument in favour of an attribution to Spain of the silk stuff at Vich just referred to, for the two resemble one another in several respects. The Spanish origin of the " peacock " stuff has been questioned, it is true, but a comparison of the wings and legs of the bird, and the foliage, with corresponding parts of the silk stuff at Salamanca Cathedral already described [PLATE 1, C] presents a strong case in favour of a common origin, and the peacocks have an obvious and close resemblance to those on one of the Cordovan ivory caskets already referred to.[11] The plinth on which the birds rest, cut away at each end, is also found on that casket, and on another like it in Pamplona Cathedral. There is a large piece of this stuff in the Cathedral of Saint Sernin at Toulouse, where it is known as the *chape du roi Robert*. In each alternate row the peacocks are in green, and there are other slight changes in the distribution of the colours.

A brocade in Mr. Kelekian's collection, which has already been mentioned in connexion with the *suaire de Saint Léon* at Sens [PLATE 3, B], is here reproduced [PLATE 5, A]. It is important to note the features in which this fine stuff resembles others attributed to Spain—for the attribution (in common with several others discussed in these pages) has not been made before. The pairs of griffins in the circles and the parrots in the intervening spaces are in green, with heads in gold thread, on a red ground. The very close resemblance of the foliations within the interlaced ornament to those in a similar position on the *suaire de Saint Léon* should be remarked. It also has an obvious relationship to the brocade reproduced on PLATE 5, B. Several attributions have been suggested for the last, though once Spain is considered it seems to rule out all others. The pattern of the circular bands is a later and modified rendering of the type exemplified in the " sphinx " stuff [PLATE 4, D]. A more conclusive argument is the relationship to Mr. Kelekian's brocade. The materials and the colours are the same, and the parrots are very closely similar.[12] A silk brocade in the Cathedral of Lérida should be compared with this group of stuffs. The pattern consists of pairs of rampant lions within eight-pointed stars, and stems in the intervening spaces recalling the ornament found on the stuffs just described. The pattern is in red and blue.[13]

The Archæological Museum at Madrid possesses the larger part of a brocade mantle removed in the year 1848 from the tomb of the Infante Don Felipe (d. 1274), son of Ferdinand the Saint, at Villalcazar de Sirga, near Palencia. The design is Muhammadan, but there is no reason to seek a place of origin outside Spain. Small geometrical forms in gold are repeated in close order with the aim of setting-off the richness of the material rather than that of leading the eye into the intricacies of a pattern. A broad band runs arbitrarily across the design, containing the word " baraka " (blessing) in bold Kufic characters continuously repeated in two lines, the lower being inverted. Another brocade, closely similar, is claimed to have been removed from the Infante's tomb at the same time. A piece of the first design is in the Victoria and Albert Museum.[14] The student of the art of the Middle Ages will not be altogether surprised to find a brocade with legible Arabic inscriptions used in the family of a royal saint of Castile, and an inveterate enemy of the Muham-

[11] Victoria and Albert Museum, No. 10-1866.

[12] The pattern of the brocade at South Kensington was copied in a slightly simplified version in the latter half of the last century, and examples are sometimes to be found in collections of old fabrics.

[13] Reproduced in " Dedalo," I, 1920, p. 105 ; G. Sangiorgi, " Contributi allo Studio dell'Arte tessile," Milan, p. 27.

madans, even though such a practice among Christians had been anathematized by Pope Innocent IV only twenty years before.[15] These Muhammadan stuffs were also used for vestments. A cope and dalmatic from the Cathedral of Lérida in Catalonia are made of brocade in some respects similar.[16]

Granada was the last capital held by the Moors in Spain, and in course of time it became their chief weaving centre. The brocade band in gold and black reproduced on PLATE 6, A, was probably woven there. It bears the well-known formula, " There is no conqueror but God," adopted by the Muhammadans of Spain and repeated profusely in the decoration of the Alhambra. Another example is seen on PLATE 6, B.

The different currents in the art of Spain betray a tendency to flow together towards the close of the Middle Ages. The progressive stages in the transformation of some of the old textile patterns may be traced. One such design is shown in an earlier form on PLATE 8, A. As this pattern becomes modified the two lions with fantastic crowns are sometimes replaced by swans or other birds, and the characteristic foliations gradually change into the typical floral motives of the sixteenth century.

While this process is going on, the animals and birds become subordinated to the other elements in the design, or they drop out altogether, and were it not for the intermediate links the origin of the later phases might easily be lost sight of. The colours are usually red, green, yellow, and white, but their allocation varies. Versions in embroidery are sometimes found, and a pile carpet of this design is in the Victoria and Albert Museum.[17]

The geometrical and interlaced patterns which form the chief feature in most collections of Spanish silk fabrics need not be described at length. Such motives have a subordinate office in many of the earlier Spanish stuffs. By the fifteenth century they have taken the first place, and their intricacy is emphasized by the brilliancy and purity of the colours, among which red and yellow predominate. The horizontal bands running arbitrarily across the design generally afford the best clue to the date of origin. They may have trees and birds of early type (Barcelona Museum), or hunting animals recalling stuffs of the thirteenth century (D. Pedro Castillo Olivares).[18] Where inscriptions fill the bands they heighten the decorative effect, though they contribute little of documentary value, as they are usually formulas giving no clue to locality or date. The group is regarded as mudéjar work of Granada.

The apparent ease with which the Spanish weaver represents these complicated interlaced ornaments is one of the indications of the continuity of craftsmanship under changing fortunes. The skill of the early Muhammadans was handed down so as to outlast the recovery of the whole peninsula for Christendom. Writers of the first quarter of the sixteenth century still speak of the silk bazaar of Granada, where the Moors sold stuffs " ouvrés à la moresque," some time after the recovery of Granada for Christian Spain.[19]

[14] " Catalogue of Muhammadan Textiles," No. 987, Plate XIX. Illustrations will also be found in L. Williams' " Arts and Crafts of Older Spain," III, p. 29 (Madrid Museum); " Museum," I, 1911, p. 432 (M. Claudius Côte); " Dedalo," I, 1920, p. 112 (Signor G. Sangiorgi); Pasco, Collection Miquel y Badia, Plate XIII, Nos. 102, 103.

[15] Saint Ferdinand's own funeral robe is in the Archæological Museum at Madrid. It has a heraldic pattern of castles and lions for his kingdom of Castile and León. (L. Williams, " Arts and Crafts of Older Spain," Vol. III; Whishaw, Arabic Spain, fig. 9.)

[16] These vestments are no longer complete. A small fragment of the cope, from a portion removed some time ago, was acquired in Spain, in 1923, by Sir William Lawrence and presented to the Victoria and Albert Museum (Victoria and Albert Museum, " Catalogue of Muhammadan Textiles," No. 988.)

[17] " Guide to the Collection of Carpets," 2nd. ed., 1920. Plate 38.

[18] " Pedro Mg. de Artiñano, " Catalogo de la Exposicion de Tejidos," Madrid, 1917. Perhaps the earliest of these stuffs with interlaced patterns belong to the fourteenth century.

[19] Voyage de Philippe le Beau, and Navagiero (see J. Riaño, " Spanish Arts," p. 256.)

The repeated inscription on the silk fabric reproduced in colour on PLATE 7, " Glory to our lord the Sultan," is more commonly found than any other in this class of weavings. Other examples will be seen in the group of woven stuffs and embroideries in the collection of Count Valencia de Don Juan reproduced on PLATE 6, B.

THE FIFTEENTH CENTURY.—Traces of the formal arabesques and Arabic inscriptions subordinated to a more fanciful conception are to be seen in the brocade illustrated on PLATE 5, C. The fabric is a white silk damask with spiders and small plant motives in gold. The attributions given to this stuff, both as regards provenance and date, are unusually varied, but the mercurial art of Spain covers a wide range of ornamental detail. There need be no hesitation in accepting the view that this fabric was produced by the Spanish weavers in the latter half of the fifteenth century, when the earlier formal patterns were giving way to a more unfettered treatment.[20] Some of the fifteenth century patterns are still true to the Oriental tradition. The silk fabric illustrated on PLATE 8, C, belongs to a well-known group of Spanish weavings of that period, generally woven in yellow on a deep blue ground. The design of this example is to be traced to Hither Asia, whence it journeyed eastwards as far as China and westwards to the Spanish peninsula. It is one of those patterns which exemplify the far-reaching influence of one locality upon another in textile art, and the distance which ornamental motives may travel.

A small silk panel in the Musée des Arts Decoratifs at Paris is reproduced on PLATE 5, D. Its nationality has been a matter of debate, and its sober colouring has led experts away from the right road, that leading to Spain, but the character of the ornament is decisive. The " palmette " motive of white curled leaves seems unfamiliar at first sight, but it is found more subordinated in the group of stuffs represented by those on PLATES 8, A, and 8, C, one of the most typical of Spanish patterns. A careful comparison of the other details with those represented among the interlaced patterns, of which PLATES 7, 6, B, and 11 are examples, can only tend to confirm the attribution. It was probably woven in the first half of the fifteenth century. The colour of the ground is deep blue; the pattern is in cream-white, bluish-white, and emerald green.

A silk fabric in which an approximation to natural forms is combined with the typical interlaced patterns is reproduced on PLATE 8, C. It is in green, yellow, and white on a red ground.

One of the stateliest of the mediæval European textile-designs derived from Oriental models consists of pairs of animals and birds supported by large palmettes. Even if a little formal, the different renderings of this pattern are always impressive. It was developed with considerable variations in Italy, its principal European home. In examples such as that illustrated on PLATE 8, B, the characteristics of Spanish weaving are plainly visible. Wyverns replace the gazelles. The rows of tiny birds outlining some of the palmettes and the small running hares help to associate this version with the Spanish peninsula. It is chiefly in green and gold, with small details in red, white, and blue.

Whether this type of design entered Spain directly from the East or through Italy may be a matter of opinion. At a later time the influence of Italy on Spanish textile-design is beyond dispute. In the fifteenth century Italy was providing the whole of Europe with the sumptuous velvets and other rich

[20] Prof. Miquel y Badia of Barcelona had a piece of this brocade in his collection. He thought it to be " Mudéjar," of the fifteenth century (Pasco, Pl. 19, No. 129).

fabrics for which its reputation was then unchallenged. Spain was not likely to remain unaffected, particularly at times when a Spanish dynasty was ruling in the south of Italy and a Spaniard occupied the Papal throne. Italian fabrics were widely used in Spain, and Italian influence spread among the local weaving establishments. Some fabrics show a variation of the well-known " artichoke " pattern, with a quasi-Gothic touch pointing to Spain rather than to Italy. The red and yellow silk shown on PLATE 9, A, is nearer than some to the Italian original, but certain features—the border of tiny leaves and pomegranates round the palmette-forms, the inessential but effective outlines marking the contours of the pattern, the general elaboration of detail—are contributions of the Spanish genius. Velvets with patterns more or less of the same type were used abundantly in Spain. Some differ in nothing from the Italian velvets, and presumably came from Italy. Others have modifications in the design showing that they were intended for Spanish use, whether woven in the country or not. The red and gold brocaded velvet on PLATE 9, B, is one of these. The pilgrim's staff and shell, emblems associated with St. James (of Compostela), as well as the bursting pomegranate, indicate that the velvet should be related to Spain. In general appearance and texture it resembles the Florentine velvets. Whether the Spanish velvet weavers were able to compete with the Italians so favourably we are unable to say. Valencia and Granada were the chief centres of velvet weaving.

Towards the end of the fifteenth century, many varieties of silk brocades with gold and silver threads were woven at Toledo. The silk manufacturers of Toledo retained their prestige until the middle of the seventeenth century, when public favour seems to have been transferred to the stuffs of Seville, Granada, and Valencia.

A factory under French direction was established at Talavera in 1748, and for more than half a century brocades following French models were woven there. The silk-weaving industries of Granada, Seville, Barcelona, Valencia, and Toledo continued to prosper throughout the eighteenth century. Those of Zaragoza, Manresa, Cardona, Mataró, Jaén, Murcia, and Requeña are also mentioned. Silk-cultivation continued to be an important industry in Spain throughout the century, and it is recorded that the prices of silk fabrics were affected by the varying results of the harvest year by year.

These later fabrics mostly follow models imported from abroad, and they lack the national character and the peculiar interest of the earlier phases of textile art in Spain.

EMBROIDERY was practised in Spain from early times. The celebrated hanging of the Creation in Gerona Cathedral [PLATE 10] conforms in its rendering of the theme to the type generally followed where Byzantine influence was felt. There is no apparent reason for denying to Spain the credit for this work, which belongs to the eleventh, or perhaps the twelfth, century. In its present state it measures 3.78 metres in height by rather more in width. The design is in coloured wools on a linen foundation. In the middle is a figure of Christ holding an open book inscribed S(an)c(tu)s D(eu)s. Within the enclosing circle are the words Rex fortis, and on the outlining band, Dixit quoque Deus Fiat lux et facta est lux (Gen. i, 3). Around are the Days of Creation—the Spirit of God moving on the face of the waters ; the creation of light and darkness ; the creation of the firmament in the midst of the waters ; the waters divided from the waters, and the creation of sun, moon and stars ; the creation of Adam ; the creation of Eve ; the creation of animals, fishes and birds.   The surrounding inscription is from Genesis i, vv. 1, 31.   In the angles are the four winds.   In the top and left borders the year (Annus) presides over the labours of the months.   The bottom border is incomplete; it represented the Invention of the Cross.   The right border is missing.

The embroidery reproduced on PLATE 11 is traditionally reputed to be a banner taken by Alfonso VIII of Castile from the Almohades at the great battle of Las Navas de Tolosa in the year 1212.   Obviously it must be attributed to a later date, somewhere within the limits of the fourteenth century.   Its size (10 ft. by 7 ft. 3 in.) and form would render it more suitable for a door-hanging than for a military banner.   The ground is crimson silk, with embroidered and woven decoration in gold and colours, chiefly blue, red, and white.   The middle contains an eight-fold repetition of a group of interlaced Kufic characters interpreted by Señor Riaño as signifying " the Empire."[21]   The other inscriptions in large blue Naskhy characters are quotations from the Koran.   Among the ornaments in the narrow band within the border, edging the inner field, is a lion in violet three times repeated.   The character of these lions is Spanish rather than Moorish, and it seems that the hanging may be an example of mudéjar art.   It is the property of the Monastery of Las Huelgas, near Burgos.

Large numbers of richly-embroidered vestments are preserved in the church-treasuries of Spain.   Sometimes the work shows the influence of the Low Countries; embroiderers are known to have been called to Spain from Brabant.   In later times there is a tendency to over-elaboration, and the questionable practice of tinting in water-colour as a substitute for needlework was sometimes resorted to.   The fine chasuble of about the year 1500, of which the back is reproduced in colours [PLATE 12] is in the Victoria and Albert Museum.   The brocaded velvet in silk and gold, with a pile of two thicknesses, shows the influence of Oriental design in the arabesque-forms issuing from the broad wavy bands.   The embroidered half-figures of angels in the orphrey are boldly designed, and the changes of colour are cleverly manipulated for distant effect.[22]

The two silk frontlets of appliqué work reproduced on PLATE 13, A, are in the collection of Mr. Archibald Russell, Lancaster Herald.   Their remarkably decorative quality needs no enlarging upon.   The pilgrim's staff and shell on the first arbitrarily punctuates the inscription, " Domine memento me " in reddish silk on a black ground.   The Cross on the second, in black and white, is that of the Dominicans of the province of Segovia.

The band of which a section is reproduced on PLATE 13, B, is considered to have been used for a canopy of State.   It is of crimson velvet, with gold and silk embroidery.   The arms are probably intended for those of the cathedral city of Barbastro in Aragon.   Another admirable specimen of Spanish heraldic design, though somewhat injured by use, is the green velvet panel for a chairback, with appliqué work in silk, shown on PLATE 13, C.   It bears the arms of Velasco, Dukes of Frias.

In Spain it has been a common practice to embroider elaborate reading-desk covers *en suite* with sets of vestments.   One of these, in the possession of the King of Spain, is reproduced [PLATE 14, B].   It is of crimson brocaded velvet, with side borders and end-panels of red velvet embroidered in gold and silver.   The work was executed by embroiderers at the Escorial for Philip II.

[21] " Spanish Arts," London, 1879, p. 254.

[22] Half-figures of angels behind battlements are to be seen on the orphreys of a cope in Burgos Cathedral; reproduced by L. de Farcy, " Le Broderie," IInd supplement, Angers, 1919, Pl. 217.

A remarkably fine silk tabard in the Archæological Museum (Abbaye de la Sainte Vierge dans la Byloke) at Ghent is shown on PLATE 14, A. It was made for the herald of the Archduke Albert, Governor of the Spanish Netherlands, and the Archduchess Isabella, daughter of Philip II. In the opinion of the learned curator of the museum, Flemish embroiderers were employed on this work. He may well be right. During the long association of the Netherlands with the ruling house of Spain, Flemish artists and craftsmen are known to have been employed both in and for Spain.

The fine hanging of green velvet, with decoration in appliqué work, patchwork and gold and silk embroidery [PLATE 15], the property of the Metropolitan Chapter of Zaragoza, is from the Monastery of Las Huelgas, Burgos. Below the figure of the Emperor Vitellius are the three Fates. It will be noticed that the elaborate ornamentation of the side pilasters with the terminal figures is skilfully counterchanged.

TAPESTRY.—The story of tapestry-weaving in Spain is not a very long one, but brief though it be, it cannot be fully dealt with here. The weaving of large tapestry-hangings originated in Flanders, and most European centres where such work was done owed their initiation to Flemish immigrant craftsmen. This was the case in Spain. There are a few notices of tapestry-weavers in the country in the later Middle Ages. A weaver of Salamanca was established in Madrid under the protection of Philip II and Queen Doña Ana. The outcome was the foundation, under his successor, Antonio Ceron, of the factory of Santa Isabel at Madrid, the interior of which is represented in Velazquez' picture " Las Hilanderas " in the Prado, painted about 1660.

Tapestry-weaving was again begun in the capital in the early years of the eighteenth century, when Van der Goten, a weaver of Antwerp, was engaged to direct operations. The factory at Seville, founded a few years after, was an off-shoot. It did not last long, and the weavers were soon transferred to Madrid. In these factories various paintings were copied and some heraldic work was done, but no national style was evolved.

The most characteristic and the most successful achievements of the Spanish tapestry-weavers were the famous series of tapestries after Goya's designs woven in the royal factory of Santa Barbara at Madrid. There were originally forty-five of these, with subjects illustrating the daily life and amusements of the people of Spain. Goya's first design was handed over to the factory late in 1776, and the last in 1791. The work thus covered the middle period of his life. Thirty-six of the designs are now shown in the Prado Museum. Most of the tapestries are still preserved in the royal residences. The tapestries here reproduced are in the Escorial. The first [PLATE 16] is entitled *A walk in Andalusia*. As it bears the date 1777, it must have been one of the earliest of Goya's designs to be completed. The other [PLATE 17] is *The Kite*.

CARPETS.—The carpet-knotting industry of Spain, gauged either from the nature of its achievements, or the duration of its operations, is the most considerable in Europe. The story begins in the fifteenth century, and it comes down to modern times. A very short summary will be deemed sufficient here. The knotting-process was borrowed from the East, but Spain introduced a variation of her own—that of making the knot on a single warp thread—presumably in order to be able to reproduce the slender lines which are so noticeable a feature of Spanish textile-design.

Many of the carpets of Spain closely copy Eastern patterns, but from the beginning (so far as we can trace it back) Spain was capable of producing work of true originality. The long narrow heraldic carpets of the fifteenth century are well known, though few only have been preserved. The shields of arms of Spanish families are disposed over the middle field on backgrounds of small diaper patterns. Thin Kufic lettering, the significance of which contributes nothing illuminating, fills the border.[23]

The carpet here reproduced in colours [PLATE 18] bears witness again to the originality of the carpet-weavers of Spain. The mediæval treatment of the lions warrants an attribution to the fifteenth century, and at latest it cannot be very far onward in the sixteenth. There are four lions on the original piece —their colours are red, green, blue and green.

Geometrical patterns recalling Spanish tilework or the tracery of the Alhambra are also found in the early Spanish carpets. A preference is shown for a few colours in bright tones, such as the silk-weavers used.

As the sixteenth century advances the carpet-weaver takes to imitating the elaborate patterns of the contemporary brocades and damasks; this he does with extraordinary skill. The use of the single-warp knot materially aids him.

The subsequent history of carpet-knotting in Spain is a further demonstration of originality in design. The weavers of the Santa Barbara factory at Madrid produced knotted carpets as well as tapestries, and they do so still.

[23] A. F. Kendrick and C. E. C. Tattersall, " Hand-woven Carpets," London, 1922, Plates 76, 77 ; " Meisterwerke Muhammedanischer Kunst," Munich, 1911, Vol. I, Plates 85, 86 ; " Museum " (Spanish), I, 1911, p. 431.

A—The " veil " of Hishâm II, Khalif of Cordova (A.D. 976-1013). Total length about 3 ft. 8 in. (Royal Academy of History, Madrid)

B—Silk fabric from a church in the Pyrenees; 9th century. Diam. of circles, 14 in. (Barcelona and Berlin Museums)

C—Brocade covering a document of the period of Fernando II, King of León (A.D. 1158-1188). 12 in. by 19 in. (Cathedral Archives of Salamanca)

Silk fabric; 12th century. 13 in. by 9½ in. (Victoria and Albert Museum)

B—The " suaire de St. Léon "; 12th-13th century. Total size, 3 ft. 6 in. by 1 ft. 7 in. (Treasury of Sens Cathedral)

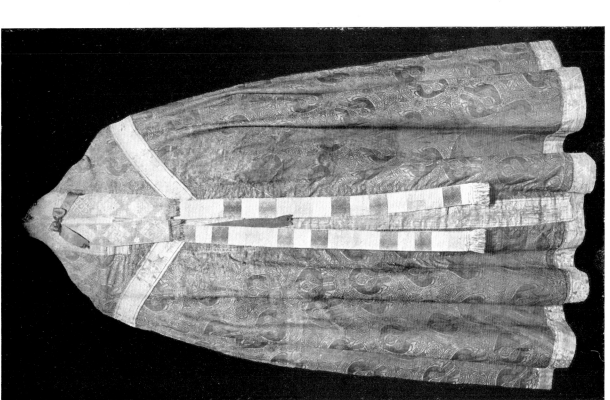

A—Chasuble of St. Edmund, Archbishop of Canterbury (d. 1241). (Church of St. Quiriace, Provins)

A—Brocade of the 12th-13th century. 5½ in. square. (Victoria and Albert Museum)

B—Fragment of a vestment " of St. Bernard Calvó "; 12th century. Diam. of circles, 14 in. (Episcopal Museum, Vich)

C—Brocade; 12th century. Total width, 2 ft. 8 in. (Episcopal Museum, Vich)

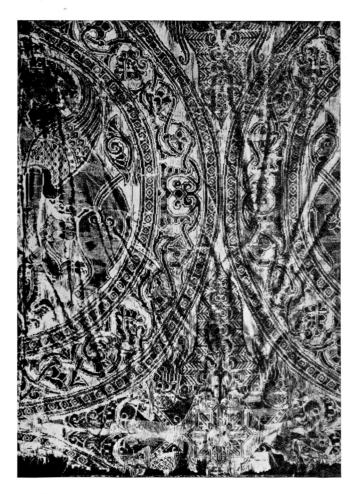

D—Fragment of a vestment " of St. Bernard Calvó." 12th century. Diam. of circles, 12 in. (Episcopal Museum, Vich)

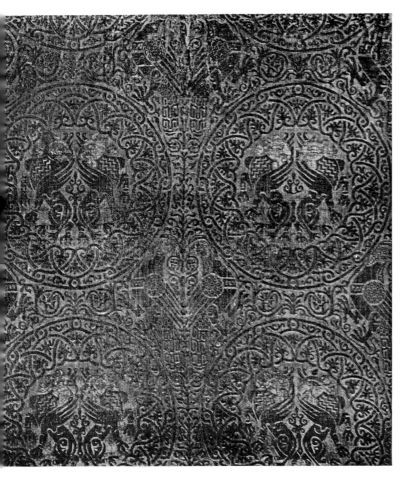

Brocade, 12th-13th century. Diam. of circles, 10 in. (Mr. Dikran [Ke]lian, Paris)

Brocaded damask, 15th century. 8½ in. by 23½ in. (Victoria and [Alber]t Museum)

B—Brocade, 13th century. About 12 in. by 9½ in. (Victoria and Albert Museum)

D—Silk fabric, 15th century. 6½ in. by 7½ in. (Musée des arts decoratifs, Paris)

A—Brocade band from Granada; 14th century. Total length about 22 in. Width, 2½ in. (Victoria and Albert Museum)

B—Group of woven and embroidered fabrics. (Collection of Count Valencia de Don Juan)

Silk fabric; Granada, 15th century. About 22½ in. by 11 in. (Victoria and Albert Museum)

A—Silk fabric, 15th century. About 13 in. by 12½ in.

B—Brocade, 14th century. 13 in. by 8½ in.

C—Silk fabric, 15th century. Full size, 3 ft. 2½ in. by 10¼ in.

D—Silk fabric. 15th century. 11 in. by 7 in.

All in the Victoria and Albert Museum.

B—Velvet brocade, with the pilgrim's staff and shell; late 15th century. Width about 22 in. (Victoria and Albert Museum)

A—Silk fabric; late 15th century. 3 ft. by 2 ft. 4 in. (Victoria and Albert Museum)

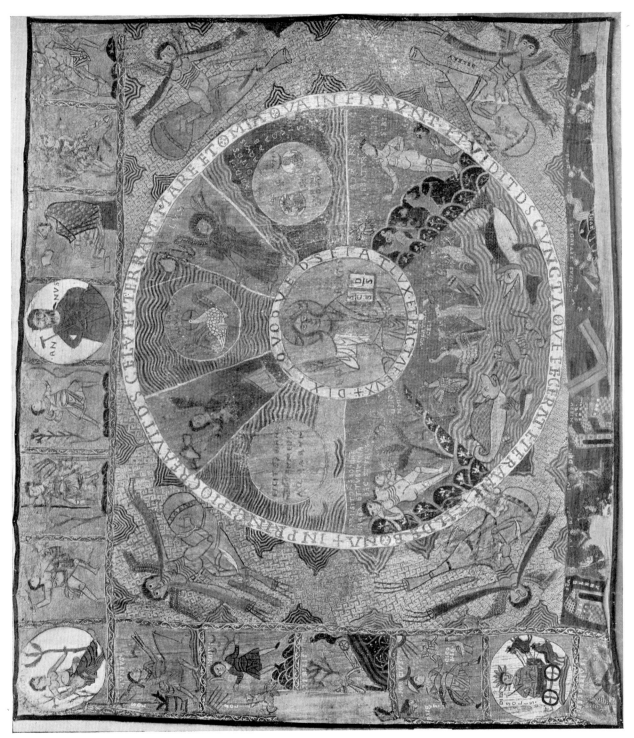

The Creation and *The Labours of the Months.* Embroidered hanging of the 11th-12th century. About 12 ft. 6 in. wide.
(Gerona Cathedral)

" Banner of Las Navas de Tolosa "; 14th century. About 10 ft. by 7 ft. 3 in. (Monastery of Las Huelgas, Burgos)

Velvet brocade chasuble, with embroidered orphreys; about 1560.   Height, about 4 ft. 6 in.
(Victoria and Albert Museum)

A—Silk appliqué work frontlets; the upper one late 15th century, the lower one 16th century.   Each about 10 in. wide. (Mr. A. G. B. Russell)

B—Band for a canopy of state, with the arms of the city of Barbastro (?);   16th century.   Width, about 11 in. (Victoria and Albert Museum)

C—Chair-back panel, with the arms of the Dukes of Frias; 16th century.   About 2 ft. 6 in. by 16 in. (Victoria and Albert Museum)

Phot. Maison Sacré de Gard

A—Tabard, appliqué work in silk. Made for the herald of the Archduke Albert, Governor of the Spanish Netherlands, and his wife, Isabella, daughter of Philip II. Late 16th century. (Archaeological Museum, Ghent)

B—Reading desk cover, made for King Philip II. 16th century. Width, about 18 in. (H.M. the King of Spain)

The Emperor Vitellius. Hanging of appliqué work and embroidery. 16th century. Height, 7 ft. 3 in.
(The Metropolitan Chapter of the Cathedral of Zaragoza)

A Promenade in Andalusia. Tapestry after Goya. (Escorial)

The Kite.   Tapestry after Goya. (Escorial)

Pile carpet; 15th—16th century. Total length,
5 ft. 2 in.; width, 1 ft. 4 in. (Victoria and Albert
Museum)

CERAMICS AND GLASS.

I. Hispano-Moresque Pottery. *By A. Van de Put*

THE range of ceramic refinements possessed by the Visigoths is obscure. That enamelling was a representative art in the Spain of Swinthila and Reccesvinthus (seventh century) is altogether improbable, although certain bronze plaques of Septimania, the Gallic remnant of the Visigothic state, which passed under the Arabs at the fall of Narbonne in 720, point to a knowledge of true enamel and, potentially, of a lead glaze. But the developments possible from this important ceramic adjunct appear to have been but timidly realized, and Visigothic pottery, with its stamped and incised dishes and lamps, is essentially at the Roman and Early Christian stage. Yet the orientalization of Spain, which it is customary to date from the Arab conquest, was to a minor extent already in progress before that event. A Byzantine occupation of the coast of Bætica from the Atlantic to the Valencian frontier of the Jucar, under Athanagild (d. 567), lasting about eighty years, until the reign of Swinthila, marks a period of direct intercourse with the Eastern Roman Empire. Of the Septimanian bronze ornaments also, some of the finest show eastern influences in their designs. Not only a strong Hispano-Roman culture in parts of Bætica brought late under Visigothic rule, but Byzantine and, probably, Near Eastern accretions were, therefore, taken over by the Arab conquerors of 711-13.

Documentary and other evidences are forthcoming for the period towards the end of the Umaiyade Khalifate of the West (—1009). Something of the state of pottery-production in the eleventh century can be gathered from two Arabic MSS. (draft-agreements for the deposit of wares for sale), drawn up by Muhammadans of Alpuente (Valencia) and of Toledo respectively.[1] The first, which embodies similar formularies of Cordova and itself dates from before 1069, mentions: jars (tinajas) of red or white ware, plain or with mouldings; glazed bowls; glazed bowls, " crystal " coated on the inside; red or white or green or yellow—glazed; white jars (alcaduces) for the norias, of clay, large, medium, and small Persian ones, etc.

And the Toledo formulary, of before 1066, includes: earthenware bowls, glazed, coated with white " crystal " on the inside, and outside with yellow " crystal," or ornamented, or golden, or cream coloured.

The first historical notice of the golden pottery which plays so large a part in Spanish ceramics thus emanates from Toledo at about the middle of the eleventh century, although its exclusively Toledan origin is not thereby implied. It should perhaps be stated that the pigment used in the decoration of the pottery which is uniformly described as *golden* (Arabic, *mudhahab*; Spanish, *dorado*) by Muhammadan and Christian witnesses, is generally accepted as a metallic compound the firing of which produced a surface iridescence or lustre, varying in different pieces as ruby, mother-of-pearl or greenish-yellow, according to the determining constituent, whether copper or silver, and to the proportion of it used. Such lustre is at times indistinguishable, except as a sheen, from the pigment itself, and is subject to deterioration. Lucio Marineo attributes to Murviedro and Toledo, in 1539, the production, for ordinary purposes, of " much yellow [ware] which looks golden " (mucho amarillo que paresce dorado).

[1] Published by my regretted friend, Don G. J. de Osma, from the MSS. preserved in the libraries of the Junta para Ampliación de Estudios, and of the R. Academia de la Historia, Madrid, in his " Apuntes sobre Cerámica morisca. Adiciones á los textos " (etc.), No. II, 8, 12, 13. Only the most important items have been selected for mention here.

ANDALUSIA.—The earliest lustred specimens so far encountered in Spain are from the ruins identified as Medina az-Zahra, the palace near Cordova commenced by Abd-er-Rahman III in 936-7, pillaged by Berbers in 1010 and already uninhabitable in the twelfth century. These sherds have a fine white, tin-enamelled body, with bold, somewhat barbaric designs in olive-brown pigment with greenish-gold lustre [PLATE 1, A]. Totally different in style from the accompanying unlustred wares, they belong unquestionably to the family of the so-called Samarra lustre (Mesopotamia) of the ninth century, found also in the district of Rhages or Rhei, north of Teheran, to which latter variety they approximate in the decorative employment of animal form. Like the mihrab tiles of the mosque at Kairwan, which likewise exhibit the Samarra ornament, this ware indicates a wave of ceramic transmission of which only the general direction can yet be surmised, and it may possibly represent an early type of Spanish lustre. To a similar but distinct current was no doubt due the Egyptian lustre of the tenth century.

The principal other wares discovered at Medina az-Zahra are : (i) of fine red body, the upper face coated with white slip, with Kufic inscriptions, plant-form, animal and human figures in bluish-green pigment, the underside coated with the transparent lead- (or *melado*) glaze[2] [PLATE 1, B]; (ii) of similar body, pale *melado* coloured, with underglaze ornament of green and brown inscriptions, the underside plain; (iii) of white body, slip-coated, having Kufic inscriptions in bluish-green with or without manganese outlines; (iv) of white body, unglazed, with Kufic inscriptions, etc., in bluish-green, outlined in black.

A fragment from Medina az-Zahra, in the Victoria and Albert Museum, each side of which is differently coloured, proves on analysis[3] to have its white face lead-glazed (and slip-coated). The impression conveyed by the Medina az-Zahra unlustred fragments is largely of a blend of Arab and Byzantine elements. Critically considered, the collection (which is still in need of detailed classification and analysis) lacks stanniferous sherds—a probable indication of the nature of the contemporary lustre ware (a slip ware?) mentioned in the Toledo formulary; and therefore of its relation to the technical combination of the fourteenth and fifteenth centuries, in which lustre pigment was applied to earthenware which had received a coat of tin enamel (i.e., a lead-glaze rendered white and opaque by oxide of tin).

In the domain of tilework the pavements of Medina az-Zahra are important as including fictile incrustations in cells and compartments of stone, of classical geometrical design; and others formed of red tiles with squares of stone.

Of purely Byzantine character is the pottery from the neighbouring site of Medina Elvira in the Granada Archæological Museum, which cannot be later in date than the early eleventh century. One piece has a design in green and dark purple of a horse with a bird upon its saddle. The evidence obtained here, at Paterna, near Valencia, in the lowest of the three deposits revealed by the excavations on the El Testar site in 1908, and elsewhere, as to the diffusion of the ornamentation from oxide of copper and manganese, is significant of its Byzantine origin. But at Paterna the contemporary derivation of certain Near Eastern animal motifs is illustrated also.

[2] From galena, otherwise lead-ore (which in Andalusia contains about 80% lead, with an admixture of other substances including oxide of iron), imparting a honey colour (*melado*) to the clay body.

[3] The report of the analysis, by the British Museum Research Laboratory, is as follows: " (a) white side: this contained no tin or borax. Found: Silica 36.7%, Oxide of lead 48.1%, Soda and Potash also present. (b) greenish-yellow side: Silica, lead and aluminium were all present in quantity, together with traces of phosphate and iron." This seems to decide what may have been the nature of the first item in the Toledo formulary quoted above.

The fall of the Umaiyades was succeeded by the rise of numerous local dynasties (" reyes de taifas ") and the inauguration of the Spanish reconquest, at the recovery of Toledo, the old Visigothic capital, in 1085. During the process—arrested by hoards from Africa in 1094 (Almoravides) and 1148 (Almohades), each of which in turn supplanted its predecessors—Muslim Spain became a dependency of Morocco, although it imprinted the Andalusian character upon the monuments of Almoravides and Almohades, and of their successors of the Marinid dynasty (1269-1470) at home. Amid the political turmoil it is difficult to discern the trend of any but the main architectural movement, and the story of ceramic activities is still a recital of isolated dates. But the tiles and pottery found in the ruined fortress of Qal'a at Bordj-bou-Areridj, situated about half-way between Algiers and Constantine, abandoned for Bougie in 1090 ; also, the roundels in the Berlin and Ravenna Museums— the last removed in 1916 from the tower of Sant' Apollinare Nuovo—deserve consideration, in the absence of anything Spanish or definitely attributable to Spain at the period. The African fragments, especially, may stand in the line of Spain's derivation of the technique : lustre upon tin-enamel. The yield at Qal'a includes stamped, green-enamelled ware ; green and brown upon slip of the Medina az-Zahra type, lustred tiles and pottery (enamel and slip) with inscriptions, approximating in decorative treatment to the Hispano-Moresque. The great variety of decorative devices includes tiles of hexagonal shapes, with the pattern " reserved " in the ground colour, the pigment actually figuring its background. The Qal'a was a centre of considerable art-activity, which Bougie became also, before the Almohades conquered the Beni-Hammad in 1152. A Genoese inventory mentions lustred jugs of Bougie in 1312.

In Spain, the geographer Edrisi attributes golden pottery (and its export thence) before 1154, to Calatayud, which had fallen to Alfonso I of Aragon in 1120, two years after Zaragoza. This is the last " ceramic " date before the armies of Castile, Aragon and Navarre, dealt the Almohade empire a decisive defeat at Las Navas de Tolosa (1212). The fall of Majorca in 1228, of Cordova in 1235, of Valencia in 1239, of Murcia in 1240, and of Seville in 1248, reduced Spanish Islam to a temporary home in the kingdom of Granada, with a frontier running almost everywhere far south of the Guadalquivir, a vassal of Castile from the fall of Jaén in 1246.

In this State, newly founded by Mohammed Ibn-el-Ahmar (1238-73), who claimed the purest Arab descent, and among a population recorded as originally from Damascus but with later Persian, Syrian and Egyptian contingents, ceramics attained eminence, exhibiting an ultimate development similar to that undergone by Almohade art from the mid-thirteenth to the late fourteenth century in the palace of the Alhambra—resulting in the zenith of elaborate but delicate ornamentation. The stages of this evolution, which took on a resemblance to Persian art of the thirteenth century, have yet to be discovered.

The historical references and monuments of the later Andalusian pottery are equally matched and important. Ibn-Said (1214-86), a contemporary of the founder of the Nasrite dynasty of Granada, records golden pottery of Murcia, Almeria and Malaga ; in the fourteenth century it is referred to Malaga by Ahmed-ben-Yaya-el-Omarí (1337), by the Egyptian Ibn Fadl Allah (1337), by Ibn-Batuta (1307-77), of Morocco, and Ibn-el-Hatib (1313-74), of Loja. The earliest record of the Andalusian production therefore connects it with two of the three seaports within the frontiers of Granada, but Ibn-Said mentions Murcia, capital of the adjacent kingdom on the east, in the first place.

The pottery of Andalusia includes vases and fragments in the **Alhambra** at Granada and in various European and American museums; a dish in the **Berlin Museum**; tilework in the Alhambra and the Cuarto Real, Granada, and a wall-revetment from Granada, now in the collection of the Instituto de Valencia de Don Juan, Madrid. The ware is decorated in lustre and sometimes blue pigment, upon tin-enamel. Varieties of polychrome tile, of which also the Alhambra contains fine examples, will be separately considered. The principal example is the famous vase of amphora shape, exhibited in the Alhambra [PLATE 2, B]. Its cream-colour body is encircled, at about the middle, by a band of cursive inscription which supports motifs of arabesque combined differently upon either side with a pair of gazelles (?) in the antithetic grouping of the Near East of antiquity; their bodies, upon a field of pale azure, are reserved in the ground colour with outlines and patterned fillings of gold—a convention derived through Persian or Byzantine art from the Sassanian method of indicating muscular surfaces. Variously shaped compartments of arabesque, inscriptions, etc., complete the decoration of the body; the neck-panels have fillings of arabesque or interlacing. In places the surface of the vase has lost its coat of enamel, and the colours having faded, the presence of lustre upon the yellowish golden pigment has been more than once questioned.[4]

The known history of the vase begins in the sixteenth century. The story of its discovery, filled with gold pieces, is told by the Abbé Bertaut, of Rouen (1659); he saw several vases which, according to Echeverria (1764), were reduced to two, with a third in a bad state of preservation. Lozano (1785), and after him Murphy, engraved the second, which had disappeared, leaving only the existing specimen, about 1814-20.

Lozano's print shows a vase [PLATE 2, A] differing materially from that under consideration. There is Gothicizing foliage upon the handles, and the main motif is a representation of the arms of the Nasrites, the Banda of Castile, charged with their Arabic motto, as in use during the latter part of the reign of Mohammed V (d. 1391).

The ornamentation of the two vases in the Leningrad Museum and in the National Museum at Palermo [PLATE 2, C], evinces a strong predilection for horizontal zones and the kufic epigraphic motif.

A vase lately acquired by the Instituto de Valencia de Don Juan, Madrid, from the Counts Burgio, of Mazzara, Sicily, combines the same bold motif, with a Solomon seal of interlacings similar to the caligraphic device in the centre of the so-called banner of Las Navas which, according to Amador de los Rios, is probably a trophy captured from the Nasrites in the fourteenth or fifteenth century. The vair pattern and roundels with inscriptions, upon the banner's lower fringe [TEXTILES, PLATE 11], are moreover comparable with like details in the upper panels and base of the vase-neck owned by the Hispanic Society of America [PLATE 3, A], which resembles the " Alhambra " vase in the employment of a pale blue in its decoration.

Whilst the ornamental schemes of the vase-group as a whole show much variety,[5] the necks of the majority are more uniformly treated with panels of interlacing and arabesque. Yet no two are the same.[6] But a neck in the

---

[4] Seco de Lucena gives the vase's measurements as: height, 136, circumference, 225, cm., or, less than 4 ft. 6 ins. x 7 ft. 5 ins. The body is cracked and most of one handle is missing.

[5] It is to be observed that the Hispanic Society's neck and the Alhambra vase show an arabesque in outline; composed of palm springing from a calyx and with curled ends, which is of an earlier type than the (post-Almohade) varieties (a) in silhouette, seen upon the Petrograd and Palermo vases; or, upon the Burgio vase, which has (b) the calyxed palm but also traces of the later hatched palm-leaf.

" Ars Classica " collection, Geneva [PLATE 3, B], and the fragment of a neck
from Fostat in the Victoria and Albert Museum [PLATE 3, D] exactly resemble
one another, but for a slight variation in the drawing of the interlacing at the
bottom.   The neck-fragment in question is of thick, red earthenware ($5\frac{3}{4}$ ×
4 ins.), with cream colour enamel and gold pigment of a pale olive shade with
red-purple iridescence.   The sides of another Fostat fragment in the Victoria
and Albert Museum [PLATE 3, C] shows motifs and execution similar to those
of the two foregoing ; it is part of a large shallow dish ; the interior has a pale
gold pigment with ruby lustre, and the outside, deeper shades of the same
colours.

The Andalusian pottery includes also the dish in the Berlin Museum [PLATE
4, A] decorated with interlacings and arabesque in lustre pigment, the base
of which is inscribed with the word Malaga—as it were, a topographical
certificate of origin to the group.

Modern criticism still attaches importance to the theory originally proposed
by De la Rada y Delgado, that the existing " Alhambra " vase was made at
Granada.[7]   The attribution was supported by an alleged differentiation between
its technique and that of Spain's enamelled and lustred pottery—an erroneous
one, albeit the vase, especially in its pristine condition, would contrast
strongly with its fellows.   Evidence of the existence of potteries at Granada
under the Nasrites was also adduced by De la Rada.   The theory's further
development, that the vase and tilework of the Alhambra are among the productions of what was in reality a court fabrique, can certainly not be described as
fantastic.   To hold that the case against Granada ceramics is unproven, is not,
however, to assign the vase to about the year 1420,[8] i.e., to a date very little later
than the reign of Yusuf III (1409-18), the king of Granada designated in the
inscription upon the revetment from a house in the Albaicín quarter at Granada,
now in the Instituto de Valencia de Don Juan [PLATE 5, A].   The silence of
Ibn-el-Hatib, vizir to Yusuf I (d. 1354), and to his successor, Mohammed V,
with regard to the alleged ceramic production at the Nasrite court, is no doubt
important, yet so only down to 1368, when the Sallust of Granada, as he has
been called, crossed to Africa, dying there in 1374. The reign of Mohammed V
lasted until 1391, and includes important architectural works stylistically akin
to the vase.   To it, or at all events to the fourteenth century belongs the flat,
enamelled tiling forming the spandrels of the Alhambra gate (alias Puerta del
Vino), in which the arabesque is designed in black upon white, with fillings of
yellow, green and azure.   A more elaborate arabesque in lustre pigment upon
tin-enamel is seen at Granada in the tiling from the Cuarto Real (de Santo
Domingo), a palace or alcázar situated near the former Potters' Gate—Bib-
Alfajjarin, reputed as of the first half of the fourteenth century [Fig. on p. 76].

VALENCIA.—The *de facto* relationship of the contemporary Valencian
lustred pottery to that of Malaga may eventually bring about regroupings
productive of greater certainty as to the dates and provenances of the pottery

[6] The Madrid (Archæological Museum) vase has no interlacing upon its neck-panels, nor has the neck owned by
the Hispanic Society ; on the example engraved by Lozano it forms a band round the middle. Lack of space prevents
other vases of the Alhambra group from being noticed here, as to which see Bibliography. No published list of
them is, however, quite complete.

[7] " Jarron árabe que se conserva en la Alhambra de Granada," in " Museo español de Antigüedades," IV, 79.
1875.

[8] Osma, Apuntes, I, 35. " La alfareria granadina florecía conocidamente, en el primer tercio del siglo XV. Son
de este tiempo la mayor parte y los más perfectos de los ejemplares que se conservan ; unos evidentemente de la
propia Granada y otro de la fabricación de Malaga ; más mentada." He adds that Yusuf III, (1409-18) is alluded
to in the (inscribed) revêtment from the Albaicín ; and that the Alhambra vase is of the same period or a little
later, in so far as the shape of the letters in the inscription and the details of the foliage in the arabesque, are
indices.

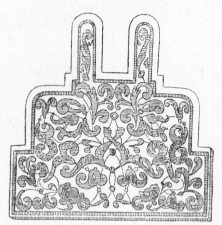

TILE FROM THE CUARTO REAL DE SANTO
DOMINGO, GRANADA.

of acceptedly Andalusian origin. Malaga was reconquered by Ferdinand and Isabella in 1487, Granada in 1492; in 1500, tiles for the restoration of the Alhambra were procured from Seville. That also, Lucio Marineo fails, in his memorabilia (printed in 1539), to mention Malaga as a pottery-centre, while awarding the palm for the contemporary golden-ware to Valencia and stating that good ware of the kind was made at Murcia, is fair testimony to the industry's decline during the reign of the Catholic kings; if by then it had not already decayed. There is practically no evidence of a flourishing ceramic art at Malaga for the period 1450-1500. Presuming its existence down to the fall of Granada as being of the nature of things, it would seem, nevertheless, that under the changed conditions and policy towards the Mudéjares ensuing upon the union of the Spains and the gradual æsthetic encroachment of the Renaissance, no such vital efflorescence of a Mussulman art was any longer possible as that which began at Valencia about a century after the reconquest. Boabdil, last king of Granada, died at Tlemcen, a voluntary exile, in 1494. The Almohade prince, Cid Abu Said, legitimate ruler of Valencia and Murcia at the fall of the city, ousted by a rival in 1229, became a Christian (by name " Don Vicente de Belvís ") and had founded feudal houses in Aragon and Valencia ere he died in 1247. His former subjects, their houses and lands partitioned among the knights, clergy and men-at-arms, of the army of James I of Aragon, became a race of suburbans and rustics, the craftsmen among whom were henceforward in contact with the art influences, especially the developing Gothic of the Aragonese states.

Little is known of Valencian ceramics of this period except that lustre production, when introduced later on from Malaga at Manises, found a craft in operation at the neighbouring Paterna, which, if indeed of Byzantine origin, was far older than the reconquest. Of great importance is a contemporary ceramic series in the Barcelona Museum, apparently from the middle El Testar deposits, with a decoration of figures and plant-form, etc., in the green and manganese technique : the dish illustrated inevitably recalls the thirteenth century figure designs of Rhages [PLATE 4, B]. Paterna's " blue and white " was found in the upper stratum. A vase in the Victoria and Albert Museum [PLATE 6, A], with simulated Arabic inscriptions in blue, probably Paterna, is at all events Valencian ; as is the series of tiles decorated in brownish red on white slip, presented by Dr. W. L. Hildburgh to the same collection [PLATE 7, D]. Some Paterna tiles have a stamped mark consisting of the quartering for Sicily from the arms of the dukes of Segorbe, titular lords of the locality for the greater part of the fifteenth and sixteenth centuries, varied with a crescent and star (or rose) in base [PLATE 6, B].

Manises itself has traditions of a great summer palace of the Moorish sovereigns, the so-called *Casa de la reina mora* or *Serallo*, as also of a castle, later belonging to the baronial family of Buyl—of intimate connexion with Manises pottery—and standing until the seventeenth century, tiles from which were, until recent times, used in houses locally. From the standpoint of free-hand design there is no finer variety of Spanish tile (or *azulejo*) than the

Valencian *rajola*, with ornament in cobalt blue and, in rare instances, in lustre pigment; or in purple and green, like the tiles of Teruel, upon tin enamel. The beauty of these tiles with their designs of interlacing, foliage, arms, and mottos [PLATE 7, A-C], and their variety—the shapes also include the oblong hexagon or *alfardon*—are alike inexhaustible; and orders for large numbers of them may be said to punctuate (1376-1494) the annals of Valencian pottery.

At the reconquest, the lordship of Manises (with Paterna) had fallen to Don Artal de Luna. It was regranted in 1329 to Philip de Buyl, son of a chamberlain to James II of Aragon, who was the husband of Teresa de Belvís. A further reference to the locality in connexion with the late royal line of Valencia occurs in 1362, in a letter from Peter IV of Aragon to his kinsman Alfonso, count of Denia (himself the husband, since 1355, of Violante, heiress of the Arenós branch of Cid Abu Said's descendants), stating that a dispute over Manises between Don Peter Buyl, son of Philip already mentioned, and Don Johann de Belvís, might assume the proportions of a civil war. The earliest records of what was undoubtedly lustre pottery in Valencia (i.e., of Manises)—for they denote its said relation to Malaga—are met with in Catalan inventories of this period. In 1343 occurs " II scutellas sive tayadors de terra de Melicha sive de Valencia," and a like entry can be cited for 1367.[9] Osma remarks that the imitation of Malagan ceramics at Valencia would appear to date at least from the first third of the fourteenth century. In the present state of the question it is easier to indicate what may have been among the earliest of such *obra de Malaga*, than to recognize in it the imitation of the style of Malaga as we know it. The sum of the data would appear to indicate that the known Valencian pottery is a collateral to, rather than a direct descendant of, the Andalusian styles represented by the wares of the " Alhambra " group. Neither arabesque nor interlacing, the ornamental factors common to the chief productions of Malaga, form distinctive elements in the earliest known Valencian pot-decoration, much less differentiate a variety of it referable to a period of imitation.

Their oriental or archaic elements distinguish certain Valencian styles as being, on the other hand, productions of the period when Eximenes testified to the " beauty of the ware of the Manises, golden and masterfully painted," and to the requests for it, on the part of pope, cardinals and temporal princes " as a special favour " (1383).

Historical and internal considerations alike indicate the lustred pottery found in 1896 at Pula, in the extreme south of Sardinia, now in the Cagliari Museum, as Manises ware of the late fourteenth or early fifteenth century.[10] This remarkable *cache* included enamelled and lustred ware of two styles: (i) combining an ornament suggestive of a section of palm-stem and its leafage, with crocketted " gable " and pierced " finial " forms ultimately derived from eighth century Persian art. In the fragment from Fostat in the Victoria and Albert Museum [PLATE 9, B] these motifs are separated by radiating blue lines. The best Pula example has also a central square of simulated Arabic

[9] " Obra de Malica " is found in a Majorca inventory of 1493. To derive the term " majolica " from Malaga (cf. Glueck and Diez, " Die Kunst des Islam," 1925, 84) is even more certainly unsound than the older, but largely discredited theory that Majorca was the original fount of production of the enamelled and lustred pottery known in Italy as majolica, a designation it received from the circumstance that it was imported in Balearic vessels. That " iscodelle di maiolica " were seen by Niccolò Frescobaldi in the house of the Prato merchant, Francesco Datini, in 1395, and that Datini opened a branch or agency in Majorca in the same year—his Valencia branch was opened in 1393—is further, if inconclusive, evidence on this point.

[10] F. Nissardi, " Scavi in Sardegna," in " Le Gallerie nazionali italiane," III, 280; until recent years similar vessels decorated the walls of village houses in the district of Oristano. It is precisely at Milis, near Oristano, that a branch of the Valencian Buyls is found, lords of Alghero, and in 1364, barons in Aragon, descended from a grandson of the first lord of Manises.

inscription. This ware has been found on the site of Theodosia in the Crimea. The second style at Pula has a principal ornament of arabesques, and "finials" alternating with the tree-of-life motif employed in one variety of the early inscribed wares. The "palm-and-finials" style itself merges into the great family of pieces decorated with the dark blue *alafia* inscription (i.e., a deformation of the Arabic word for grace, benediction, etc.), and spirals, to which belongs the dish (British Museum) with the arms of the counts of Ribagorza and Prades, extinct in the male line in 1434. A fine example in the Wallace Collection [PLATE 9, A] has the inscription, four trees-of-life, the palm ornament and the arms of the king of Castile and Leon; almost certainly, that is, of John II (1406-54), the letter of whose sister Mary, consort of Alfonso V of Aragon, to the Buyl lord of Manises, ordering a service of "obra de melica" or Malaga ware, is on record. Equally important, if less circumstantially interesting, is a document showing that an earlier queen of Aragon, Maria de Luna, purchased earthenware of a Moor of Manises—"Mohamet Abdulasi, moro del loch de Manises "—in 1404.[11]

Belonging to this period is the unique bowl in the Victoria and Albert Museum [PLATE 8], painted upon its sharply sloping inner surface with a ship that displays upon its mainsail the arms of Portugal, as borne by the kings of the house of Aviz, but without the bordure, and a school of porpoises or dolphins below; the ornament, including trees-of-life on the exterior, is in copper lustre. But for the absence of the two ravens which, at stem and stern, accompany mediæval delineations of the so-called *nau de Sao Vicente*, otherwise the ship of the arms of Lisbon, the vessel's identity with the latter would be beyond question.[12]

Possibly the rarest Valencian-Moresque style, at present dated by a fine example in the Victoria and Albert collection, bearing the arms of Alfonso V's consort, 1415-58, is illustrated in the dish (diam. 0.435 mm.) from the Engel-Gros Collection [PLATE 9, C]. The insignia, which are a perfectly correct dimidation, or impalement by halving, of the arms of Aragon and of the cadet line of the house of La Cerda (by marriage lords of Lara and Vizcaya), appear to refer to the daughters of Isabella, wife of John of Aragon, lord of Elche, slain by Peter the Cruel in 1358, in whom the line ended about or after the third quarter of the fourteenth century. The ornament, except here for the ring of blue lines round the middle, is in lustre pigment, as is the eagle upon the back; the motif was possibly derived from the vair seen in the Hispanic Society's vase neck or its textile original.

An early fifteenth-century style dated by a dish in the Wallace Collection with the arms of Burgundy, 1404-30, has a sparse foliage ornament upon a dotted ground, in most examples also an animal figure in blue and an inscription in Gothic lettering. The contemporary diffusion of motifs drawn from Manises lustre is illustrated by the drug-vase (*tarro*) with ornament in blue, attributed to Catalonia, in the Instituto de Valencia de Don Juan [PLATE 11, B].

For the variety of wares produced throughout the fifteenth century reference must be made to the documents (Osma, especially II and Adiciones); laconism is of the essence of trade descriptions, and majolica was being produced by the dozen or, unlustred, by the gross, and packed in large earthenware jars

[11] Published, from the Archives of the Crown of Aragon at Barcelona, by A. Rubió y Lluch, " Documents per l'historia de la cultura catalana mig eval," II, 373.

[12] The body of Saint Vincent the deacon, who was martyred at Valencia probably in A.D. 304, was according to one legend, transported by sea to the Algarve (Cape St. Vincent) and thence in 1173 to Lisbon; cf. " Terra Portuguesa," I, 37, for the Lisbon ships; and, for further remarks on the vessel and illustrations of similar ships in Catalan ' Consolats' of the early XVI century, the writers' " Supplementary Studies," 32, 1911.

for export. The existence, at the port of Valencia, of a warehouse kept (1451)
by a notary, Felipe Francés, in which he stocked pottery, shows the importance
of the Valencian oversea trade at that time, if it leaves one to imagine the
machinery by which dishes were purveyed for Italy in such profusion *c.* 1470,
in the blue or golden foliage styles, or in them combined. The pitcher illustrated, from the collection of Mr. H. Avray Tipping, with the I H S monogram
in lustre is, of extant shapes, most unusual [PLATE 10]. A difference between
the contemporary Italian and native tastes is, it would seem, reflected by the
rarity of Spanish arms upon such pieces, as witness also the dishes made for the
Buyls, now in the Victoria and Albert [PLATE 9, D] and Lyons Museums.

If boldness and vigour are the note of ceramic ornament under Alfonso V,
richness and finish may be claimed for the foliage with incised venations, under
his successor, John II (1458-79) ; and elaboration, under Ferdinand II (1479-
1516), with whom closes the series of grand styles. Adaptations of Renaissance
ornament and the disuse of heraldry characterize the advancing sixteenth
century, so that less exact evidence for style is discernible from about 1550 to
1600, than from the expulsion of the Moriscos in 1610 and the reorganization
of the industry at Manises under the Buyl patronage (1614), until about 1650.

The enamel and lustre technique flourished also at lesser centres, such as
Mislata, Muel, near Zaragoza, whose technical process has been preserved in
the simple narrative of the Dutchman, Henry Cock, and Calatayud. In green
and manganese, the combination favoured at Teruel, monumental tilework can
be shown dating from the thirteenth or fourteenth century. A jug in the
Plandiura collection illustrates a striking phase of the local ornament in blue
on white [PLATE 11, A].

Two of the earliest groups of tiles dating from after the reconquest proceed
from (i) the Church of Santa Marina, Seville, and (ii) Cordova Cathedral. The
first are of lozenge shape, *melado* glazed, stamped in relief with a triple-towered
castle and an eagle, the insignia of the Infante Philip, brother of Alfonso X,
dating 1252-69 (?) ; similar tiles are located in a chapel of the Lagarto cloister
of Seville Cathedral. The Cordovan group show, in various combinations of
enamel, *melado* and manganese, the arms of the first dean of Cordova, Ruiz
Fernández (d. 1293), and of allied conquistador families.

SEVILLE.—At Seville the ceramic note is for the most part polychromatic.
The wall-lining or dado of tile mosaic (*alicatado*) in its primitive form is entirely
composed of small sections of earthenware (*aliceres*) enamelled in monochrome : white, green, blue, purple, or *melado*, cut after firing, to form both
the white, radiating interlacings (*lacerias*) of right lines and the fields they
enclose [PLATE 12, B]. This process—the comparatively rare specimens of
which assign it to the Almohade period—can never have been other than
laborious ; it is yet obviously an advance upon the inlays of Medina az-Zahra.

A further step was a tilework of very similar pattern with geometrical interlacings of narrow, white enamelled fillets (*cintas*) forming series of detached
star-rosettes, the whole composed of separately fashioned and enamelled *aliceres*.
The dado of the Patio de las Doncellas, in the Alcázar of Seville, is a fine
specimen of this technique, *temp.* Peter the Cruel.

About the middle of the fifteenth century the design was obtained by
impressing the interlacing fillets by means of a stamp or mould ; these then
received a filling of grease tinted with manganese, which dried in the firing.
Hence the term *cuerda seca*, applied to such tiles ; the " dry cord " preventing
intermixture of the glazes [PLATE 12, C].

Varieties of *cuerda seca* were obtained by stamping interlacings of lesser depth, or by drawing them freehand. Finally the hollow tile (*de cuenca*) was produced with a stamp which left edges, etc., in relief, the shallow sinkings displaying Gothic or Renaissance designs, plant-form as well as geometrical interlacings [PLATE 12, D]. This technique, which obtained from the late fifteenth to the end of the seventeenth century, was employed in the Casa de Pilatos, built by the Enriquez de Ribera family, in the early sixteenth.

But the great treasure-house of mosaic and stamped tilework is the Alhambra, whose walls exhibit magnificent specimens of all the techniques described, including also more than one style of painted tile or *azulejo*. According to Seco de Lucena the incrusted frieze to the *alicatado* of the Mirador de Lindaraja and Torre del Cautivo, is unique.

Executed by the *cuerda seca* process is the well-known enamelled ware of the fifteenth-sixteenth century, formerly attributed, upon the strength of a problematical inscription or signature, to the town of Puente del Arzobispo, near Toledo. The principal pieces are dishes, roundels, armorial panels, and even architectural adjuncts. The final [PLATE 12, A] in the Victoria and Albert Museum, is probably from San Juan de la Penitencia, Toledo, a Franciscan convent founded by Cardinal Ximenes in 1514, and it would appear to date from about 1520. Osma considered the technique to have been practised as late as 1540-50, for designs which (e.g., extending over adjoining surfaces) would have required more than one stamping.

There remains for mention the class of imposing works in terra-cotta with incised or stamped ornament, made especially in south and central Spain since mediæval times, including amphora-shaped jars (*tinajas*), well-heads and baptismal fonts. The finest specimens of the latter, enamelled in green, with modelled surfaces, were produced at Triana, the pottery suburb of Seville, from the fifteenth to the seventeenth century, and are technical masterpieces.

II. RENAISSANCE AND MODERN POTTERY. *By Bernard Rackham*

RENAISSANCE POTTERY.—The year 1503 may be taken as a landmark in the history of Spanish pottery, for to that year belongs the earliest of a number of surviving works in which the influence of the Italian Renaissance suddenly makes its appearance. The works in question are pictures made up of painted maiolica tiles by one Niculoso Francisco. Nothing is known about this artist beyond what his paintings tell us, but their style is an unmistakable witness to his Tuscan origin. This testimony is borne out by his signatures in which he calls himself variously " Italiano " and " Pisano." That the technique, which is in fact that of Italian maiolica, polychrome painting before firing on a ground of tin enamel, was an innovation in Spanish tilework is shown by the fact that from his time onward such tiles were known as *azulejos de pisano*; we find them so described, for instance, in documents of 1584 and succeeding years. Niculoso Francisco came therefore from Pisa, and his tilework shows in certain particulars a close resemblance to contemporary Tuscan tiles, notably those which once formed the pavement of the chapel in the Petrucci Palace at Siena and are now distributed in various European Museums. There is one feature of the Spanish tiles which is of great importance—they indicate the first appearance of the *tile-picture*, that is a representational painting carried over a number of square tiles laid together. In Italy such pictures are unknown; the tiles of the Italian pavements, whether purely decorative or pictorial, are at this early stage each complete in themselves, forming a unit of design, and when, later, compositions continuing from one tile to another were introduced, they were purely decorative and not of a pictorial character. The tilework pictures of Niculoso are the first of their kind, and were followed by a numerous offspring both in Spain and Portugal, and in the Netherlands, where towards the middle of the sixteenth century this method of decoration attained a wide popularity. In another respect the Spanish maiolica tiles differ from the Italian; following the tradition of the *cuenca* tiles of the fifteenth century, discussed in the preceding article, they were used for covering walls as well as for paving, whereas in Italy wall-tiles are of the greatest rarity, such examples as the band of tiles painted each with a rose, introduced in the external walls of the Rocca Malatestiana at Rimini, being quite exceptional.

The tile-pictures of Niculoso are of such importance in Spanish ceramic history that it will be worth while to give a brief survey of them. Most of them are found in or near Seville, so that we may conclude that he worked at that place. The earliest extant, dated 1503, is a tomb-slab of tilework painted with a recumbent figure in the church of Sta. Ana at Triana. The most important are the wide frieze set with medallions containing figures in relief in enamelled terra-cotta like that of the Della Robbia (the work of the sculptor Pedro Millán), which forms the archivolt of the main doorway of the church of Sta. Paula, Seville, and the "Retable of the Catholic Kings," dated 1504, in the oratory of the Alcazar of the same city. This retable is in the form of a recess with a painting of the Visitation surrounded by a "Tree of Jesse," beyond which is a "plateresque" border with grotesques of the *candaliere* type common in Italian maiolica of the period (as in the Sienese pavement already mentioned). The altar frontal is also of painted tilework, showing a wreathed medallion depicting the Annunciation, flanked by female centaur-dragons carrying torches. There is a marked difference in manner between the Annunciation, which like the grotesque designs completing the frontal is thoroughly Italian in character, and the Visitation of the retable, in which Señor J. Gestoso y Pérez, who has described the work of Niculoso in detail, sees a "Gothicism" betraying German or Flemish influence; he suggests that in neither case was Niculoso his own designer, and that in the Visitation he was following an original by one of the Northern artists then working at Seville. The design of the "Jesse" is also purely Northern, with the various personages of the lineage represented by half-figures issuing from formal blossoms. Later tile-pictures by Niculoso and his followers are to be seen at Tentudia (Estremadura), and the Rijks Museum at Amsterdam possesses a signed panel of the *Visitation* [reproduced on PLATE 5, B], from a church in Portugal, which in the main follows the design of the Seville retable. This panel shows the strong colouring characteristic of Faenza maiolica of the end of the fifteenth century, with drawing in a heavy dark blue, a few thin washes of manganese-purple and greenish-blue, and details in yellow and orange. In the Victoria and Albert Museum is a fragment of a sixteenth-century maiolica floor-tile from the church of St. John the Baptist, Bristol, which may also be attributed to the kilns of Seville.

After the beginning of the sixteenth century the Valencian potteries, which had been the great centre of the industry, began to be outstripped by those of Talavera de la Reina and the neighbouring town of Puente del Arzobispo. Pottery of a kind had been made in these places from early times, but it was only with the spread of the Italian influence introduced by Niculoso Francisco that the wares began to be artistically important. The earliest literary evidence of Talavera pottery is that of Marineo Siculo in 1484. In 1536 the industry had advanced so far that one Garcia Fernández, in a history of the town, speaks of pottery exported thence not only throughout Spain and Portugal but also to the Indies, and during the sixteenth century potters from Talavera were sent out to Mexico to found the industry still flourishing at Puebla de los Angeles in that country. In 1545 we find mention of vessels of all kinds in Talavera ware in an inventory of goods belonging to the Duchess of Medinaceli. The productions of Talavera and Puente del Arzobispo are, with the rarest exceptions, unmarked, but excavations in the *casqueras* or rubbish-shoots of both places have been a help in identification and chronological classification.

From their first artistic emergence in the sixteenth century the wares of these two places (they are hard to distinguish one from the other and must be treated as a single group) begin to show a strongly individual character, a wild virility of design which gives them a very definite æsthetic value. We find large dishes painted in blue with vigorous figures of animals or birds enclosed by borders of rough foliage and tendrils; similar designs occur in another class in which the blue is closely intermingled with short strokes of manganese-purple and reddish orange, with good chromatic effect [PLATES 13; 14, A]. Alongside this thoroughly native mode may be noticed in certain pear-shaped polychrome jars with heraldry set among symmetrical " *ferronnerie* " and strapwork designs, a conscious effort to fall in with the fashion of the time as dictated especially from Antwerp. In tilework, of which there was a prolific output at Talavera, there are evident traces, in the ambitious tile-pictures and decorative panels, of the same Netherlandish influences blended with an Italian strain coming through the channel of Niculoso Pisano and his Sevillian school; but in the pottery proper this seems to have been no more than a passing phase, and in the seventeenth century the native stock blossoms in the full strength of its development. It is noteworthy that a large proportion of the output consisted of vessels of exceptional size, dishes, two-handled jars, barrels or cisterns and great basins for *limonadas*, as well as articles of fanciful shape such as jugs, candlesticks and inkstands modelled in the form of animals or human figures. The drug-jars which figure largely among the productions of Talavera, as of most Spanish potteries, were in the seventeenth century generally painted with a boldly-drawn imperial eagle. In the colour scheme the keynote is struck by a copper-green, intense almost to the degree of harshness, reinforced by shades of strong yellow [PLATE 15]; a heavy manganese purple plays the leading part in holding in check this green tonality, the blue which completes the palette being of a weak greyish tone and used in relatively small quantity. In the monochrome blue-and-white wares which were made concurrently with the polychrome the blue is of the same somewhat ineffective quality. The designs employed at this time consist predominantly of landscapes covering the whole surface and serving, in a manner which almost at first sight suggests the theatre, as the scene for vigorous movement either of human figures—horsemen in combat, hunters in pursuit of their quarry or children in lively play—or of wild beasts and their prey [PLATES 14, B; 16, A]. These motives were doubtless prompted by contemporary engraving—the influence of Tempesta is apparent—but in their coloured rendering at the hands of the Talavera pottery-painters, they took on a strongly personal and masculine character which is their title to estimation as an original body of work. The drawing is loose but never languid; it is instinct with a wild luxuriance which, together with the pungent colouring, makes of Talavera ware the most truly Spanish of all Spanish pottery. In the eighteenth century the rise of the Alcora factory drove Talavera, and the neighbouring Puente del Arzobispo, into the second rank; their wares, as " peasant pottery " have retained in an unassuming way the individual character which they took on three centuries ago, dominated by the green pigment which was still, until recent times at least, prepared from copper coins by a quaintly primitive process described in the monograph of Paramó. The Victoria and Albert Museum possesses a good modern example in a deep basin with a design, incoherent as representation, of which nevertheless the sweeping brushwork and powerful colouring have real decorative worth.

ALCORA POTTERY.—A new foreign strain was introduced in Spanish pottery when in 1727 Don Buenaventura Pedro de Alcantara, Count of Aranda, founded a faïence factory on his estate at Alcora, in the province of Valencia. The purpose of this young nobleman in establishing the factory seems to have been equally to give scope to his own interest in art and to exploit for the benefit of his vassals the industry, purely local in its scope, already carried on in the place. Among the chief painters engaged by the Count to control the decoration of the wares were two Frenchmen, Edouard Roux and Joseph Olerys (the latter by birth a Marseillais) from Moustiers. To these artists is due the pronounced French character of the designs, which bear a close resemblance to those of Moustiers faïence. We find either in blue monochrome or in a combination of blue, orange, green and purple, dominated by orange, borders of lacework or of sprays of flowers, small groups of figures of a grotesque type in the manner of Callot scattered inconsequently over the surface [PLATE 16, B], and airy constructions of architecture, busts, garlands and baroque scrollwork derived from the engravings of Bérain. Flower-painting at Alcora took on a very distinctive fashion of its own in large bouquets and closely massed borders of blossom treated in a full-bodied manner verging on the naturalistic but never losing their decorative quality. In due course the rococo appeared, under the influence of the Buen Retiro porcelain factory, in the turgid, somewhat bombastic form which it assumed in Spanish art. At last, when in 1749 Don Buenaventura died and was succeeded by his son Don Pedro Pablo, the faïence to which the factory owes its chief title to consideration took a place of secondary importance and the manufacture of porcelain began to be its chief preoccupation. A final development came about after the death of Don Pedro Pablo in 1798, when competition with imported English earthenware compelled Alcora in common with most Continental potteries to make lead-glazed *terre de pipe* or cream-coloured ware its staple product.

Neither the porcelain nor the lead-glazed ware of Alcora is of much artistic interest. The faïence, on the other hand, even in its greatest extravagances, has decided attractiveness. It was produced in many ambitious and grandiose forms, such as life-size busts, elaborate chandeliers, large wall-cisterns and basins [PLATE 17, A], centre-pieces in the form of an openwork pyramid with a figure on the top, and particularly the earthenware pictures with rococo framework of almost violent contortion made for hanging on the wall. These pictures are either scriptural or mythological in subject, and often bear the signature of a Spanish painter, Miguel Soliva. An example of one type of his work, in which a dense crowd of little figures is introduced in a wide landscape or an elaborate architectural setting, is to be seen in the British Museum. Two pictures at South Kensington with mythological subjects treated in a broader and more effective manner, are unsigned but may be attributed to this painter [PLATE 17, B]. At the same place there are good examples of the figures in cream-coloured ware, particularly some groups of children in the dress of the last decade of the eighteenth century, belonging to the last stage in the career of Alcora.

BUEN RETIRO PORCELAIN.—Spain was no exception to the rule by which, in the eighteenth century, a porcelain factory became an indispensable adjunct to a Continental Court. It was, however, only on the succession to the Spanish throne in 1759 of the Infante Charles, King of Naples, that this came to pass. This sovereign appears to have been won to the fascinations of porcelain by his marriage with a Saxon princess, familiar with the wonders that came from her father's factory at Meissen. In 1743 Charles founded the famous Capo di Monte factory at Naples, and on his migration to Madrid he must needs take with him to his new capital the entire establishment, with nearly all its Italian staff. The new factory at Buen Retiro began work in 1760, and at first its various departments were almost entirely controlled by Neapolitans or other foreigners, the most influential being José Gricci, in charge of the modellers and throwers. Pupils in sculpture and painting were taken from the Academy of San Fernando. All the work of artistic significance of the factory was done before 1803, when its direction passed into the hands of Bartolomé Sureda and commercialism became the order of the day, its activities being no longer limited to supplying the demands of the Court.

The productions of Buen Retiro at first showed a strong similarity to those of Capo di Monte, and indeed are not always easy to distinguish from them. They must, however, soon have developed the distinctively Spanish quality by which at their best they are marked [PLATE 19, A]. The porcelain was, during the eighteenth century, a variety of soft paste and generally shows a mellow wax-like consistency by which it differs perceptibly from any other kind. It was found eminently suitable for figure-modelling, but on account of its liability to crack less fit for "useful" wares; for this reason the proportion of figures and ornamental vases is greater than in the output of most other porcelain factories.

It is indeed by the figures produced during the first two or three decades of its existence that Buen Retiro establishes its title to consideration among the leading porcelain factories of Europe. Its ambitions were high from the very first. In 1763, in emulation of an achievement of the Capo di Monte factory during the residence of King Charles at Naples, porcelain decorations were put in hand under the direction of José Gricci for the entire lining of walls and ceiling in a saloon of the Royal Palace at Aranjuez, and shortly after a similar scheme was carried out in the palace at Madrid. These decorations consist of groups of figures in high relief connected by rococo scrollwork and festoons. To Gricci may undoubtedly be attributed the bulk of the figures and groups which at this time were turned out by the factory. Many of these draw their subjects from the repertory of classical mythology to which in all countries porcelain modellers were all too prone to turn for a supply of ready-made themes. In their strongly realistic treatment they are not widely dissimilar to their Neapolitan forerunners; they may, however, be best distinguished from them by a certain full-blooded lusciousness. A class apart is formed by a number of figures and groups, apparently the work of another modeller, representing peasants and fisherfolk in lively movement, often with a decided touch of the burlesque [PLATE 19, B]. In the careful suppression of fidgety details and the easy flow of form their modelling is quite admirable; not less so is the wise restraint, in strong contrast with the over-painting of Capo di Monte, shown in the extent and choice of the colouring used. This latter excellence the Buen Retiro figures share with the early Chelsea figures of the "red anchor" period [PLATE 18]. The less common specimens which have been left entirely without enamelling have an even greater charm [PLATE 19, C]. The vases and other vessels produced at the same time have pronounced merit as embodiments of the rococo.

Towards the end of the century a less satisfactory development set in. The lively earlier forms were abandoned in favour of a staid classicism [PLATE 20]. Dignity became the aim of the figure modellers; vases were condemned to take on severe antique shapes sometimes made tolerable by a graceful " Pompeian " decoration of pleasant colouring encompassing a panel with a landscape or a literary scene to meet the tastes of the time for topography and the classics. The jasper ware of Wedgwood, with its reliefs in white on a blue ground, was even imitated in porcelain. But it is hard to feel any warmth of enthusiasm for these later creations of the factory, and it would be unkind to its reputation to dwell on the dreary things that came from its kilns in the last years of its career. It is to the vigorous models of its prime, in which we see a Neapolitan stranger healthily acclimatized on Spanish soil, that Buen Retiro owes its merited renown.

III. GLASS. *By Bernard Rackham*

GLASS-BLOWING is a minor art which only here and there, and at a few periods—in the days of the early Roman emperors, at Damascus in the Middle Ages, and a little later in Venice—has risen to the heights of dignity reached by the arts of the goldsmith, the weaver or the potter. In Spain the craft would seem to have been practised from Roman times onwards, and the produce of it, though making no pretensions to distinction, shows for the most part a pleasant and strongly individual quality. The glass made under Roman rule seems to have shared the character common to that of other parts of the empire, and does not call for special comment here. Nor is it possible to speak with certainty as to the nature of mediæval Spanish glass. It may be well to refer here to the glass vessels found in the recent excavations on the site of Medina az-Zahra, near Cordova. One of these in particular, a noble round-based beaker cut with symmetrical volutes and cone-ornaments, is described by Don Ricardo Velázquez Bosco in his work on the excavations as showing motives entirely of Greek tradition. He goes so far as to suggest that this glass may have formed part of a gift to the Caliph from the Greek emperor. He seems to have overlooked the strong similarity between this glass and the so-called " St. Hedwig glasses " to be seen in several German Museums, which are now recognized as being closely akin to Egyptian crystal carvings of the Fâtimite period; the ornament on the glass, though doubtless ultimately of Hellenistic derivation, finds its nearest analogies in Egyptian art of the period, and no presentation of gifts from Constantinople is needful to explain its presence at the seat of the Caliph.

It may safely be said that very few of the Spanish glasses to be seen in museums or collections can be dated before the sixteenth century. Their precise classification is difficult, in spite of the fairly frequent mention in written records of glass-making localities, but it is possible to group them round three main centres of production, corresponding with three strains of derivation. The first of these is Almería in the south-east of Andalusia, in which, as might be expected, Saracenic influence is dominant, the second is Barcelona, where types were determined by the influence of imported Venetian glass, and the third the factory established in the eighteenth century under royal patronage at La Granja de San Ildefonso in the province of Toledo, where German and Bohemian fashions made their appearance in the hands of immigrant foreign workmen.

Of the three types, that of Almería with its Eastern traditions, is certainly the most interesting. The " metal " is always more or less deeply coloured, in various shades of green derived from iron in its composition, from a watery blue-green to a dark brownish olive. The vessels are generally of small size, jugs, flasks and vases, and show a feature which distinguishes them from all other glass whatsoever, the extraordinary exuberance of their decoration with applied threads, serrated ridges, spines, and festoons of glass worked up with the pincers, and sometimes a multiplicity of crinkly handles [PLATES 21, B; 22, A]. In spite of their very bizarre shapes and embellishments, these wildings of the glass-blowers' craft have an attractiveness in their fresh spontaneity rivalling that of the beautiful but more serious work of the Venetian artists. They are the instantaneous expression of a happy thought caught and crystallized in endur-ing though fragile form. The parentage of this most Spanish type of glass is perhaps to be traced in a long-necked vase illustrated by Srta. Teresa Amattler in the catalogue of her collection. This vase, decorated with small loop handles and an urchin-like array of pinched-up prickles, is classed as " Hispano-Arab " and attributed to the thirteenth or fourteenth century; it seems to provide the needful link with the glasses from the Syrian coast-towns which are similarly distinguished by the ingenious and beautiful use made of the physical properties of the material in its molten state. This Andalusian group, from the glass-houses of Almería and other places in south-eastern Spain, is better represented at South Kensington than in most museum collections. Some of the specimens there shown are believed to go back to the sixteenth and seventeenth centuries; it is likely, however, that the wares of this region maintained their character with little change until recent times.

The second group, from Catalonia, shows marked affinities with Venetian glass, the traces of which were not lost in the offshoot of the Catalan industry at Cadalso, in the province of Toledo. At Barcelona a glassblowers' guild was established in 1455 under the patronage of San Bernardino, whilst the glass of Cadalso was already renowned early in the sixteenth century. From these two districts we have vessels in clear or coloured glass (especially dark blue and opaque white), the former often decorated in the Venetian manner with bands or reticulated threads of white glass enclosed in its substance. Peculiar forms are those of the *porron* or drinking-vessel with long tapering spout and the *borracha*, a jar used for sprinkling rose-water at religious ceremonies, with a tube for filling, a narrow spout, and at the top a ring-shaped handle.

Barcelona is believed to be the place of origin of certain glasses—including two-handled vases, bowls, and standing dishes—which are decorated by the Venetian technique with painting in coloured enamels [PLATE 21, A]. They are readily distinguishable by their dominant green and yellow, the only additional pigments employed, sparingly, in their decoration being a dull opaque white and a greyish lavender-blue. The resultant colour-scheme combines with the spirited drawing of the animal and plant motives to give a pleasant air of fresh-ness to this rare group of glasses.

In the eighteenth century the native types of glass seem to have fallen from favour, and an effort was made to compete with the glasshouses of Northern Europe by the establishment of a factory under royal patronage, which after a short career at a place called Nuevo Bastan in the province of Madrid, was transferred about 1728 to La Granja de San Ildefonso, near Segovia. The glass made in this factory, which was carried on chiefly by foreign operatives, is a clear crystal similar to that of Silesia and the Netherlands, suited for cutting and engraving on the wheel. The decoration sometimes rivals in elaboration that practised by the German glass-cutters. The most distinctive form, how-ever, consists of simple floral sprays, festoons or small sprigs deeply engraved and afterwards gilded, or executed in gold on a flat surface. Occasionally as in the standing cup shown on PLATE 22, B, the exuberance of the Spanish temperament asserts itself even in this glass of exotic character, but in general the glass of La Granja is less engaging than the native types which were at that time playing a humbler rôle in the sphere of what is called " peasant art."

B—Fragments of unlustred ware, Medina az-Zahra

A—Fragments of lustred ware, Medina az-Zahra
(From drawings by Mr. R. P. Bedford)

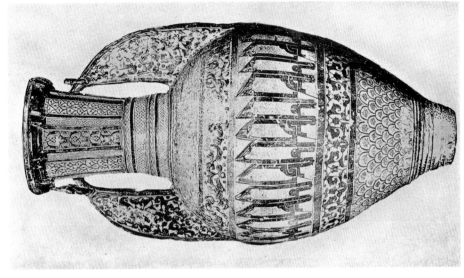

C—Vase; lustre on tin enamel. (Palermo Museum)

B—The "Alhambra" Vase; probably late 14th century. Painted in blue and lustre on tin enamel. Height, under 4 ft. 6 in. (Alhambra, Granada)

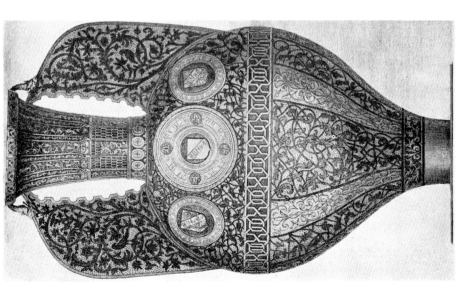

A—Vase, formerly in the Alhambra; (after Lozano)

A—Vase neck; 14th or 15th century. Lustre and blue on tin enamel. (Hispanic Society of America)

B—Vase neck. (Ars Classica, Geneva)

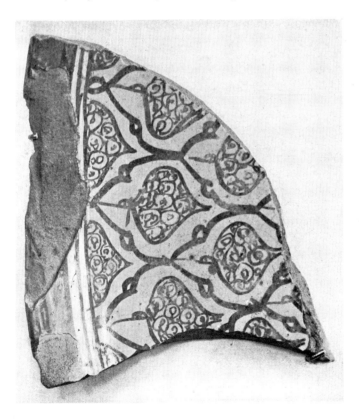

C—Lustred fragment; 14th or 15th century. (Victoria and Albert Museum)

D—Fragment of a lustred vase neck; 14th or 15th century. (Victoria and Albert Museum)

A—The Malaga dish. Andalusian. Diameter, 9 in. (Kaiser Friedrich Museum, Berlin)

B—Dish (restored) from excavations at Paterna. 14th century. Green and manganese brown on white. Diameter, 15 in. (Barcelona Museum)

B—*The Visitation.* Tile-picture, painted in blue with washes of purple, greenish-blue, orange and yellow; signed NICULOSO ITALIANO ME FECIT. Seville, early 16th century. (Nederlandsch Museum, Amsterdam)

A—Albaicín revetment; early 15th century. (Instituto de Valencia de Don Juan, Madrid)

B—Tiles; various colours; Paterna ware. (Spanish Art Gallery)

A—Drug vase; blue on tin enamel. Paterna ware. (Victoria and Albert Museum)

A, B—   —C

A, B—Tiles, Valencian; blue and white. (Victoria and Albert Museum)   C—Tile, blue and white.   (From Font y Gumá)

D—Tiles, dark red and white; probably Valencian. (Victoria and Albert Museum)

The " Ship bowl," lustre and blue on tin enamel; Manises, early 15th century. Diameter, 20 in. (Victoria and Albert Museum)

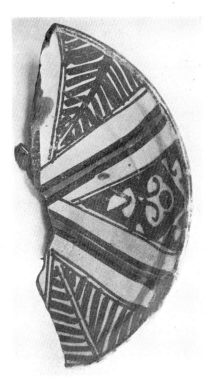

A—Dish, lustre and blue; Manises, 1406-54. (Wallace Collection)

B—Fragment, lustre and blue; Manises, early 15th century. (Victoria and Albert Museum)

C—Dish, lustre and blue; Manises. (Formerly Engel-Gros Collection)

D—Dish, lustre and blue, with arms of Buyl; Manises, c. 1475. (Victoria and Albert Museum)

Pitcher, lustre and blue on tin enamel; Manises, *c.* 1475. Height, 12¾ in. (H. Avray Tipping Collection, Victoria and Albert Museum)

A—Pitcher of Teruel (Aragon) Ware; blue on white. 15th century. Height, about 15¾ in. (Plandiura Collection)

B—Drug Jar, Catalonia; blue on white. 15th century. (Instituto de Valencia de Don Juan, Madrid)

A—Cuerda seca finial. Toledo. *c.* 1520.

B—Primitive tile mosaic
C—Cuerda seca tile, polychrome
D—Cuenca tiles, polychrome

(All in the Victoria and Albert Museum)

A—Plate, Catalonian, painted in orange, blue and green. Diameter, 13¾ in. 16th century. (Plandiura Collection)

B—Catalonian Plate, painted in blue, orange and green. Diameter, 15 in. 16th century. (Plandiura Collection)

C—Talavera plate, orange, brown, dark and light blue. Diameter, 15¾ in. 16th century. (Plandiura Collection)

D—Catalonian Plate, blue on white. Diameter, 15 in. 16th century. (Arxiu Mas Collection)

B—Jar, earthenware, painted in blue.   Talavera.   17th century

A—Dish, earthenware, painted in dark blue and reddish orange.   Talavera.
16th century

(Both in the Victoria and Albert Museum)

Large bowl, earthenware, painted in colours, with a bull-fight. Talavera. 17th century. (Victoria and Albert Museum)

B—Dish, earthenware, painted in blue, green, orange and purple. Alcora, 18th century

A—Shallow bowl, earthenware, painted in green, orange and brown. Talavera, 17th century

(Both in the Victoria and Albert Museum)

B—*The Triumph of Galatea.* Wall-panel, earthenware, painted in colours. Alcora, 18th century

A—Cistern and basin, earthenware, painted in blue; touches of red on the figure. Alcora, 18th century
(Both in the Victoria and Albert Museum)

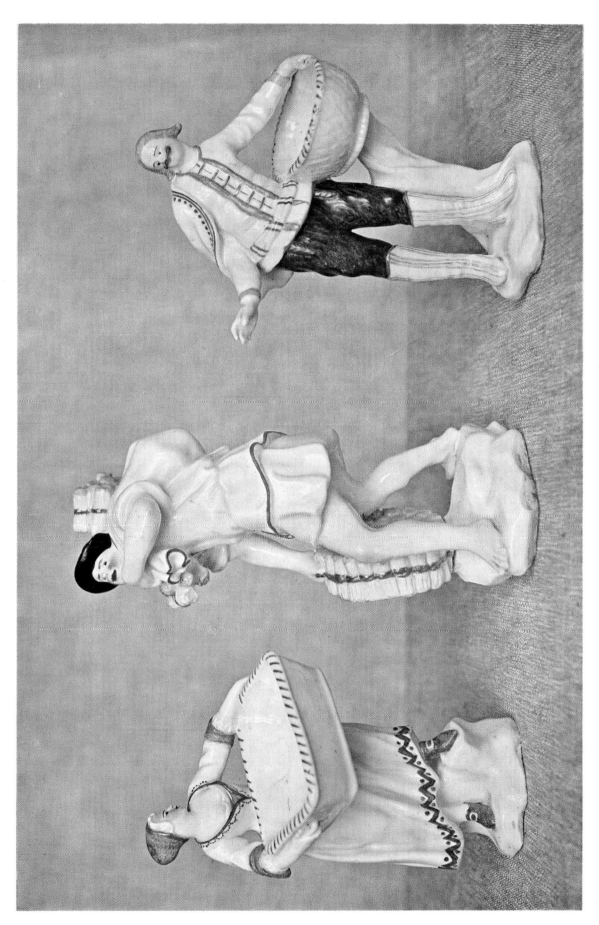

Figures of peasants, porcelain. Buen Retiro. About 1765. Actual size. (Mr. A. H. Bunford)

A—Tray, porcelain, painted in colours and gilt.   Buen Retiro.   About 1765

B—Group, porcelain, painted in colours.   Buen Retiro.   About 1765

C—Figure of a man, white porcelain.
Buen Retiro, about 1765

(All in the Victoria and Albert Museum)

—C

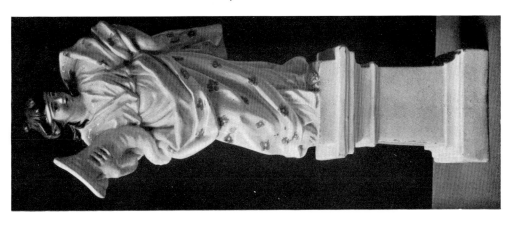

A, C—Pair of allegorical figures, porcelain, painted in colours. B—Vase, porcelain, painted in colours with mythological scenes in panels. All Buen Retiro; about 1780. (Victoria and Albert Museum)

A, B—

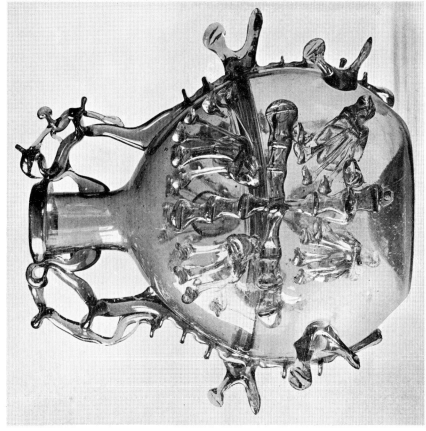

B—Flask, brownish-green glass. Province of Almeria. 17th century

A—Dish on foot, glass painted in enamel colours. Barcelona. 16th century.

(Both in the Victoria and Albert Museum)

B—**Goblet**, with engraved ornament. La Granja de San Ildefonso. 18th century.

A—Vase, pale brownish glass. Province of Almería. 17th century
(Both in the Victoria and Albert Museum)

WOODWORK. *By Bernard Bevan*

EARLY INFLUENCES.—During the Middle Ages no part of Europe was subject to so many foreign and conflicting influences as the Iberian peninsula. They affected the arts and crafts in Spain no less than the daily life of the people. Moreover they overlapped each other and so cannot be accurately described in chronological order. The Moorish influence, for instance, though it was the first to appear in woodwork, is still to be found, reduced to minor decoration, it is true, as late as the eighteenth century.

The five undercurrents which most affected the trend of Spanish design were Moorish, French, Netherlandish and German, Italian, and, with the accession of the Bourbon dynasty, French again. To these must be added certain Dutch, native American, and Portuguese influences, and indirectly through the last, Persian, Indo-Chinese, and English. The position therefore of Spanish furniture in the history of art is a hybrid one, and possibly for this reason has claimed far less attention than it deserves. The Northern influences merely filtered in, in comparatively small proportions, chiefly through the Church. The alien styles were received very late into Spain owing to her isolation, and fashions persisted long after they had been superseded in the countries of their origin.

The Moors, though they lost the greater part of Spain during the campaigns of Ferdinand III, and were finally conquered after the fall of Granada in 1492, remained on in large numbers for more than a hundred years, pursuing their various callings as craftsmen, including that of carpentry, in which they greatly excelled the Spaniards. It is to these subdued Moors, or Mudéjares as they were called, as well as to their long mastery over the country in more fortunate times, that we owe the continuance and overwhelming importance of the Moorish style in Spanish art.

It should be remembered that the Oriental mode of existence had sunk far more deeply into the life of Spain than would have at first been deemed possible. As I have already stated the Moors remained on in Spain, occasionally even intermarrying with the Europeans, long after the conquest of Granada. Though compulsory baptism was forced upon them in 1525 by Cardinal Ximénez (Cisneros), after which they were contemptuously named Moriscos—" little Moors "; and though large numbers were slaughtered or sold into slavery in Castile after the rising of 1568 and the persecution of Archbishop Ribera, many still survived. It was not in fact till 1609 that the final blow came. Envy and religious bigotry, suspicion of sympathy with the Barbary Corsairs, and finally the mean betrayal of our James I of an earlier correspondence with Queen Elizabeth, sealed their fate. Thus it fell to Philip III to hasten the ruin of his country by the expulsion of half a million of its most industrious inhabitants. Their customs, however, remained.

Throughout the sixteenth and seventeenth centuries women sat on low cushions or stools (which accounts for the very low tables occasionally met with); and in Portugal as late as 1820 women of an older generation might sometimes be discovered furtively sitting cross-legged on chairs with their skirts arranged to disguise the fact. Mudéjar furniture is now exceedingly scarce, but a large wardrobe (one of a pair) was exhibited at Madrid in 1912.[1] The entire exterior,

---

[1] In the Exposición de Mobilario Español, by the Sociedad española de Amigos de Arte; illustrated in " Spanish Interiors and Furniture " by A. Byne and M. Stapley.

as well as the inner faces of the doors, are covered with strips in a geometric star pattern, and the whole technique is that of the "artesonado" ceiling.

In constructional woodwork the Moors reigned supreme, and their methods were followed with only slight deviation due to change of ornamentation, even after the tide of the Italian Renaissance had swept over the country.

CEILINGS.—The ceilings,[2] some of them veritable masterpieces, were called "artesonados" from the word "artesón" meaning a trough, but whether this refers to each separate coffer, or to the trough-like shape of the whole is a matter of doubt. The Spaniards use the term indiscriminately— almost any wooden ceiling being called an "artesonado." Structurally they may be divided into six classes: (1) crossed-beam; (2) crossed-beam, with the structural members hidden; (3) peaked, with an open timber framing exposing the rafters; (4) in the form of a vault, usually three-plane in section, with the rafters hidden; (5) polygonal and domical, the outcome of number four; (6) coffered, really an elaboration of class one.

Amongst the very few old books on this subject which have come to light, is a "Cenninesque" treatise, published in 1633 by one Diego Lopez de Arenas, a ceiling-maker of Seville. In it careful directions are given for the construction of all types of "artesonados" (many of the author's are still extant), and the fact that the book abounds with Moorish technical terms is sufficient proof, if indeed any were needed, of the origin of this craft. Diego was a member of the Carpenters' Guild (whose patron saint was Joseph), a large and prosperous body which met once a year at Corpus Christi in the Hospital of Santiago. Mr. Byne has shown that the carpenters not only made the ceilings but designed them. Usually it was, however, another craftsman who executed the painting.

The wood most often used was the so-called Spanish cedar, really a pine (the "pino alerce"), a tree rather like our common pine, only redder in colour. It is still fairly plentiful in the scanty forests of Spain, in the neighbourhood of Valladolid for example, and was probably to be seen in abundance a few centuries ago in the now treeless environs of Seville.

Somewhat similar ceilings are to be found in Sicily, dating from the Saracenic invasion, but here they never achieved lasting popularity, and are not so well preserved as those in Spain, which, owing partly to the heavy gilding and staining, have not succumbed to the ravages of worm or beetle. Belonging to the first category is a late fifteenth-century crossed-beam ceiling (with, however, certain Gothic details) in the Casa de las Dueñas at Seville, and another in the Palacío Infantado at Guadalajara. The old ninth-century ceiling in the Mosque of Cordova was also of this type, and now that the hideous early eighteenth-century vaulting is being done away with, it has lately been rendered visible again, though in many places wholly reconstructed.

Crossed-beam ceilings with the structural members hidden did not appeal to the Spaniards as did the other types, though there is a fine example in the Dormitory of Isabel the Catholic in the Alcázar of Seville, and another in the Salone di Maria Pradilla [PLATE 1, A], subtly decorated in "lacería" or interlacing patterns with strips of light wood giving the effect of inlay. In the great Palace of the Archbishops of Toledo at Alcalá de Henares (incidentally the birthplace of Cervantes and of Catherine of Aragon) is a vast hall, the Salon de Concilios, well over a hundred feet long, built in the fourteenth century by Archbishop Tenorio with the aid of Mudéjar workmen. The ceiling, though

[2] For a full account of which see A. Byne's and M. Stapley's "Decorated Wooden Ceilings in Spain."

drastically restored and repainted in the same glaring colours as those employed at the Alcázar at Seville, is still the finest example of the open-rafter type. It is three-plane in section, with coupled tie-beams brilliantly coloured. In some cases,[3] the tie-beams of these open-rafter ceilings were not only painted or carved but pierced with holes, a decoration more quaint than beautiful, commoner in Andalucía than elsewhere.

Ceilings in the form of a vault were used over long rooms or the aisles of churches [4] and are usually three-plane, though occasionally when greater height was required, more planes were introduced. Ceilings in five planes are not unusual, and in the Casa de Mesa, a fifteenth-century palace in Toledo, is a ceiling of seven. A unique specimen in the Salón de los Cazadores in the Infantado Palace, Guadalajara, is carved all over with fruit and flowers in such profusion as to remind one of baroque work. As a rule, however, all " artesonados " were crudely built. In the case of crossed-beam ceilings the transverse members were never let into the master-beams and large nails were left visible in panelling. Even the final painting is coarse when viewed closely, but the poor quality of the workmanship is scarcely discernible from below.

The most ingenious of the Mudéjar ceilings were those called " media naranja "—half-orange, in which the intersection of the beams produced the effect of a dome. One of the finest in Spain, though it has suffered from repeated restorations,[5] is that in the Hall of the Ambassadors in the Alcázar of Seville. It is made of cedar wood, the myriad ribs inlaid with box, while the interstices between the panels are filled with tiny mirrors. A scarcely less beautiful example is over the staircase in the Casa de Pilatos, the ancient home of the Riberas ; and in the South Kensington Museum is a late fifteenth-century " media naranja " [PLATE 1, B] from Torrijos (some twenty miles west of Toledo) made for Gutierrez de Cardenas and his wife Teresa Enríquez, whose arms appear in the spandrels.

The " half-orange " being admirably suited as a ceiling for grand staircases, was much copied by early sixteenth-century architects of the Renaissance, but without conspicuous success. For though imposing from their height—the cupola of the " Archivo de la Corona de Aragón " at Barcelona is nearly seventy feet above the pavement, and at Zaragoza, in the Royal Jockey Club (the old Palacio Ayerbe), the dome is of great magnitude—it was found wellnigh impossible to blend Italian and Moorish principles in dome-building. A brilliant example, however, covers the stair-hall in the Archiepiscopal Palace at Alcalá de Henares, and was erected by Alonso de Covarrubias, with the sculpture entrusted to Berruguete. The hall is rectangular, but by canting the corners (with the shell motif) the ends were made semi-hexagonal. The cupola, or rather vault, for it is three-plane, is divided into octagonal coffers. " Italo-Moorish " domes are also common in Portugal, and in the cathedral at Lamego the decoration is carried out in the most sumptuous Baroque.[6] The germ of the coffer may be traced in a curious ceiling in the monastery of La Sisla, near Toledo, where the beams are of immense thickness, simply moulded with the small transverse members carried on a double stepping with carved brackets. The great ceilings of the time of Ferdinand and Isabella in the Aljafería at Zaragoza are coffered, but show no signs of the departure from Moorish technique. That in the throne room is divided into thirty coffers, with pendant

[3] As at Santa Clara, Seville, and Santa Isabel, Granada.
[4] As at San Pablo, Cordova, where the " vault " is held together by twisted iron tie-rods.
[5] Erected in the 13th century by Pedro the Cruel ; rebuilt in 1427, again restored 100 years later under Charles V, and finally after a fire in 1760.
[6] For an illustration of this cupola, see " Mobilario Artístico Portuguez," by Sardœira and Guimaræz.

pineapples, by massive beams, unmoulded, and with narrow strips nailed to the soffits in intricate geometrical designs.

In the cabinet of King Ferdinand is a ceiling of unique composition with the decoration arranged round a central panel framing the Royal Arms. The heraldic motif is seldom found in Spanish ceilings as the carpenters were usually Moors, in whose art the escutcheon played no part.[7] The coffered ceilings of Spain, which were erected in large numbers by Renaissance architects, are as a rule heavier in style than those in which Mudéjar influence is more apparent. Sometimes they are of real magnificence, the main coffers becoming of great size and depth. These in their turn enclose secondary coffers set diagonally. The splendid cedar wood ceiling of the Salón de Cortes in the Audiencia or Law Courts at Valencia is of this type. The coffers here are cavernous and some six feet across, with the beams richly moulded and ornamented, the general effect being that of overpowering majesty. The many fine examples in the palace of Charles V in the Alhambra are too well known to need description.

DOORS.—The construction of doors was another branch of woodwork in which the Moors were peculiarly able. The old Moorish doors were of three distinct types. The earliest has the " lacería " carved out of the solid plank. The second, with its " lazo " work and " ensamblaje," was a simple form of joinery, and in the third the strips were applied (sometimes with nails) to the main body. There are several fine examples in the Alhambra, and one (Mudéjar) at the entrance to the Hall of the Ambassadors in the Alcázar of Seville. But geometric designs were not used for doors in Christian Spain to the extent that they were in ceilings, and it was the panelled type which was latterly more in favour. There is, however, an interesting Gothic-Mudéjar door in the little cloister at Guadalupe.

Church doorways in Spain are often of immense size, quite out of proportion to the buildings into which they lead, but usually of great strength, many confining their decoration to the studs, those (late Gothic) at Tarragona cathedral being amongst the finest. Gothic and Renaissance doorways are rare in Spain, and perhaps the two most celebrated are the Puerta del Claustro, Burgos (Teutonic fifteenth century), and that (Renaissance) in the Capilla del Obispo, Madrid.

DOMESTIC WOODWORK.—Of great importance is the simplicity of the Moorish interior, almost the sole article of furniture being the chest or arca, in which everything is kept, which serves as a seat by day, as a bed by night, and as luggage on a journey. A poor man has but one or two, a rich man several more. From this lack of ostentation is derived the simplicity of the Spanish interior. It is one of the peculiarities of the Spanish temperament that anything new and modern is discountenanced as effeminate or unnecessary. The Spaniard was slow to see the advantages of cupboards with shelves or drawers which the more practically minded nations, the Italians and French, adopted with such readiness. It is this which accounts for the continued popularity of the arca, as well as the scarcity of Spanish furniture other than beds, tables, chairs, and vargueños.

In the thirteenth and fourteenth centuries a French element had appeared in Northern and Eastern Spain, due to the presence of the great ecclesiastical Orders, especially that of Cluny. These oases of French culture in the midst of the Spanish desert were architecturally of great benefit to the country and

---

[7] Another example, however, may be seen in the Prætorium in the Casa de Pilatos, Seville, where the ceiling is set with square panels, some containing heraldic devices, carved and painted in black and gold.

woodwork was also probably affected, though examples of this date are exceedingly rare. This Gothic influence, however, prepared the way for the vast colonies of artists and workers of all trades, who in the fifteenth century came down from the Netherlands and Germany. From the old pictures of the Hispano-Flemish school we can gather some idea of their furniture; the huge four-poster beds, and the long, narrow chests, after the pattern of the Italian cassoni, usually carved with flamboyant tracery. An example of this type is the chest on PLATE 2, A, which, though of the early sixteenth century, retains much of the Franco-Netherlandish spirit.

Towards the end of the fifteenth century Gothic art was on the decline in Northern Europe, but in Spain it was by no means played out. The pulpit of hammered iron[8] in Avila cathedral and another of wood in Santa Tomás, are alone sufficient to prove the vitality of the style, although perhaps these last are the translation of a Renaissance idea into a Gothic language. However, purely Northern decoration was sometimes used in conjunction with the new forms as late as the seventeenth century. It is surprising, therefore, that Italianism, the " Obra del Romano " as it was called, should have taken such a hold on the country. The new style, nevertheless, introduced in the last decade of the fifteenth century, by the great ecclesiastical princes and powerful families such as the Fonsecas of Coca, the Mendozas of Guadalajara, the Riberas, and Velascos, proved irresistible. The Renaissance may have been introduced a little earlier into Catalonia by way of France, but its effect was insignificant in comparison with the direct Italian influence.

TABLES.—Furniture was less speedily transformed than architecture, and PLATE 2, B, shows a sacristy table with canted legs of the first quarter of the seventeenth century, the middle drawer of which is decorated with formal sprigs (carved out of the solid and not as in later work, applied) that still hark back to the days of flamboyant Gothic. On the two side drawers are carved the Keys of Heaven and the Instruments of the Passion, a most unusual decoration. The table on PLATE 2, C, though probably of about the same date as the preceding one, has lost all trace of the Gothic, and is thoroughly Italian in design. It is possible the drawers and consoles were recarved at a later date, for the stretchers are plainer than one would have expected. The four corner legs are deeply turned, and the fifth is twisted, a feature essentially Spanish, or rather Iberian, for it was greatly used in Portugal; and incidentally one can scarcely recall a baroque or Churrigueresque retablo in either country devoid of the spiral column. It might be concluded that important differences of style would exist in the scattered provinces of so vast a country, and one in which communications were so difficult, but on the contrary there was little provincial originality. Chisel cuts or mouldings were employed in distant parts of the peninsula identical to those introduced as much as forty years before, and for this reason it is impossible to date Spanish furniture with the same precision as we can English or French, by the use of certain decorative motifs.

The Refectory Table on PLATE 3, A, dates from the middle of the seventeenth century, and probably came from Pamplona. The stretchers are left unornamented and the turning of the legs is of the simplest. This example is only eleven feet nine and a half inches long, but in some cases these tables reach a length of over twenty feet. The tops are magnificent slabs of walnut, and the edges are never bevelled or even moulded as in the contemporary work of other countries. Another feature common to many Spanish tables, and

[8] There is a good illustration of this in " Segovia, Avila, und el Eskorial," by Dr. August Mayer.

well illustrated on PLATE 3, B, is the dovetail groove in the underside of the top, the aim of which was to obviate the use of nails and render the table more easily dismountable. Tables with bracing irons were nearly always fitted with this device, and were thus collapsible. Bracing irons were only used in conjunction with splayed legs (these were sometimes turned [9]), and the ironwork was often of great beauty. Occasionally, in the case of long tables, there were three pairs of splayed legs and two sets of bracing irons. The walnut table on PLATE 3, C, also of the late seventeenth century, exhibits the ponderous solidity characteristic of the late Renaissance in Spain. Chisel cuts in great variety took the place of mouldings, and the heavy panelling which was copied so profusely in the Netherlands made its appearance.

CHAIRS.—The oldest form of chair in Spain was probably that with the X or scissors-frame, and like other early Spanish furniture, was decorated in the Moorish style. In the Victoria and Albert Museum is a chair of this type [PLATE 4, A] of the late fifteenth or early sixteenth century, the whole frame of which is inlaid with wood and ivory in star patterns. Often, however, the stiff geometrical designs gave place to tiny dots of inlaid bone or ivory like Goa work, known as " grains of wheat." The seat, of cloth or leather, was hung, as was the back, and the Italian solid form of X chair is scarcely ever found in Spain. In fact at the very moment that the scissors-framed chair had reached the height of its popularity in Italy it was discarded in Spain, and superseded by the more ordinary quadrangular form.

Arm-chairs and high-backed chairs were common towards the middle of the sixteenth century. The seats were made of leather, sometimes covered with velvet, or quilted like scales, held down by large studs. Bone and ivory inlay was discontinued, and the front stretcher became flattened [as on PLATE 4, B, and C], richly carved, and occasionally showing traces of the contact of Spain with her newly-won American possessions. The arm-rests (and " remates ") either terminated in grotesque masks, or in simple scrolls. In Colonial furniture, Peruvian, Mexican, etc., the latter became disproportionately enlarged, and the arm-rests, as much as five inches in width, were often grooved. The sixteenth-century arm-chair on PLATE 4, C, if not actually of American origin, is characteristic of the Colonial influences. It is made of chestnut, the front stretcher carved, and the heavy scroll feet painted red and gold. It retains the original leather seat and back, painted with the arms of the Franciscan Order. The " remates " are typical of native American influence. Late in the seventeenth century much of the furniture was painted, in the South red, and in the North white and gold. There were five-backed settees, and the chairs assumed weird baroque forms[10] which persisted until the reaction brought about by the arrival of the Bourbons and the taste for French culture. I give an example of a typical Spanish Louis XVI chair [PLATE 4, D] to show how completely French fashions had undermined the design of furniture in Spain. Even the Balearic islands came under the spell, and at Palma in Majorca there lived one Adrian Ferran who did fine work in the Empire style, which however could not possibly be mistaken for real French. At Port Mahon on Minorca, however, much English furniture, pseudo Chippendale and Sheraton was made, but this is directly attributable to the long periods of British rule between 1713 and 1802.

---

[9] There is a good example in the Casa del Greco, Toledo.

[10] The example par excellence is the great arm-chair with its eerie personality, said to have belonged to Fra Antonio de Sotomayor, now in the Provincial Museum, Salamanca.

LEATHER.—I have already said that leather was used for chairs, but in Spain it also served the purpose of covering arcas, coaches,[11] travelling chests, benches, cushions, the walls and floors of palaces; and in churches it took the place of altar-fronts, tapestries, carpets, crowns for images, and upon it even pictures were painted. Undoubtedly the tanning of leather was originally a Moorish industry, and the word " guadamecíles," " guadamecí," or " guadamecíes " is usually traced to the town of Ghadâmes in Tripoli, where it is said, leather was made in the twelfth century. In Spain it was prepared at Granada, Seville, Toledo, Barcelona, Lérida, Ciudad Real, and Valladolid, but above all at Cordova.

The leather was at first quite plain, usually black, and used solely for utilitarian purposes, but later incised, or cut and punched decorations were introduced, and were much resorted to by the Spaniards in Mexico. Stamped and painted leather came into vogue in the early sixteenth century, but it was not till 1529 that gilding was practised, when the Ordinances of the Industry were confirmed by Charles V at Cordova. By this time embossed leather had been introduced, and not only were " guadamecíles " made in great quantities, but the leather was cut into the forms of columns, pilasters and friezes in the plateresque style, heavily embossed. But by the middle of the century the quality of Spanish leather, even at Cordova, had deteriorated, and Mr. Leonard Williams quotes [12] an ordinance of 1543 describing the leather then produced as " wretched, the colouring imperfect, the pieces undersized." An official licence was demanded of all " guadamecileros," who had to show that with their own hands they could mix their colours and make a cushion. But still the art degenerated. Pictures grew popular, and finally the industry was killed by the taste for French fashions. Early in the seventeenth century great numbers of the leather workers had already emigrated to Italy, France, and above all the Netherlands, where they produced a great deal of what is erroneously known as Spanish leather work. In fact, it is a moot point whether any good leather was made in Spain after 1650.

CABINETS.—The only indigenous piece of Spanish furniture is the vargueño, a species of cabinet with a drop front hinged at the bottom which could be used to write upon. The inside contained tiers of drawers, often richly gilded, inlaid with bone or ivory, or painted in polychrome—a veritable blaze of colour. Though the vargueño is pre-eminently Castilian—its name is said without much foundation to have been derived from Vargas, a desolate hamlet near Toledo—it was probably of Moorish origin, for a few early specimens have been found with scissors-stands, inlaid with " grains of wheat." The commoner stands are of several different types, the earliest being the box stand, a cupboard of four divisions, that is with two drawers above, and a cupboard with doors below, as on PLATE 5, B. The bottom portion, however, of the mid-sixteenth-century vargueño on PLATE 5, A, is composed of six divisions, and is probably unique in this respect. The two upper and lower divisions are cupboards with hinges placed at the side, while those in the centre are drawers.

Ironwork was much used as an embellishment to Spanish furniture, and most of the earlier drop fronts are faced with pierced iron mounts on a background of dark red velvet to show them up. These plaques assumed every conceivable variety of design, and later examples are often edged with the cable border, a motif really borrowed from the Portuguese, who being the most enter-

[11] For instance, the coach of Philip II, of black leather, studded with nails in the Museo Nacional dos Coches at Belem.
[12] In his " Arts and Crafts of Older Spain."

prising navigators of the age, naturally favoured a design reminding them of the sea. We see the cable in most specimens of Manueline architecture.

The vargueño locks were of very special construction and consisted of a hasp of great length, dropping from the top and sliding into the face of the patterned lock plate, which, like the mounts, is of perforated iron. These latter were sometimes gilded. The hinges of the drop front were placed inside, but the nails were driven in from the exterior, where the heads are carefully concealed by little scallop-shells usually three in number. The two heavy shells [PLATE 5, A] at the point of junction of the two parts of the vargueño are the heads of the pulls (sliding into slots), upon which the drop front rested when open or used for writing. In later days when Italianism had gained a stronger hold on the design of these cabinets, the pulls were often terminated with masks.

There can be no doubt that the vargueño is the direct ancestor of our modern drop-front secretaire, but the importance of its position in history as a " transitional " article of furniture is not generally understood. In reality it is derived from the " arcón " (a large " arca "), and its relation to the chest, primarily an article of practical use, not " de luxe," is confirmed by the long survival of ironwork handles at the sides—embellished, but ever strong and massive. Like the old Moorish arca it was not only used in the home but as luggage, a fact substantiated by its less well known name, the mule-chest. The example shown on PLATE 5, B, is a little later than the preceding specimen. The drop front has been opened to show the wealth and magnificence of the interior, with its many drawers and miniature arched portals flanked with spiral columns. The two sunk panels to each drawer are decorated with floral designs in colours on ivory, each framing a tiny landscape also painted on ivory. The same floral designs are repeated on a larger scale in the circular panels of the base— a common feature—and in this case show well the curious combination of Moorish and Italian ornament prevalent at this time. The other two forms of stand are (1) the trestle or " puente " and (2) the narrow table with turned splayed legs and bracing irons. Examples of the first type may be seen on PLATE 6.

The vargueño from the Salting Collection is made of walnut, and in the drop-front, which is decorated with inlaid strips of light wood in Moorish " lacería " or interlacing patterns, are sunk circular medallions, typically Italian in design. This is but another example of the blending of the " Obra del Romano " with the older influence, and this cabinet is not very much later than those with the box stands mentioned above. It is fitted, however, with a hinged top (not an early feature), which in the illustration is lifted to show the appliqué carvings in pear wood, of the interior. These, executed in the same style as those on the outside, but with far greater delicacy than most work of this date, consist of open arcades on a background of red velvet, also enclosing circular medallions with bearded heads. The hinged top was not commonly used for vargueños, and is generally found in connexion with " papeleras," little cabinets without drop-fronts or stands.

The cabinet on PLATE 6, A, is an example of the influence that the style of Berruguete and the Plateresque sculptors had upon furniture. It is of chestnut, the open front carved with medallion heads, demi-figures, and other grotesques. Despite the fact that vargueños were made in considerable quantities in Spain, cabinets were largely imported from abroad, Italy, Flanders, and Germany being the most prolific cabinet-making countries. By the end of the century this importation of foreign furniture had reached such a pitch that the prices of Spanish vargueños had fallen to half that realized by their alien competitors. Protection of the home industry was urgently needed, and at last, in 1603, Philip III passed a sumptuary pragmatic at Valladolid forbidding the admission of cabinets from Nuremberg. However, the foreign infiltration had done its work, and foreign peculiarities, especially Italian, are much to be found in later Spanish furniture. The drop front of the vargueño was discarded. Cabinets came architecturalized, and treated, in Neapolitan fashion, like miniature classic temples. The " portals " noticed in connexion with PLATE 5, B, were no longer blind, but gave entrance to little halls, surrounded with mirrors in gilt frames, and paved with black and white tiles. The tops became crested; the use of ebony and ivory inlay was much countenanced, also tortoise-shell for the panels of the little drawers. The sacristy cupboards, as well as the doors, in the Cartuja at Granada are perhaps the finest examples of this peculiarly un-Spanish phase in the furniture, but these are of far greater merit than most of the works of this epoch.

Following upon the conquests of Mexico, Peru, and Chile, in the early years of the sixteenth century, and the resultant glut of silver brought from America, repoussé work was used extensively, in fact to such a degree that towards the end of the century silver became relatively scarce, and its use on furniture was eventually prohibited.

BEDS.—Beds on the other hand were not equally sumptuous, at least in their woodwork. The frame was set high, and steps [13] were sometimes necessary. In Gothic days the beds were hung with damask curtains, vallances, and canopies in such profusion that most of the woodwork was hidden. In the winter, skins lined with cloth were used as bedclothes, and the number of different hangings used on the bed was quite extraordinary.[14] PLATE 7, A, illustrates an early sixteenth-century bed with spirally scored posts painted in polychrome, a favourite mode of decoration, particularly in Catalonia, though the use of colour was by no means confined to this region. Usually, it may be added, the brightest colours are to be found in the South, in Andalucía and Estramadura, while more sombre tones, black and dull gold were employed in the North. The amazingly coarse workmanship and lack of refinement common to all early Spanish furniture may be noted in connexion with this bed. Huge nails, apparently driven into delicate pieces with the utmost carelessness are allowed to pierce right through the wood, the truth of the matter being that the Spaniard cared more for strength and durability than for external appearance. In a decree published at Granada, commenting upon the defectiveness of the chairs then produced—I quote Mr. Williams—it was expressly ordained that the nails which fasten the seat of the chair to the legs must traverse the frame completely and be hammered back upon the other side.

During the seventeenth century Catalonia evolved a form of bed peculiar to herself. The head was made quite separate from the frame and hung on the wall. It became very elaborate as the century advanced, and often took the form of an architectural pediment, painted with a religious scene, or a heraldic device supported by cherubs, angels, satyrs, etc., rendered more life-like by flesh-coloured paint. As time wore on the structural beauty of the frame had also become accentuated in other parts of the country. In Castile beds were made with pediments and pyramidal finials in the stiff Herrera style, but

---

[13] Occasionally made of silver.

[14] For a full list of which see " The Arts and Crafts of Older Spain," by Leonard Williams, Vol. II, where is also given a detailed description of the bed and bedclothes of Princess Juana, extracted from an inventory made upon her marriage with the Count of Foix in 1392.

more often the heads were essentially baroque. Little arcades with arches supported by coupled columns were a common feature.

These fashions survived until an entirely new influence, Portuguese, appeared in the West and curiously enough in Majorca. Scores of wavy spindles took the place of the arcades and coats of arms. The tall posts, called " salamonicas," were now made with double twists, and crowned with tapering finials [PLATE 8, B]. Possibly the style may have been inspired by the graceful ironwork " rejas " in the churches. In Portugal[15] (though there is little to distinguish between the forms of the two countries) a distinct Persian influence may be discerned.

ECCLESIASTICAL WOOD-CARVING.—In ecclesiastical wood-carving Mudéjar workmanship is scarcely ever found,[16] most of the early artisans coming from Holland, Flanders or Germany. PLATE 9, A, illustrates a late fifteenth-century Paschal candlestick, which though found in the south, shows very distinct traces of Flemish design, particularly in the stiff finialed canopies over the saints. These are painted in tempera on a background of gold leaf. The whole is decorated in polychrome and richly gilt. Choir-stalls of this date were of two distinct types, those " a fenestrajes," and those in which an important part in the decoration is played by figures, either singly or in groups. Of the first type are the stalls of 1485-1487, in the Cartuja de Miraflores near Burgos, by Martín Sánchez, the very similar ones of Santo Tomás at Avila, finished in 1493, and those in the cathedral of Segovia.

One of the great wood sculptors of his time, and one of the last to work in the Gothic style was Rodrigo Alemán, to whom we owe the " sillerías " at Zamora (1490), Ciudad Rodrigo (in which, however, he showed himself slightly susceptible to Portuguese influences), and Plasencía [PLATE 10, B]. These last, with their Biblical scenes intermingled with the most ironical and profane subjects, were executed in 1520. The celebrated choir-stalls (the lower row) in Toledo Cathedral, with their great series of reliefs representing the Fall of Granada, dated from 1495, and are also Gothic, but were left unfinished owing to the death of the donor, Cardinal Pedro de Mendoza.

Of the " figured " choir-stalls the most important are those in León Cathedral, which, although probably begun (in 1467) by Jean de Malines and a Dutchman named Copín, are in the purest German style [PLATE 9, B], and we owe the greater part of the work to a German, Theodoric, who completed it in 1481. The outstanding characteristic of later Spanish wood-sculpture, namely, the striving after complete realism, is already apparent. The one thing necessary for a Spanish statue was that it should imitate life as nearly as possible,[17] and the most prosaic German work (even at Ulm) was hardly more successful in this admittedly low ideal. However, the standard of Teutonic workmanship in Spain was high, and Burgos, which had been a centre of German influence ever since the erection of the cathedral towers by Hans of Cologne, retains a unique series of late Gothic retablos in this northern style, there being three in San Gil, and others in the cathedral, San Nicolás, San Lesmes, and the Cartuja de Miraflores, the last by Gil de Siloe, possibly a German by birth. But it was a Burgundian, Philip Vigarni,[18] born at Langres, who brought in the Renaissance and executed the Passion sculptures on the Trassagrario, in a style

---

[15] There is a Portuguese bed somewhat similar to that reproduced in PLATE VIII in the Bethal Green Museum.

[16] The one exception being the early 15th century choir-stalls of La Seo, Saragossa, where the high backs were decorated by Moriscos. The stalls are of Flemish oak.

[17] Zarcillo the Guido Mazzoni of Murcia is a typical though late example.

[18] Also spelt Viguerny, Biguerny, and known in spain as Felipe de Borgoña.

not far removed from the contemporary Burgundian screen at Albi, as well as the cathedral choir-stalls. These last [PLATE 11, A] form a fine ensemble, but have been spoilt by later additions. Amongst Vigarni's other work may be mentioned thirty-five stalls of the upper row at Toledo,[19] and the large altar-piece in the Royal Chapel at Granada, with the kneeling figures painted and gilded, of Ferdinand and Isabella. Polychrome decoration was much resorted to, as was only natural in a country so addicted to Realism, and the finest retablos in the country, those at Seville and Toledo, are a perfect riot of colour. Even the greatest sculptors, Berruguete, Gregorio Hernández, Montañés, and Alonso Cano, did not scorn its use.

In the south wood-carving showed a later development than in the north, owing to the widespread use of Moorish ornament.

Amongst the earlier carvers were Nefro Sánchez, a pupil of the Breton Mercadante, who designed the monument of Cardinal Cervantes at Seville, and Dancart, who executed the Altar Mayor. But the glory of the school of Seville came when Miguel, the Florentine, had established the Italian style. Torrigiano was at work and the Malaga choir-stalls were then completed. But the school was short-lived, declined in the late seventeenth century and finally died out, though we find Pedro Cornéjo, a pupil of Roldán, when over eighty years old, at work at Cordova, as late as 1757, on the carved mahogany choir-stalls [PLATE 11, B]. The carving suffers from over-elaboration, but nevertheless the ensemble is impressive and typically Spanish.

There is nothing tawdry or cheap in Spanish Art from the austere fanaticism of El Greco to the bitter sarcasm of Goya.

The national temperament, sombre as it is, is a Baroque temperament, full of fancies and extravagances, war-like, religious to the verge of superstition, yet inconsequential, and in Spain even the baroque style, carried to a degree of ornateness unparalleled elsewhere in Europe, compels admiration for its dignity and splendour.

[19] The others were by Berruguete.

A—Crossed-beam ceiling with structural members hidden. (Salone di Maria Pradilla, Alcázar of Seville)

B—Mudéjar " media naranja " ceiling from Torrijos; late 15th century. (Victoria and Albert Museum)

A—Chest, early 16th century, showing flamboyant Gothic influence.

B—Sacristy table, 1600-25, with canted legs; drawer fronts decorated with the Keys of Heaven and Instruments of the Passion

C—Five-legged table, early 17th century, showing Italian Renaissance influence and use of the spiral column.
(All in the collection of Mr. Lionel Harris)

A—Refectory table, mid-17th century, from Navarre. Length, 11 ft. 9½ in.

C—Walnut table, late 17th century, richly carved and decorated with chisel cut ornament, etc.; top unbevelled

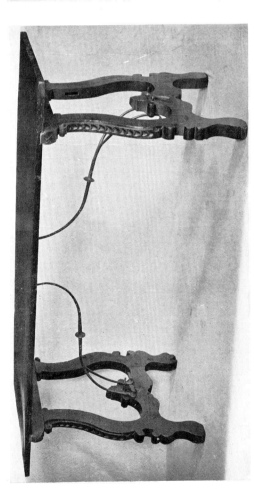

B—Table, late 17th century, with splayed legs and bracing irons. Dovetail grooves on underside of top.

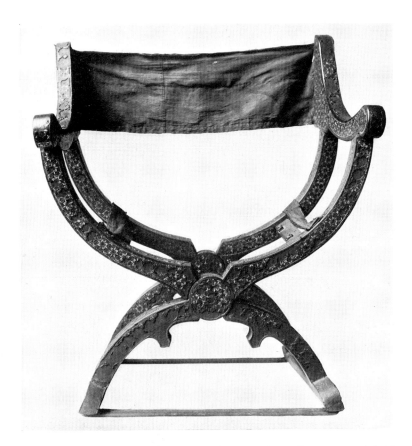

A—Scissors-framed chair, late 15th or early 16th century, inlaid with wood and ivory in star patterns

B—Walnut chair, 1540-50, upholstered in quilted velvet, with figured " remates "

C—Chestnut armchair, 16th century, from Holme Lacey, with the arms of the Franciscan order, painted in red and gold, with scroll arm rests, feet, and " remates " of native American type. (Victoria and Albert Museum)

D—Spanish Louis XVI chair, upholstered in Louis XIV French silk damask

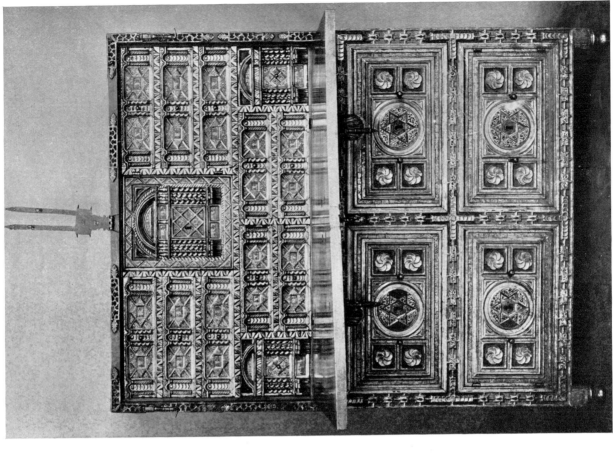

B—Vargueño, late 16th century, open to show combination of Renaissance and Moorish design

A—Vargueño, 16th century, with three-tiered box stand, the drop front ornamented with pierced iron mounts

B—Walnut vargueño, 16th century, the drop front inlaid with light wood; pear wood appliqué carvings inside the lid. (Salting Collection, Victoria and Albert Museum)

A—Open front vargueño, 16th century, carved with demi-figures and grotesques in the style of Berruguete; trestle or columnar stand

A—Bed, early 16th century, with spirally scored posts, decorated in polychrome

B—Bed, early 17th century, with arcaded head, and heraldic device

B—Walnut bed, early 18th century, with double-twisted posts and
light finials in the Portuguese style

A—Bed, mid-17th century, with arcaded head and tall " salamonicas "

A—Paschal candlestick, late 15th century, decorated in polychrome, showing Flemish influence

B—Choir stalls, German in style, by Jean de Malines, Copin, Theodoric, and others, 1467-81. (León Cathedral)

A—Choir stalls, early Renaissance, with older Gothic ends, from Huesca

B—Choir stalls, Gothic, by Rodrigo Alemán. (Plasencia Cathedral)

A—Choir stalls, Renaissance, by Philip Vigarni, with later additions. (Burgos Cathedral)

B—Choir stalls, Baroque, by Pedro Duque Cornéjo, 1757. (Cathedral Mosque of Cordova)

METALWORK. *By Pedro M. de Artiñano*

GENERAL REMARKS AND ORIGINS.—Metalwork, from the beginning, has been a sure and precise measure of Spanish culture and of Spanish greatness: and there is nothing strange in this, for Spain has always been pre-eminently a mineral land. The first germs of civilization were implanted by the Phœnician and Greek colonists, who came exclusively to trade in metals, principally silver, gold, lead, and iron; and references to the mining of these metals may be found in the classical writers.

In caves and the rudimentary dwelling-houses of the age in which these first elements of civilization made their appearance, one finds dross and other indications of the mining of the precious metals, chiefly of silver. There is, however, the noteworthy fact that no object made of such metals has been found among the household furniture of these dwelling places; nor are there any scraps of the metals themselves. This indicates that during the neolithic period the metals were worked by foreigners alone, and that they worked them solely for export; the natives having realized their commercial value.

In spite of this, it was actually in the Cave of the Bats (Murciélagos), belonging to the neolithic period, that the first Spanish ornament in precious metal was discovered; a smooth gold crown, undoubtedly made from pure metal, which appears to have been worked into a sheet of practically uniform thickness, by being hammered upon a stone, and then trimmed with a stone hatchet, producing a section thicker in the centre than at the edge.

Later, both the conditions of mining and the customs of the natives changed: plates of silver, or iron, or sometimes copper or bronze, are found among their household goods. This shows that, in this second period, the people either had learnt the use of metals and worked them for themselves, or that foreign metalworkers, for the most part Phœnicians, had settled in Spain.

What the working of metals in those early ages really signified for Spain may be gathered from the fact that whilst, throughout the rest of the world, in Austria, Poland, Switzerland, France and elsewhere, some 4,000 burial places belonging to the Hallstatt period have been found, in one Spanish necropolis of this period, that of Aguilar de Anguita, no fewer than 5,000 burial places were discovered, nearly all containing very interesting specimens of iron work.

The greater number of the objects found in cemeteries of this description, numerous in Spain, are the weapons typical of that civilization; chiefly swords with upturned hilts, of which the two ends are finished with a ball; but there have also been found arrows, spears, shield bosses, and other objects then in ordinary use, such as bits for horses, hammers, and axes. And, as a curiosity, may be mentioned some iron hoops forming two vertical superposed arcs, which, in the opinion of the Marquis of Cerralbo, were used by the Iberian ladies to bear the mantle which covered their heads, and developed with time into the comb which now supports the Spanish mantilla.

IRON.—The history of Spanish ironwork may be divided into three main epochs: the first from prehistoric times to the end of the Visigoth monarchy; the second including the Reconquest and the Renaissance; the third covering the period from the War of Independence till the present time. In the first, objects in metal are manifestly utilitarian; in the second, essentially decorative and artistic; and in the present, they are industrial, thus losing the elegance and charm so characteristic of the preceding period.

In the first period a very interesting class of exceptions is that of arms ornamented by the inlaying of gold or silver, such as those found in the north of Spain by the Marquis of Comillas, and those discovered by Cabré in the necropolis of Mirabeche on the border of Cantabria. Arms inlaid with silver have also been found in Granada; indeed, weapons with inlaid iron hilts and scabbards are found practically all over the peninsula. The decorated arms of this period are more frequently of bronze than of iron on account of the former's greater durability.

It is worth mentioning that, after careful examination, it has been demonstrated that during the Roman period arms were only steeled on the surface. It follows that this was managed by a superficial carbonization, which gave the necessary degree of hardness whilst avoiding risk of breaking; this process implies a by no means common knowledge of metallurgy, and confirms the reputation of Spanish swords and other arms during the Roman period.

Very few objects of the Visigothic period have survived. In the necropolis of Carpio del Tajo, numerous trinkets were found which must have been made of iron as they did not resist the action of time and were completely pulverized by exposure to the air when they were discovered: they were, indeed, thin shells of rust rather than solid objects. However, a certain number of Visigothic objects which may be regarded as works of art have been preserved: very rich pieces, the primary element of which, iron, was rendered capable of resistance. In such a case the article was made of iron, with its proportions, measurements, and polished surface exactly adapted to its purpose; it was then enriched by decoration of a decadent Roman character; volutes and geometrical designs, inlaid with gold or silver, filling or covering the whole surface, following the tradition of the swords of the earlier period. As an example, there survives a bit in the Royal Armoury on which are some letters, the same as those found on coins of the Visigoth King Witiza. Moreover, all this ornamentation has a well-defined character, which corresponds with that of the architectural ornament seen on the remains of existing Visigothic buildings. Undoubtedly many things of a purely utilitarian character which have been classified as Roman were in fact Visigothic, possibly even as late as the period after the Reconquest: however, as the dimensions and the technique of these objects differ in no wise from those of the Roman period, they have been taken for Roman; a confusion which is difficult to avoid, for they differ neither in their artistic value nor in their technique.

Ironwork is mentioned in the oldest Christian manuscripts of the Reconquest period; for example, in the codices of Sahagún (A.D. 1059), León (A.D. 1090), and Vich (A.D. 1100). On the other hand, the excavations of Medina az-Zahra, Alamirilla, and Elvira show clearly that the Arabs at the time of their highest culture, when the caliphate was at the zenith of its splendour, did not use iron for artistic but for other purposes; and the finding at Elvira of the complete ironwork of a door, cut from a plate, must be regarded as something exceptional. This is, perhaps, the earliest known example of this kind of technique.

Here it must be said that in Spain at this period the type of grille or *reja* formed of repeated double volutes arranged lengthwise on parallel axes was very common; this type is believed to be of French origin, but it was most common in Spain, and it is in Spain that one can trace a real evolution which began to show itself in Upper Castile, in the second half of the eleventh century. Many have been preserved; for example, those in San Isidoro of León, in the church of the Virgen del Mercado, at Palencia, in the chapel of the Holy Cross in Pamplona, in the cathedral of Zamora, a door in San Juan de las Abadesas, etc. In the kingdoms of Castile and León the *rejas* have a special feature in that the volutes tend to cover the whole surface, whilst in the north of Spain, that is to say in Navarre and Catalonia, they are elaborated and open; and in the later examples one finds symmetrical branch forms, as if an effort had been made to conventionalize plant form and to find a way to conform to the outlines of the new Gothic style rather than the Castilian. This decorative idea could not fail to impose itself gradually on every kind of work, and the iron candlesticks forged at that time were inspired by contemporary architecture.

A proof of the importance of ironwork during this period in Spain may be seen in the facts that in Barcelona the smiths were formed into a guild which had become very important by the year A.D. 1200, when they were mentioned by King Peter II; and that in the *Ordenamientos de Posturas* of King Alfonso X in the Cortes of León and Castile, held at Jerez in 1268, very detailed regulations were made for the iron trade, dealing especially with the place of origin of the metal and with the conditions of its working, not forgetting the question of transport by land and sea. Then, too, some smiths, as representatives of their guild, had a seat in the Cortes, known as the *Consejo de Ciento*, the Council of the Hundred, which governed Barcelona from A.D. 1316. At Valencia the brotherhood of smiths was dissolved in 1298 for political reasons, but was again admitted by Don Alfonso II to the Cortes of 1329. These facts are of considerable interest when one remembers that at Paris, for example, there was no guild of smiths before the year 1411.

During nearly the whole of this period the ore was obtained from the Basque provinces and Catalonia, in which the Catalan forges were developed. This became of considerable importance, especially in the Basque provinces. There was detailed legislation regarding the working; and the rights and privileges of the foundries were set out in the privilege granted at Burgos, on May 15, 1366, by King Alfonso XI.

The first modification that the Gothic imposed upon the Romanesque was a fundamental change in proportion: in candlesticks and similar objects the thickness of the bars which formed the tripod was reduced, and from them sprang a stem, which might be from fifty to eighty times higher than thick. The entire design was inspired by plant forms, ornamented with a number of rings. They welded on the topmost section of the candlestick lance-shaped plates, which bent capriciously to emphasize the pricket of the candlestick, irrespective of its proper function which was to support the candle, so that in the ornamental whole it took the place of the stamens of a flower; whence this form became known as the lily-shaped candlestick [PLATE 1, A]. It was slender in form and proportion, full of harmony and poetry, as would be expected in the work of guilds seeking their strength in the latest architectural novelties of our Gothic cathedrals.

Another feature found in ironwork from the beginning of the Gothic period is the plate, applied as a decorative element to give the whole solidity and architecture. In the oldest examples this plate is a polished sheet, either straight or curved; but at a quite early date these components were modified in one of two ways, either by raising the plate or by stencilling it. The former system was in fact rudimentary repoussé work, since the heightening hardly extended to more than a couple of millimetres above the general level of the plate; when this was stencilled, or silhouetted, it was generally done by making arches, or repeating some motif of small dimensions.   Later on this technique developed into that of the double plate, which was commonly employed from the fifteenth century.   The system of double plates consists in superimposing two or three plates each with the same outline, but on lessening scales, each being progressively less broad; so that when they are superimposed the motifs or parts of them coincide in such a way that each plate serves as an exactly centred base for the following one, giving the whole an aspect of relief, the design being worked out not by a monotonous silhouette, but by multiple lines, producing the necessary effects of light and shade.

This technique was common throughout Europe, and in Spain was practised with real mastery.   Many examples of it are now taken for the work of French smiths; and if in the ironwork of our old chests the towers of Castile were not seen above the minutely fretted iron border, with the shells of the Apostle St. James above the four angles of the locks, and if in many of the objects with network designs, a marked Arab influence is not noted, a very considerable portion of our fifteenth-century ironwork would be looked upon as foreign.

Contemporaneously with the use of the open work plate in its last stage of evolution, there appeared another method, in which the surface of the plate was in several degrees slightly raised; the resulting decoration being softened by two or three incised lines, traced with a chisel, following the whole motif, having for its aim the fusion of each of the smooth surfaces with that on which the adjacent decoration is worked.   We might say that this undulating work was a commercialization of the previous type, the aim being to produce a sense of depth which was brought about very curiously by means of these repeated undulations.

The full maturity in the art and technique of working iron is reached about the end of the fifteenth and beginning of the sixteenth centuries in the reign of the Catholic Monarchs.   The minute work of the twin open-work plates and embossing disappears, the latter becoming rarer till the end of the first third of the sixteenth century.   In design, the motifs of the Renaissance make an appearance and with them the human figure, which till then had only been clumsily treated in some forged door knockers and other small articles; and with the human figure repoussé work unexpectedly reappears, after having all but disappeared during the Middle Ages.   The Spanish conquests in the north of Italy during this period without doubt introduced Spaniards to the art of the North Italian designers and workmen.   Ironwork embossed with minute Renaissance motifs is very frequently met with: motifs which are very small in relation to the whole work and to the dimensions of the surface on which they appear; whilst, on the other hand, the relief is high in relation to the motif itself, giving an appearance of rubbed silver to the worked surface.   This spread to the other arts, to architecture as much as to iron work; and, for the reason just given, this technique has become known as the plateresque style, the " style of the silversmith."

However, as time passed, little by little the figure stood out in higher relief, being worked with a vigour, a grandeur, and an apparent simplicity that is the real characteristic of our art at that period.   Plate was seldom used; only for the embossing either of the figure, or of the emblems and the shields with which the great screens were crowned.   Later on, though still in the full Renaissance period, the plate was used for furniture, or figures of men or animals; as, for instance, the eagles that serve as lecterns in many of our churches and cathedrals, or the figures on the top of our *rejas*.   At this moment for the first time appears work done on a lathe, and also cast iron pieces such as the backs of fireplaces; but neither attains any importance till well on in the seventeenth or the beginning of the eighteenth century.

During the whole of the first half of the sixteenth century the *rejas* constantly expressed a certain Gothic tradition, and therefore were not quite up to date with the general taste of the period. The idea of the whole was architectural, and the decoration in the first years of the century was in the form of borders of long ribbons hanging in curved festoons, crossing and recrossing each other. These ribbons were open-work plates, whilst the festoons or bands that divided them into rectangular sections were generally of repoussé work, decorating them with castles, on plates which were cut away and curved, hanging at regular distances to break the monotony of the border. The principal columns and bars, of suitable proportions, are square, and their flat surfaces are embossed with grotesques in relief. The bars that fill in the design although, as has been said, square in section, are arranged with salient angles, so that looking at the *reja* the spectator sees two sides, naturally with different illumination, producing a very interesting play of light and shade. From the end of the fifteenth century they are often twisted, being shaped round their middle into curved figures, or volutes, or inverted hearts; decorations which are sometimes alternated, being distributed symmetrically. The top sections which, as has already been said, are composed of ribbons or open-work borders, such as Fray Francisco of Salamanca made them in his first period, are completed with round bars on which are soldered shorter embossed plates with figures and decorations; however, the bars are often left uncovered, giving the whole the aspect of tree trunks, the short plate being suitably annexed to give the idea of leaves, more or less roughly; but there is no approach to the Renaissance grotesque. Sometimes these small bars form volutes ending nearly always with the figure of a saint. Frequently, too, the top section contains a complete story; for example, the genealogical tree of the Virgin [PLATE 2, A], or some similar theme. This school, which was originated by Muñoz of Cuenca, is found in Jaén and all over Central and Southern Spain.

As the century advanced *rejas* became more architectural, and constituted in themselves an independent construction which in some cases tends to create an impression of depth; that is to say something more than the smooth surface or curtain which was the initial aim. The classical example of this type of screen is that of the Constable's chapel in Burgos cathedral [PLATE 4, C], which was finished in 1523, the work of Cristobal de Andino. It is perhaps the most perfect example of all known *rejas*, in spite of the fact that it is not large, nor was any attempt made to accumulate an excess of detail, such as is found in other works of the same Andino which are heavier and less graceful.

For the very reason that the *reja* at this time became architectural in its construction, the main columns, the frieze, and the whole framework took on dimensions and a thickness that were not in harmony with the quality of the material employed; so that, because of its intrinsic resistance, and because moreover it was all but impossible in that age to work and emboss very thick pieces of metal, the plan was adopted of constructing the whole architectural framework of wood, and then covering it with gracefully embossed plates. By this method an adequate distribution of the mass was procured, and the working of the material in columns, of apparently considerable dimensions became possible.

The *reja* that gives access to the side door of the cathedral of Cuenca is an admirable example of this last method of construction. Contemporary with it, following, however, the ancient idea of the *reja* being simply a curtain separating the altar and the presbytery from the part destined for the faithful, is the *reja* of the chapel royal in Granada, made by Master Bartolomé, in which the last memories of Gothic are mixed with square columns and graceful friezes of embossed plates; this screen has three rows of figures in addition to that on the top, figures intermixed with a row of flaming cressets, ornamented with grotesques, that make up the top row, crowned by a monumental Christ between two figures.

During the second third of the sixteenth century, that is to say during the reign of Philip II, the ornamental decorative details, the grotesques, were abandoned, and a frankly architectural tendency was followed; this was inspired by Greco-Roman models and was extraordinarily severe. The work is divided into sections in which a collection of columns is usually found, apparently supporting a part of the work; these at first were forged but later they were turned, so proclaiming the change of technique. At this period beauty was sought in general effect rather than in detail, in the weight and proportions of the whole, and in a fitting distribution of the mass. They cut off, as has been said, the ornamental details, characteristic of the plateresque period, which are not always distinguishable at any considerable distance; and in place of these strove for a more adequate outline. As a consequence embossing lost its importance, and there appeared a tendency towards something conventional and cold, mainly, perhaps, for economic reasons. This was marked late in the sixteenth century by a geometrical attitude which left the surface undecorated but distributed the mass harmoniously, and produced its effect by outlines and contrasts.

The early seventeenth century brought in a reaction against these tendencies. A return was made to the imitation and copying of Nature, though not to the variety and taste which was so typical of the Renaissance; and the decoration was sumptuous. It was almost exclusively floral, and was worked in such detail that it acquired an extraordinary importance; the root idea being lost in the effort to cover the whole surface with an excess of detail. On the other hand, at that same period was developed the locksmith's art: which, however, in the main imitated French work. However, interpreting it in view of the geometric school of Philip II or of the baroque extravagances which followed it, this acquires an individuality distinguishing it from French work: for example, not uncommonly the loop or handle of the key is covered with lineal lace-like decoration closely related to our fifteenth-century *mudéjar* work.

Our eighteenth-century *reja* makers copied the French rococo volutes, and our *reja* work had but little individuality, for everything was borrowed from France. In spite of this, however, there was some interesting work even when devoid of individuality: as instances of this there are the grilles of the palace of the Marquis of Dos Aguas in Valencia and the balconies of some of the public buildings in the Basque provinces, for example, those of Mondragón and Oñate.

Towards the end of the seventeenth century a popular style of ornament made its appearance; because popular, a style born without great pretensions and at first chiefly used for the humblest articles, which perhaps accounts for its grace and spirituality. This style arose in Estramadura, whence it spread to the region of Salamanca and Zamora; thence turning south it annexed Guadalupe to invade all Andalusia. At present it is common in the south of Spain, having its principal centres in the mountains round about Granada, and it has been persistently stated that there are details derived from Moorish tradition. Its decoration consists of volutes frequently repeated and imposed in a single arc of a circle; concentric circles, like those of the Romanesque type, are rare. Occasionally figures are used as ornamental details, but they are always comic and silhouetted, never modelled or embossed; the articles always have a flat surface, upon which the volutes are worked and the sheet cut away. Perhaps the most important work of this school is a lamp bracket in Coria cathedral, and one of the best known is the cross known as the Cross of the Locksmiths of Seville made by Sebastian Conde at the end of the seventeenth century.

During the eighteenth century our smiths were inspired almost exclusively by French models, and during this period more interest is to be found in the minute work of the engravers and locksmiths who established a real school of locksmiths' work in Madrid; of this the masters and inspirers were Alonso Martinez and two of his chief workmen, Antonio Gutiérrez and Pedro de Pastrana, who in 1738 did the artistic ironwork for the door of Sigüenza cathedral.

The story of Spanish ironwork may be regarded as coming to an end with this period. From the year 1768 onwards a number of fresh starts have, it is true, been made by the Basque society " Amigos del Pais " which is greatly interested in everything relating to the encouragement and the future of the iron industry; but its object is rather industrial and economic than artistic.

Finally, with the War of Independence at the beginning of the nineteenth century, Spanish locksmiths and engravers all but vanished. There was a revival during the romantic period, but little collective work was done, the greater part being individual. But in some cases there has been a continuance, and local schools have been formed: as, for example, that of Don Plácido Zuloaga, who has been successful in establishing at Eibar a school of decoration, where iron is damascened.

TOLEDO BLADES.—Though the famous steel weapons made at Toledo hardly come within the scope of this article, no account of Spanish ironwork could be regarded as complete without some reference to them; and for that reason it may be worth while to add a few notes regarding their manufacture. The industry was a very ancient one. Gratius Faliscus, a contemporary of Ovid's, praises the Toledo weapons; while, somewhat later, the Kings of Castile exempted the Toledo armourers from taxation.

From time immemorial Spanish armourers disliked working with new iron. They insisted on using old oxidized metal, more especially iron that had been battered by long service, the ideal material being the iron from old horseshoes which had been worked and worn by the labour of the horses.[1] But the crude steel for the strengthening strips[2] was from the earliest times imported into Toledo from Mondragón, in Guipúzcoa, where it had been manufactured out of metal from Monte Udala.

The industry reached its greatest development in the sixteenth and seven-

---

[1] The same practice was later on followed by the Madrid arquebuse makers with the greatest success. This gave rise to the popular song :—

> Pues todas las naciones
> admiran el primor de mis cañones
> comprando la hermosura
> que fué carbon y callos de herradura

All the nations admire the excellence of my guns, buying the beauty which once was charcoal and calkers.
[So nearer home shoe-smiths like to make new shoes from old ones, the battering of use making the metal harder.—ED.]

[2] *Calees.* [A Toledo blade had an iron core, called the *alma*, i.e., soul, and on either side of this a steel plate, the three being welded together.—ED.]

teenth centuries. At the beginning of the eighteenth, the popularity of the thin, light French sword brought about a rapid decay, so much so that when in 1780 the Government made a serious effort to establish a factory of swords and other steel weapons, with a view to reviving the old and famous industry, only one master of the art could be found to superintend the workshop, an old man eighty years of age, Luis Calixto by name, then living in Valencia. On the other hand, during the sixteenth century, about the year 1560, Spanish cutlers founded workshops in America. The most famous seems to have been the workshop at Puebla de los Angeles, in Mexico, if we may judge by the output.

All the processes of manufacture were surrounded by traditional and mysterious practices. One of the principal accessories of the craft of forging was the fine white Tagus sand, and every forger had his supply of it constantly at hand. Directly the iron which was being forged or strengthened with the steel became red hot, the operator took it from the fire and, throwing a little sand on the hot metal, arrested the sparks. Only then was the sword ready to be hammered on the anvil. Having in this way shaped the blade, the next process was to temper it. For this the craftsman formed a trench in the forge, a narrow line of fire little more than three-fourths the length of the blade, leaving outside both ricasso and tang. In this position the blade was heated, and as soon as it acquired a cherry-red colour, it was placed perpendicularly, point downwards, in a tall narrow wooden pail filled with water from the Tagus. For this operation it was the custom to choose the deepest obscurity and an overcast darkness of night, in order that the expert might the better appreciate the colourization due to the action of the fire, but no doubt also to surround the process with greater mystery.

This work was accompanied by the singing of prayers, followed by the repetition of certain formulæ and weird invocations, the grammatical sense of which was anything but clear, the object being to regulate the length of the immersion. The following is an example of these invocations: " Blessed be the hour in which Christ was born "—" Saint Mary who bore Him "—" St. John who baptized Him "—" The iron is hot "—" The water hisses "—" The tempering will be good "—" If God wills."

The care with which these operations were conducted will be realized if we note that to avoid the cooling of the piece as it passed from the forge to the water, no work was done when a north wind blew in Toledo, and tempering was never done save when the air was warm and the wind from the south, preferably if the sky was overcast.

The operation of annealing was also curious. The blade was heated till it was liver coloured; it was then lifted with pincers by the tang and ricasso, and smeared with raw unmelted fat taken from the parts about the kidneys of a sheep or male goat; after this it was placed point uppermost against a wall and left there till the flame from the fat had died away and the blade had slowly cooled down. It was then ready to be sharpened and mounted.

Some of the pre-eminent Toledan master sword makers, such as Hortuño de Aguirre, Julián del Rey, Sahagún el Viejo, Menchaca and Juanes de la Horta, were accustomed to stamp their swords with their own punch, which was usually kept in the city hall. Thanks to this circumstance, the marks of a large number of craftsmen have been preserved. They were published in 1760 by Don Francisco de Santiago Palomares, chief clerk of Toledo and its archbishopric, when the Government organized the new factory. This factory is still flourishing; but in place of the curious and mysterious old recipes, there has been established a well-appointed laboratory for study of the resistance of metals and the microscopic analysis of steel.

BRONZE.—The earliest Spanish bronze work belongs to the same culture as that of the Halstatt iron period, and consists of domestic utensils and arms in which are seen Iberian decorative motifs. But the oldest bronzes which can be regarded as real works of art are certain heads of bulls, which belong to Cretan art, some of them with an axe between the horns. These were found in Majorca and are now preserved in the National Museum of Archæology. Several of these figures are of natural size, their execution, realism and power, combined with a naïve and almost barbarous style, reveals the indigenous hand that worked them.

In a considerable number of deposits, some of them explored by the Government, as, for example, that of Despeñaperros, a considerable number of votive bronzes, nearly always representing figures, have been found, together with the stone moulds that served for the casting of the objects. And the abundance of these objects is notable as showing the existence of a popular industry. These figures, though made in Spain, show in general two oriental influences: that of Phœnician bronzes and even of some Egyptian types; and of Greek bronzes, representations of gods, men and women, warriors on horseback, a motif often found in brooches and buckles, and representations of animals, more especially of the bull, which in Spain certainly bears direct relation to the story of Hercules.

During the Roman period Spanish bronzes were absolutely perfect in their working. The examples of that period are in fact as interesting and perfect as the best of those found in Italy; but our art does not show the individuality which was a characteristic of Iberian work before the Roman domination. Specimens of bronze work from various excavations, of the greatest interest as a measure of the general culture of the period, may be seen in the National Museum of Archæology and in Tarragona Museum.

The case of the bronzes of the Visigoth period is similar. There remains little on which to form a judgment regarding that period: however, during the recent excavations made by his Majesty the King in Carpio del Tajo a considerable number of specimens were found, chiefly belt buckles worked in bronze and not infrequently gilt. This points to an advanced stage of the industry, but there is no marked difference between these specimens and those found in other localities of the same period. At the present time various Visigoth deposits are being investigated, and the objects met with are, from an artistic point of view, very like those found at Carpio del Tajo, though less rich.[3]

The Arabs were fond of the working of bronze on iron, silver, and gold. Some very interesting specimens were found during the excavations at Elvira, a little town near Granada, destroyed before the caliphate reached its full splendour; consequently these are specimens of the earliest Spanish-Arab bronzes. Various writers of the earliest period of the Christian Reconquest also speak of bronze works, which shows that the Arabs were not alone in their love for this metal. In the museum at Cordova there is a hemispherical bell which, according to the inscription, was made in the year 875; and in the same museum there is a bronze stag, with gold inlay completely covering the surface; this was

[3] Bronze working in Spain is referred to in the "Etymologies" of St. Isidore in Book XVI, Chapter 20, and Book XX, Chapters 7 and 8 (Migne, "Pat. Lat." 82).

found during the excavation of Medina az-Zahra, a palace built by Abd-er-Rahman III in 961 and destroyed half a century later; it appears to have served as the spout of one of the many fountains that adorned the palace.

An open-work lamp of much later date in the National Museum of Archæology shows that the bronze industry continued to develop in the hands of the Arabs: it bears an inscription to the effect that it was made for King Mohammed III of Granada in the year 705 of the Hegira, that is to say in A.D. 1305. There are also boxes of the same technique but of much finer workmanship that must have served as jewel cases, since in all of them the bronze is strengthened or ornamented with silver plates, bone, and ivory.

There is one specimen of this kind of work known as the Box of Cuellar [PLATE 7, D], which belonged to the well-known collector, Don Alejandro Pidal; this, like others of the same size and richness, has survived because it was kept in a church to contain the hosts to be used at Mass.

In connexion with this period notice must also be taken of the interesting use made of bronze embossed by a die for the adornment of the great doors of the principal public buildings. These doors, which were made of wood, were sometimes covered in iron, but for the most part in bronze, and the plates which covered them were ornamented with reliefs made with a die, which often enough were stamped in various directions, some perpendicular and others sloping, in fanciful arrangement. This custom and this technique which we find in some Arab buildings, were common in the Christian kingdoms; as an example, there is the Gate of Pardon in Toledo cathedral, the plates of which have Arab and Castilian inscriptions alternately. And on the Gate of Pardon in Cordova cathedral we find the same thing, salutations in Arab characters alternating with inscriptions in Gothic: these give the date 1377, and specify that the High and Mighty Don Enrique was then King of Castile. Frequently either castles and lions alternate with the inscriptions, or the motto of the Nazarites: " God alone is the Conqueror." We might say something similar about the Gate of Pardon in Seville cathedral [PLATE 9, C].

This technique of superficial decoration by die stamping appears to have originated in Spain in Visigothic goldsmith work, and then to have become popular both with Christians and Arabs; plates of either bronze or silver being used indifferently. A most important example, the so-called " tablas alfonsinas " (the Tablets of Alfonso), is a wooden reliquary, covered with stamped silver plates, made in Seville for Ferdinand III in the middle of the thirteenth century [PLATE 8, B]; and another is the small box in the Instituto de Valencia de Don Juan in Madrid [PLATE 8, A].

The Archæological Museum in Madrid possesses one or two small well buckets, some lamps, and other objects of less importance found in Cordova. The industry has lasted to the present day, producing, during the Renaissance, braziers, mortars, and lamps that kept their traditional form. During the Renaissance period many silversmiths worked in bronze: very frequently they used this metal when they had in hand a piece of work which on account of its great size could not be done in silver. This was done, for instance, in the case of the great candlesticks used in the ceremonies of Holy Week, altar screens when they were not made of iron, pulpits, etc. For example, in 1543 Francisco Villalpando made the ambos, one at either end of the *reja*, in Toledo cathedral, ambos which are marvels of the art of the Spanish Renaissance, notwithstanding the fact that he was by trade a blacksmith and not a worker in bronze. About the same time Juan López, a silversmith, made the screen in the chapel of the Virgen del Sagrario in the same cathedral; whilst Nicolás de Vergara and his son, of the same name, also silversmiths, between 1571 and 1574, founded and finished the bronze plates for the lectern in the choir. And it would be easy to add to the list.

The sepulchral groups of the Escorial were cast in bronze by Pompeo Leoni, and his work serves for an example; its artistic interest is as great as that of the praying statue of Cardinal Don Cristóbal de Rojas in the collegiate church of Lerma, in the province of Burgos, made by the last of the Arfes (Juan). The statue on the top of the Giralda of Seville, the lectern, and the tenebræ candlestick in the same church were the work of Bartolomeo Morel, and were made in the year 1562. The pulpits in the cathedral of Santiago de Compostela [PLATE 9, A] are also very important works; they are signed in 1563 by the Aragonese artificer, Juan Bautista Celma, who shortly after also signed a beautiful gilt *reja* for a chapel in the cathedral (La Seo) of Zaragoza.

During the seventeenth century, surrounded by the baroque taste of the time, they continued to work in the style of the Renaissance. A number of *rejas* and large candlesticks were made, but it must be said that, as with ironwork, so with bronze, this period was one of decline: however, during this century, developing upon the lines of the preceding, they cast statues. As examples, there are those of Philip III and Philip IV on horseback; for the latter of which the Sevillan sculptor, Juan Martínez Montañés provided the drawings and perhaps the model for the head.

At the beginning of the eighteenth century bronze working received a fresh impulse, chiefly from the influence of King Philip V, who ordered a considerable number of statues for the gardens of La Granja; and shortly after, when his son Charles III transferred from Naples to Madrid the factory known as Buen Retiro, they set up in it foundries and workshops for bronze workers: they were already at work in 1778, and henceforward turned out a considerable number of objects, all of which, however, were inspired by French taste, which predominated in the Spanish court during the second half of that century. Bronze working went on in Buen Retiro until its destruction in 1808; and then in the nineteenth century the story of bronze in Spain followed the well-known evolution of all our industrial arts during the Romantic period.

SILVERSMITHS' WORK.—Silversmiths' work in Spain in ancient times was, as has already been said, of extraordinary importance, for the crown found in the Cave of the Bats was only the first of a considerable number of others, such as the one found at Montilla, which was $15\frac{3}{4}$ ins. in length by $1\frac{3}{8}$ ins. in breadth, that of the quinta of Agua Branca, a crown formed from a plain rectangular plate $23\frac{5}{8}$ ins. long, that of Sambento, the silver crown found by Siret at Fuente-Alamo, to say nothing of those showing markedly Greek influence, such as the crown in the treasury of Jávea.

During this period two distinct influences were at work—the Phœnician and the Greek. Of the first class there have been preserved amongst others a considerable number of jewels found in excavations made at Cadiz: these objects are chiefly rings, pendants of different kinds, gold necklace beads, and some ornamented amulets. In the island of Iviza, Señor Vives found a considerable number of objects with Phœnician characteristics, perhaps even more markedly Carthaginian: and among these, on account of its artistic character, stands out a large pendant or ear-ring decorated with lotus flowers, very like those found later at Aliseda, where the most important of the treasures of ancient times still preserved in Spain were found. Of this find the most interesting objects are the pendants and a belt : the pendants consisting of a hoop that thickens in the central part, from which irradiates a series of lotus flowers separated by palm trees and vultures ; whilst the body of the belt is a granulated work, the same subject, a fight between a man and a lion, stamped with a die, being repeated on each of the small component pieces.

Of the objects showing Greek influence, found for the most part on the Mediterranean littoral, perhaps the most important are those recovered at Jávea, which include coins earlier than the Roman domination of Spain, struck at Ampurias, Arco-Gadir, and New Carthage. The most important jewel is a crown, consisting of a central band with two triangular terminals which undoubtedly hung on the temples of the head. The gold base has been decorated with wire, on a system which was the precursor of filigree. This wire must have been applied by first etching with a graver on the smooth surface, and then placing the wire on the groove thus formed. Inasmuch as this preparation with the graver was sometimes too violent, it resulted in cutting through the sheet in places, so giving the impression of open work. The decorative details were displayed in bands, following the Greco-Oriental method ; the bands being formed of waves, stalks, snakes, or lozenges, of the same kind of work as is seen in some of the crowns on the statues found at El Cerro de los Santos.

The Roman period was plainly a colonial period. Our gold and silver was for the metropolis : our industry took its life from Rome, and the commonest objects, as well as the most important, display the fashions and the civilization of the Empire. It is commonly known that there was no great quantity of silver and gold in Rome before the third century, and that following on their conquests in Spain and Africa, the Romans thoroughly exploited the natural deposits of those colonies, which resulted in a great love for sumptuous table services and jewellery ; and these became lavish and exaggerated during the period of the decadence of the Empire.

The technique of Roman silversmiths' work is markedly characteristic. The objects are formed of two plates, one of which serves for the setting, the other for the device. This device is the outer part, which was worked and embossed. The setting was another sheet which formed the underside of the plates or the inside of the cups, and was not worked but left smooth. Device and setting were joined together by means of a thick tendon, and as between the two there was a hollow space, to avoid denting they filled this with some composition or metallic substance, sometimes tin, the resulting combination being less heavy than would be expected from its volume.

One of the objects which has been known and studied for some time past is the Otáñez plate, a complicated composition which points to highly developed local manufacture. The treasures found in Santisteban del Puerto, those of Mogón and those of Cordova, which are entirely of the technique just described, all indicate the height of perfection to which Spanish silversmiths' work had then reached. The silversmiths of that age had their guilds, and some memorial stones have been preserved ; for instance, there is the example in Valencia, dedicated by his wife to the memory of Julius Apolaustus, maker of silver vessels.

The Roman Empire fell, and upon its ruins there arose a new civilization, impressed only by the size of a work of art and by its value as a show piece. It was only during the last period of the Visigothic domination that Spanish goldsmiths' work became more individual, and at the same time was enriched by the use of decorative motifs taken from the architectural ornament of its buildings in a style which persisted until the Arab invasion.

In the jewels found at Guarrazar [PLATE 10, B] are found the same decorative details as are seen later on in, among other great works, the Victory Cross of Oviedo, at San Miguel de Linio: large flowers, leaves of winding foliage, roses, etc. The treatment is always simple, almost mere outline, such as a child might sketch. And it should be noted that, not even accidentally, does one find these motifs either in the work of Central and Northern Europe, or in French work, which is not naturally related to this art.

The smooth surfaces are decorated in various ways. When the articles are neither gold nor silver, the decorative work is done by casting as in the bronze objects found at Carpio del Tajo. Then the lines are retouched with a chisel, and more often than not the decoration is completed by inserting in the ends garnets, or stones, or glass, so producing a good polychromic effect.

Another way of decorating the surface was to emboss it (but not embossing as the Romans understood the term—because by this only lineal design can be obtained) producing in addition to lineal designs the effect of considerable thickness by stamping a simple geometric line which, monotonously repeated, covered the whole surface, giving an idea of thickness which in truth did not exist and at the same time producing a motive of conventional floral design.

A third way was to inlay lines of different metals, that is to damascene the surface. There are some curious specimens of this, as, for example, the horse bit called after King Witiza, which is kept in the Royal Armoury. In general these objects were iron, since the use for which the article was destined required this, and the decoration was, as has been said, of gold and silver.

Spanish silversmiths' work at the beginning of the Middle Ages was mainly inspired by the Byzantine tradition. The Cross of the Angels, made in Asturias in the time of Alfonso II, and the no less important Cross of Victory, now both in Oviedo, record the Visigoth technique, and much of the Byzantine taste popular in Christian Spain in those times. The latter of these two objects was made in 908 in the castle of Gauzon, and in it are seen cloisonné enamels, which show the existence of a Spanish workshop, perhaps the first in Western Europe.

The records of our monasteries show clearly that during the eleventh and twelfth centuries kings and magnates made them gifts of valuable objects in gold and silver.

Filigree work and stones were used in Spain to enrich the objects in like manner as throughout Western Europe, but the lines of decoration were peculiar to Spanish art because it was influenced by the Oriental taste introduced by the Arabs. Thus, for example, the cup, or chalice, of Santo Domingo de Silos is of great interest: it is decorated with filigree work tracing the horseshoe architectural motives characteristic of the period. So the great altar frontals, for example, the one made of enamel in the Burgos museum, which formerly belonged to the monastery of Santo Domingo de Silos, reproduce between the arches that cover the figures horseshoe constructions that show quite clearly that the work is markedly Spanish. During this period, especially in the Christian kingdoms, decoration took two forms, filigree and repoussé. And the embossing in some cases was in such high relief that the figure seems completely to leave the plane of the plate, the relief often exceeding half the thickness of the figure. However, our silversmith work of the Romanesque period differs comparatively little from that of the rest of Europe.

Very few specimens of Arab work have survived: such as have, are characterized by being striking and showy rather than of positive worth, this being true both of intrinsic value and artistic interest. Generally speaking they are hollow objects worked from a plate, and for the most part are such that the filigree work is exaggerated, completely covering the surface, with a resultant appearance of monotony.

Arab work of this kind attains its greatest interest and its greatest force in the decoration of weapons, the hilts and even the blades being covered with a combination of filigree, enamel, and chiselling, alternating with work done on other materials such as ivory and bone; as a result of the minute work, the whole object presents an extraordinarily rich appearance, giving the impression of lace-work.

Gothic silversmiths' work developed more slowly in the Christian kingdoms than either architecture or the other arts, so that at the beginning of the fourteenth century many things were still made in the Romanesque style, and to-day are sometimes classified as belonging to the thirteenth century. The characteristic of every existing specimen is that it is based upon something architectural: the leading idea being a Gothic building, a reminiscence of some cathedral or a detail from some chapel. Subject to this primary idea, numerous secondary themes inspired by nature are developed with floral motifs, introducing round lines within the general proportions of Gothic art. In this period nothing is seen of repoussé work. But on the other hand, in many cases the silver was cast, and then plates were added; and with these plates they built up veritable edifices, finishing up with chisel work on the original casting, so doing what the mould could not reproduce. Filigree work also disappeared during this period, double or triple open-work plates taking its place.

The work of this period shows the development of a certain religious idealism, which interprets the human figure in an especial manner; dealing with it as an auxiliary decorative element, with an absolute absence of the nude, which was unknown to the Gothic silversmith.

There are a certain number of very interesting things in Spain which, though intended for ordinary use, are so impregnated with religious sentiment that they seem to be rather objects connected with religious worship, than objects having no connexion with it. For example, there are a certain number of bookbindings of this nature; and chairs, such as the throne of King Martin of Aragon, now in Barcelona cathedral [PLATE 11, B], and other things in the same style: all of which show the architectural characteristics of the period.

It must also be said that work was done in translucent enamel of the Italian type, as perfectly as in France or Italy. In the specimens of Gothic silversmiths' work we find enamel medallions often so pictorial that they take the place of the coloured glass in a cathedral.

During the second half of the fifteenth century artists from two different quarters are met with in Spain: some coming from Lombardy in consequence of her political relations with Italy, and others from the south of Germany, possibly also for political reasons. Those of the former class brought in the motifs of the Renaissance; but of a special Renaissance, the characteristic of which was work in flowers and small grotesques; very small, in fact, in comparison with the object in its entirety, but with a relief which was very high compared with that of the motif itself. Independently of this style, the German artists who settled in Spain brought in an exaggerated florid Gothic ornamentation which also consisted of minute designs. In Spain, however, both styles acquired two characteristics : one, resulting from the *mudéjar* art having taken so firm a root in the peninsula, consisted in the covering of the whole disposable surface with decoration ; in one case this decoration may be geometrical network, whilst in the other it may consist of grotesques, or figures of fauns or bacchantes, which likewise cover the whole disposable space. The second characteristic affects the whole peninsula, and is that exaggerated naturalism which in the case of architecture is known in Portugal as " Manueline " after King Manoel, and in Spain is called the " Isabelline " style, after Queen Isabella the Catholic.

During the first years of the sixteenth century artists continued to work in the Gothic style, so far as the outline and the general idea of the work were concerned, but many of the details were frankly renaissance. It was at that moment that the repoussé work with vines, bunches of grapes, fauns, bacchantes, animals and vases reappeared : and it is extraordinarily curious to note how these details, belonging absolutely to the Renaissance, interchange with and complement each other, resulting in a style, the general impression of which is Gothic.

In this manner were made the most important specimens of silversmiths' work now existing in Spain, perhaps the most important and finest in the world. The monstrance in Cordova cathedral and that in Toledo cathedral are examples : they are the work of Enrique Arfe, who was domiciled in León at the beginning of the sixteenth century and may be regarded as a genuine Spanish artist, though his work is very reminiscent of the school of Cologne. In the greater part of his works appear details made by the *cire perdue* process; with the peculiarity that some of them were polished, others unpolished, and some chiselled, so that they give a series of varying light, colour, and reflection which constitutes one of the most striking characteristics of his work.

The proportions of these monstrances are gigantic. That of Toledo contains more than 330 lbs. (avdp.) of silver, and on it are 260 small statues with pillars, the greater number of which are covered with precious stones. The height is about 8 ft. 6 in. In consists of more than 5,000 pieces, kept together by 12,500 screws. It was begun in 1515 and finished in April, 1524.

One of the peculiar features of the works of that period is that in spite of their complexity the objects are extraordinarily slender and transparent : they are, as it were, metal lace floating in space. The whole work is perfectly harmonious, but on approaching it the details acquire importance and the thing is as marvellous when looked at close as when it is seen from a distance. In the general outline of these examples of Gothic taste, Renaissance motifs are seen in constantly increasing proportions; the same artist, Enrique Arfe, for example, during the years 1518 to 1520, that is to say whilst he was finishing the Toledo " Custodia," constructed the shrine of San Froilán in León cathedral, a work which is absolutely Renaissance in style, in that the whole surface, all the pillars, all the intervening spaces, are covered with ornamental detail of the renaissance type—volutes of flowers, nude figures, animals, fruit, urns, etc., so that the only part remaining smooth is the groundwork from which rise repoussé figures in twin arcs. Perhaps work of this kind may be regarded as the most typical example of the style called later on " the plateresque."

In the middle of the century, silversmiths adopted with some strictness the architectural types; which in truth they had never abandoned even when working in the style of the Renaissance; in the specimens of this work a very great elegance in the distribution of the ornamentation will be seen, and no less so in the proportions of the component parts. In the figures an extreme naturalness was aimed at: this resulted in a certain affectation, and frequently there is a certain audacity in the matter of movement, the action of the figures and the movement of their dress being exaggerated. At this point the classical reaction set in, cold and severe, from the court of Philip II, extolled by the pedantry of the humanists and perhaps in harmony with the political reverses and national sorrows of the age, which the public symbolized by the severe lines of Greco-Roman art; an austere ideal which appeared in the last period of the reign of Philip II. The Greco-Roman was frequently called the Herrerian style, after Herrera, the architect of the monastery of the Escorial. The transition to it from the plateresque was made easy by a large number of works having a smooth surface, sometimes decorated by graven lines, and only adorned by medallions in relief, rings, elements more or less constructive, or enamelled medallions distributed geometrically over the object. A number of relatively small pitchers belong to this period, cylindrical in shape, with a domed top, and a foot of smaller proportions. The spout is very often embossed with a mask or some more or less grotesque figure: and the handle is very large and in the greater number of cases is worked out in geometrical forms. The dome with which the cylindrical body ends is nearly always supported by braces in relief. The whole is interesting and pleasing. A considerable number of such pitchers of varying form were made in Spain, and especially in Toledo [PLATE 12, A].

In the seventeenth century a reaction set in against the severe taste of the time of Philip II: this took the form of a return to floral ornamentation, with which circular or rectangular spaces were filled by details monotonously repeated over the whole surface. During this time silversmiths' work lost much of the high finish of the preceding century. No such important works were undertaken as had then been done: but on the other hand, a considerable number of embossed trays, lamps, mirror frames, basins, brasiers, pitchers, etc., were produced. The ornamentation is excessive; often its turgid superfluity creates a feeling of oppressive sumptuousness. Withal there is no sign of either genius or inspiration, and very often the motifs are repeated, especially when the structure of the piece lends itself to this; as, for example, the repetition of arms or feet of a fixed pattern.

At the beginning of the eighteenth century silversmiths' work followed French taste absolutely: but in the second half of that century, in consequence of the impulse which Charles III tried to impart to all the industrial arts, the celebrated workshop of Martinez developed in Madrid. Martinez, a native of Huesca, was sent by the Government to Paris and London, and thence returned to the capital with a perfect knowledge of the most recent mechanical improvements in the working of the precious metals. His taste and style influenced all Spain. His work was inspired by an almost too severe classical taste, and the pieces produced by him recall something of the hardness of the too mechanical processes to which they were subjected. His workshop was a place of considerable importance, especially when account is taken of the period, for he employed as many as 500 workmen.

During the nineteenth century Spanish silversmiths' work followed almost exclusively French taste and French methods, being an art and an industry which in relation to French, English, Italian, and German work must be held to have lost in individuality what it gained in extension.

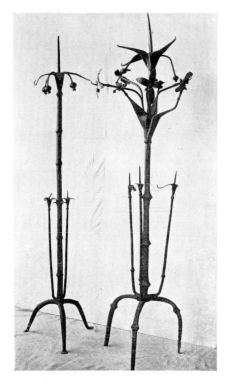

A—Iron torch-holders; 14th century   *B*—Iron grille; Romanesque.   (S. Vincente, Avila)

C—Iron grille, late 14th century. (Siguenza Cathedral)   *D*—Grille, plateresque style

B—Grille, mid-16th century, of a Chapel. (Cuenca Cathedral)

A—Grille, mid-16th century, of a chapel. (Cuenca Cathedral)

B—Grille; 16th century. (Cuenca Cathedral)

A—Iron Grille by Maestre Bartolomé (1523) of Jaén. (Cathedral of Granada)

B—Iron grille; first part of 16th century. (Condestable
Chapel, Burgos Cathedral)

A—Iron pulpit; early 16th century. (Cuenca Cathedral)

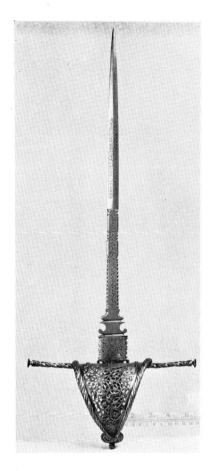

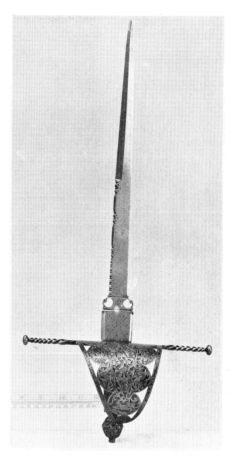

A—Left-hand dagger, inscribed DIDACUS A CVENCA FACIE-BAT; Toledo, about 1650

B—Left-hand dagger; Toledo, about 1650

C—Left-hand dagger, Toledo, about 1650

D—Inscribed rapier; Toledo, about 1640 (All in the Wallace Collection)

E—Rapier with basket handle; Toledo, about 1640

A—Cabasset; Toledo, about 1590.

B—Cabasset; Toledo, about 1600-10. (Both in the Wallace Collection)

B—Gothic iron knocker; 15th century. (Gerona)

A—Gothic iron knocker; 15th century. (Barcelona)

C—Bronze knocker. (Tarragona Cathedral)

D—Casket in pierced and gilded bronze; Hispano-Moresque of 14th century. (Don Alejandro Pidal)

A—Silver Casket of repoussé work; 13th century. (Instituto de Valencia de Don Juan)

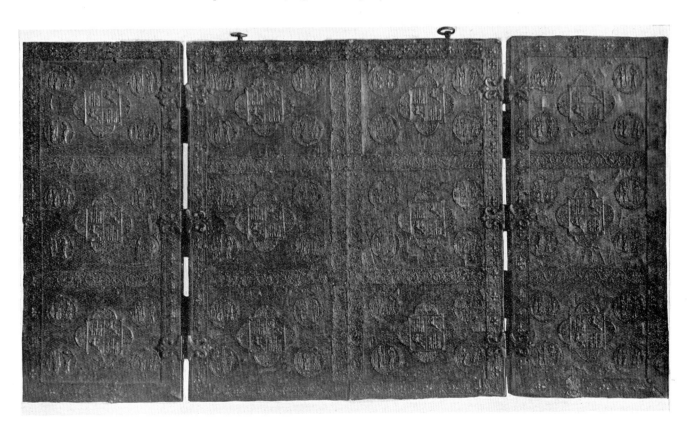

B—Silver reliquary of repoussé work; 13th century. (Seville Cathedral)

C—Bronze door; Moorish-Christian. (Sacristy of the Sacrarium of Seville Cathedral)

B—Copper panels of the doors of the Alhambra. (Granada)

A—Bronze pulpit; 14th century. (Santiago de Compostela)

A—
B—

A—Crowns of Gothic kings; gold and precious stones. (Cluny Museum)
B—Visigothic jewellery found in Guarrazar

B—Silver throne of King Martin of Aragon; early 15th century.
(Barcelona Cathedral)

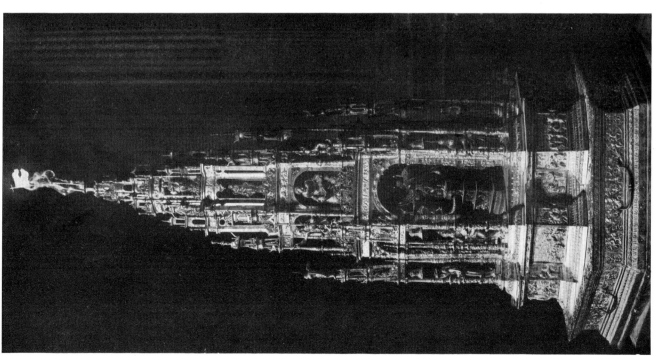

A—Silver shrine in the plateresque style.   (Jaén Cathedral)

A—Silver jugs, 16th century. (Instituto de Valencia de Don Juan)

B—Silver trays, 18th century. (Instituto de Valencia de Don Juan)

REFERENCES to the older authorities, as well as to the very numerous articles on artists, local schools, and special topics of the art of Spain, will be found in many—especially the more encyclopædic (e.g., Section I)—of the works enumerated. But article-references are included when required for the presentation of the subject. Section XV of the bibliography gives the titles of the better-known Spanish art-reviews; others primarily of local scope are classified in Section III.

PLACES OF PUBLICATION.—In order to avoid repetition, it is understood that Spanish, English and French works, are published at Madrid, London and Paris, respectively, unless specified to the contrary. A. Van de Put.

I.—GENERAL ART HISTORY.

Histoire de l'art, depuis les premiers temps chrétiens jusqu'à nos jours. Publié sous la direction d'André Michel. 1905-24. Most of the volumes specified below contain special sections on different periods of Spanish art, with bibliographies :—

I.—Carlovingian; Visigothic—by P. Lafond. Oriental Influences—by J. J. Marquet de Vasselot. Romanesque Architecture—by C. Enlart.
II.—Gothic Architecture—by C. Enlart. Sculpture—by E. Bertaux.
III.—Painting and Sculpture, down to Ferdinand and Isabella—by E. Bertaux.
IV, V.—The Renaissance—by E. Bertaux.
VI.—The Seventeenth Century—by P. Paris.
VII.—The Eighteenth Century—by P. Paris.

CABROL, F. AND LECLERCQ, H.	*Dictionnaire d'archéologie chrétienne et de liturgie.* 1903— Numerous critical articles upon Spanish art-antiquities, with full bibliographical apparatus; e.g. vol. V, *Espagne;* VI, Guarrazar (Couronnes de)—By H. LECLERCQ.
*DIEULAFOY, M.	*Art in Spain and Portugal.* (" Ars Una " series.) 1913.
JUSTI, C.	*Miscellaneen aus drei Jahrhunderten spanischen Kunstlebens.* 2 vols. Berlin, 1908.
*TYLER, R.	*Spain. A study of her life and arts.* 1907.
*WILLIAMS, L.	*Arts and Crafts of Older Spain.* 3 vols. 1907.
*MAYER, A. L.	*Alt Spanien.* (Architektur und Kunstgewerbe.) München. 1921.
*HIELSCHER, K.	*Das unbekannte Spanien. Baukunst, Landschaft, Volksleben.* Berlin, 1922.
KEHRER, H.	*Spanische Kunst von Greco bis Goya.* München, 1926.
PÉREZ-VILLAMIL, M.	*Artes e industrias del Buen Retiro.* 1904.
BABELON, J.	*Jacopo da Trezzo et la construction de l'Escurial. Essai sur les arts à la cour de Philippe II.* 1922.
SÁNCHEZ CANTÓN, F. J. (Editor).	*Fuentes literarias para la historia del arte español.* (Junta para Ampliación de Estudios) 1923. *Datos documentales ineditos para la historia del arte español.* 1914. *Las Joyas de la Exposición Historica-Europea de Madrid, 1892. El arte en la Tauromaquia. Catálogo de la Exposición, Madrid,* 1918.
FRY, ROGER	*A Sampler of Castile.* 1923.

II—MUHAMMADAN SPAIN—GENERAL.

(See also in Section I, the items marked *)

Manuel d'art musulman. I—*L'architecture,* par H. SALADIN. II—*Les arts plastiques et industriels.* 2 vols. 1907. New edn.—*L'architecture,* par G. Marçais. Vol I. 1926.

SARRE, F. AND MARTIN, F. R.	*Die Ausstellung von Meisterwerken muhammedanischer Kunst in München, 1910.* 3 vols. 1912.
	The Encyclopædia of Islam. Edited by M. T. Houtsma, T. W. Arnold, R. Basset and R. Hartmann. 1913— Inter alia, the articles : *Alhambra*—by J. STRZYGOWSKI; *Arabesque* —by E. HERZFELD; etc., etc.
GLÜCK, H. AND DIEZ, E.	*Die Kunst des Islam.* Berlin, 1925.
RICARD, P.	*Pour comprendre l'art musulman dans l'Afrique du Nord et en Espagne.* 1924.
WHISHAW, B. AND E. M.	*Arabic Spain. Sidelights on her history and art.* 1912.

III.—REGIONAL ART AND ARTISTS.

El arte en España. Barcelona. (Published under the patronage of the Comisaría Regia del Turismo y Cultura Artistica.) Illustrated booklets upon important towns and edifices, etc., with text in Spanish, French and English, by recognized authorities. The Comisaría publishes also the series : Spain. Pamphlet guides to Spanish art and history, with text by R. Tyler. (Comisaría regia del Turismo.)

Castile

HUIDOBRO SERNA, L.	*Contribución al estudio del arte visigotico en Castilla : Burgos.* Valladolid, 1916.
MAYER, A. L.	*Toledo.* Leipzig, 1916.
LAMBERT, E.	*Tolède.* 1925.
RAMÍREZ DE ARELLANO, R.	*Catálogo de artifices que trabajaron en Toledo, y cuyos nombres y obras aparecen en los archivos de sus parroquias.* Toledo, 1920. *Notas del archivo de la catedral de Toledo.* 1914.
PÉREZ SEDANO, F.	*Documentos de la catedral de Toledo. Colección formada . . . por Don M. R. Zarco del Valle.* (Datos documentales ineditos para la historia del arte español, I, II. Junta para Ampl. de Est.) 1914.
AGAPITO Y REVILLA, J.	*Del Valladolid monumental; la iglesia de San Pablo y el colegio de San Gregorio.* Valladolid, 1911.
AGAPITO Y REVILLA, J.	*De arte en Valladolid.* Notas sueltas. Valladolid, 1914.
COLORADO Y LACA, E.	*Segovia. Ensayo de una critica de sus Monumentos.* Segovia, 1916.
MAYER, A. L.	*Segovia, Avila und el Eskorial.* Leipzig, 1913.

GUERLIN, H.   *Ségovie, Avila et Salamanque.* 1914.
JAÉN, A.   *Segovia y Enrique IV.* Segovia, 1917.
SAN ANDRÉS, MARQ. DE   *Guía descriptiva de Avila y sus monumentos.* Avila, 1922.
    VII. Centenario de la catedral de Burgos, 1921. *Catálogo general de la Exposición de Arte retrospettivo.* 1926.
LAMPÉREZ Y ROMEA, V.   *Los Mendoza del siglo xv y el castillo del Real de Manzanares.* Madrid (R. Academia de la Historia), 1916.
VIELVA RAMOS, M.   *Monografía acerca de la catedral de Palencia.* Palencia, 1923.
AGAPITO Y REVILLA, J.   *La basílica visigoda de San Juan Bautista en Baños de Cerrato (Palencia).* Valladolid (19—?).
RINCON LAZCANO, J.   *Historia de los monumentos de la villa de Madrid.* 1909.
TORMO Y MONZÓ, E.   *En las Descalzas Reales : estudios . . . iconograficos y artísticos.* 1917.
POLENTINTOS, CONDE DE   *El monasterio de la Visitación de Madrid. (Salesas reales.)* 1918.
CALABUIG REVERT, J. J.   *El real templo basilical de San Francisco el Grande, en la historia y en las artes.* Valencia. 1919.
ESTEBAN, E.   *La Sagrada Forma de El Escorial.* El Escorial, 1913.

León
PÉREZ LLAMAZARES, J.   *El tesoro de la real colegiata de San Isidoro de León (Reliquias, relicarios y joyas artísticas.)* León, 1925.
DIAZ-JIMÉNEZ, E.   *Historia del Museo Arquelógico de San Marcos de León. Apuntes para un catálogo.* 1920.
ANTON Y CASASECA, F.   *El arte romanico Zamorano : monumentos primitivos.* Valladolid, 1919.

Andalusia
VELÁZQUEZ BOSCO, R.   *Arte del califato de Córdoba. Medina Azzahra y Alamiriya.* (Junta para Ampliación de Estudios.) 1912.
GESTOSO Y PÉREZ, J.   *Guía artística de Sevilla.* 6th ed. Sevilla, 1913.
GESTOSO Y PÉREZ, J.   *Ensayo de un diccionario de los artífices que florecierion en Sevilla desde el siglo XIII al XVII inclusive.* 3 vols. Sevilla, 1899-1909.
GESTOSO Y PÉREZ, J.   *Catálogo de las pinturas y esculturas del Museo Provincial de Sevilla.* 1912.
WHISHAW, B. AND E. M.   *Descriptive account of the Museum of Andalucian pottery and lace, antique and modern.* Seville. 1913.
VELÁZQUEZ BOSCO, R.   *La Rábida, Palos y Moguer : el monasterio de Nuestra Señora de la Rábida.* (Junta para Ampl.de Est.) 1914.
GUTIÉRREZ DE QUIJANO Y LÓPEZ, R.   *La cartuja de Jerez.* Jerez, 1924.
SALADIN, H.   *L'art ornemental hispano-moresque. L'Alhambra de Grenade.* 1920.
SECO DE LUCENA, L.   *La Alhambra.* 2nd edn. Granada, 1920.
GÓMEZ-MORENO, A.   *Arte cristiano entre los moros de Granada.* Zaragoza, 1904.
RAMOS LÓPEZ, J. DE   *Carácter de los monumentos artisticos granadinos del siglo XVI.* 2nd edn. Granada, 1900.

Murcia
BAQUERO ALMANSA, A.   *Catálogo de los professores de las bellas artes murcianos, con una introducción historica.* Murcia, 1913.

Estremadura
MONSALUD, MARQ. DE   *Arqueologia romano-visigotica de Extremadura.* 1900.
MÉLIDA, J. R.   *Catálogo monumental de España. Provincia de Cáceres.* 1914-16. Ministerio de Instrucción Publica y Bellas Artes (1926). 2 vols. and portfolio of plates.
VILLACAMPA, C. G.   *Grandezas de Guadalupe.* 1924.

Galicia
    Galicia Historica. Santiago. 1901-3.
DEL CASTILLO LÓPEZ, A.   *Riqueza monumental y artistica de Galicia.* Coruña, 1921.
HARTLEY, C. G.   *The story of Santiago de Compostela.* 1912.
LÓPEZ Y LÓPEZ, R.   *Santiago de Compostela. Guía.* 3rd ed. Santiago, 1920.

Asturias
REDONDO, I.   *Iglesias primitivas de Asturias.* Oviedo, 1904.

Navarre
    Comisión de Monumentos históricos y artísticos de Navarra. *Boletín.* 2nd series. Pamplona, 1910—
ITURRALDE Y SUIT, J.   *Las grandes ruinas monásticas de Navarra.* Pamplona, 1916.

Aragon.
ABIZANDA Y BROTO, M.   *Documentos para la historia artistica y literaria de Aragón. procedente del Archivo de Protocoles de Zaragoza. Siglo XVI.* 2 vols. Zaragoza, 1915-17.
    Zaragoza. Exposición retrospectiva de arte, 1908. Texte historique et descriptif par E. Bertaux. Saragossa, 1910.
DEL ARCO, R.   *Guía artistica y monumental de Huesca y su provincia.* Huesca, 1910.
DEL ARCO, R.   *La catedral de Huesca.* Huesca, 1924.
LÓPEZ LANDA, J. M.   *El monasterio de Ntra. Sra. de Rueda.* Calatayud, 1922.
    Arte Aragonés. Zaragoza, 1913—

Catalonia
INSTITUT D'ESTUDIS CATALANS.   *Anuari.* Barcelona, 1907.
GASETA DE LES ARTS.   Barcelona (Junta de Museus), 1924—
RUBIÓ Y LLUCH, A.   *Documents per l'historia de la cultura catalana mig-eval,* publicats per. Barcelona (Inst. d'estud. cat.), 1908, 1921.
GUDIOL Y CUNILL, J.   *Nocions de arqueologia sagrada catalana.* Vich, 1902.
GONZALEZ Y SUGRANES, M.   *Contribucio a la Historia del antichs gremis dels arts y oficis de la ciutat de Barcelona.* Barcelona. 1915.

DESDEVISES DU DEZERT. *Barcelone et les grands sanctuaires catalans.* 1913.
BASSEGODA, B. *Santa María de la Mar.* Monografia historico-artística. Vol. I. Barcelona, 1921.
IRANZO Y EIRAS, V. *El claustro del monasterio de San Pedro de las Puellas.* Barcelona (Asoc. de Arquitectos de Cataluna, 1903).
FOLCH I TORRES, J. *Museo de la Ciudadela. Catálogo de la sección de arte romanico.* Barcelona, 1926.
SOCIEDAD ARQUEOLÓGICA TARRACONENSE. *Boletin arquelógico.* Tarragona, 1901—
DEL ARCO, L. *Guia artistica y monumental de Tarragona y su provincia.* Tarragona, 1906.
DEL ARCO Y MOLINERO, A. *La primitiva catedral de Tarragona. Santa Tecla la Vieja.* Tarragona, 1914.
DOMENECH Y MONTANER, G. *Historia y arquitectura del monestir de Poblet.* Barcelona, 1925.
PUIG Y CADAFALCH, J. *Santa Maria de la Seu d'Urgell.* Amb. la collaboracio de P. Pujol. Barcelona, 1918.
FALGUERA, A. DE *Sant Pere de Roda.* Barcelona. 1906.
SANTACANA ROMEU, F. *Catalec del Museu Santacana de Martorell.* Martorell, 1909.

Valencia

Archivo de Arte valenciano. Valencia. (R. Acad. de Bellas Artes), 1915—
Guia del Museo de Bellas Artes de Valencia. Valencia, 1915.
ORELLANA, M. A. *Valencia antigua y moderna.* 3 vols. Valencia (Acción bibliografica valenciana), 1923-4.
SANCHIS Y SIVERA, J. *La catedral de Valencia; guia historica y artistica.* Valencia, 1909.
SANCHIS Y SIVERA, J. *La iglesia parroquial de Santo Tomás de Valencia; monografia histórico-descriptiva.* Valencia, 1913.
GAY, M. G. *Monografia histórico-descriptiva de la real parroquia de los Stos. Juanes de Valencia.* Valencia. 1909.
SOLÁ, J. M. AND CERVOS, F. *El palacio ducal de Gandia.* Barcelona, 1904.
SARTHOU CARRERAS, C. *El alcazar setabense.* Valencia, 1922.

Balearic Islands

SOCIEDAD ARQUEOLÓGICA LULIANA. *Boletin.* Palma, 1886—
CHAMBERLIN, F. *Guide to Majorca.* Palma, 1925.

IV.—ARCHITECTURE.
(See also III. Regional Art.)

Monumentos arquitectónicos de España. 8 vols. fol. Madrid, 1859-85.
    Continuation : Amador de los Rios, R. Toledo. 1905-08.
JUNGHAENDEL, M. *Die Baukunst Spaniens dargestellt in ihren hervorragendsten Werken.* Text von C. Gurlitt (also in Spanish by P. Madrazo). Vols. I and II, Dresden, 1889-93 ; vol. III (supplement by P. Madrazo), 1898.
LAMPÉREZ Y ROMEA, V. *Arquitectura civil española de los siglos* I al XVIII. 2 vols. 1922.
GÓMEZ-MORENO, M. *Iglesias mozárabes : arte español del siglo IX al XI.* 2 vols. (Junta para Ampl. de Est.) 1919.
KING, G. G. *Pre-Romanesque churches of Spain.* Bryn Mawr, 1924.
PUIG Y CADAFALCH, J., FALGUERA, A. DE, AND GODAY Y CASALS, J. *L'arquitectura romànica a Catalunya.* 3 vols. Barcelona (Institut d' Estudis Catalans), 1909.
STREET, G. E. *Some account of Gothic architecture in Spain.* New ed. by G. G. King. 1914.
WHITTLESEY, A. *The Renaissance architecture of Central and Northern Spain.* A collection of photographs and measured drawings. New York, 1920.
BYNE, A. AND STAPLEY, M. *Spanish architecture of the sixteenth century; general view of the Plateresque and Herrera styles.* New York (Hispanic Soc. of America), 1917.
BRAUN, J. *Spaniens alte Jesuiten Kirchen.* Freiburg i B., 1913.
WHITTLESEY, A. *The minor ecclesiastical, domestic and garden architecture of Southern Spain.* New York, 1917.
BYNE, A. AND STAPLEY, M. *Spanish gardens and patios.* New York, 1924. *Provincial houses in Spain.* 1925.
BOTTOMLEY, W. L. *Spanish details.* New York, 1924.
LAMPÉREZ Y ROMEA, V. *El bizantinismo en la arquitectura cristiana española* (siglos VI-XI). 1900.
LAMPÉREZ Y ROMEA, V. *Arquitectura española en la Edad Media.* (Madrid. 1908.)
GROMORT, G. *Jardins d'Espagne. . . . Vues des jardins anciens et modernes de l'Andalousie et des deux Castilles, . . . accompagnées de 20 plans.* 2 vols. 1926.

V.—PAINTING.
(Including monographs on individual painters.)

MAYER, A. L. *Geschichte der Spanischen Malerei.* 2 vols. Leipzig, 1913. 2nd edition in one vol. 1922.
THE STUDIO Special number. *Spanish Painting.* [With special reference to the Burlington House exhibition, London, 1920-21.] Text by A. de Beruete y Moret. 1921.
BERUETE Y MORET, A. DE *Conferencias de arte.* 1924.
Les pintures murals catalanes. Barcelona (Inst. d'Estudis Catalans), 1908.
SANPERE Y MIQUEL, S. AND GUDIOL Y CUNILL, J. *La pintura mig-eval catalana.* Vols. I and II published. Barcelona. 1908, '25.
SANPERE Y MIQUEL, S. *Los cuatrocentistas catalanes.* 2 vols. Barcelona. 1906.
TORMO Y MONZÓ, E. *Jacomart y el arte hispano-flamenco cuatrocentista.* 1913.

TORMO Y MONZÓ, E.   *Un museo de primitivas. Las tablas de las iglesias de Játiva.* 1912.
SÁNCHEZ-CANTON, F. J.   *Los pintores de cámara de los reyes de España.* 1916.
MAYER, A. L.   *Die Sevillaner Malerschule.* Leipzig, 1911.
BERUETE Y MORET, A. DE   *The school of Madrid.* Translated by Mrs. S. Erskine. 2nd ed. 1911.
SENTENACH, N.   *La pintura en Madrid desde sus origenes hasta el siglo XIX.* 1907.
CIERVO, J.   *Pintores de España. Narraciones biográficas y de investigación.* 1480-1874. 1925. *Catálogo de la colección de pinturas del Excmo. Señor Duque de Berwick y de Alba.* (Privately printed.) 1913.
VEGUE Y GOLDONI, A. AND SÁNCHEZ CANTÓN, F. J.   *Tres salas del Museo Romantico* (Donacion Vega-Inclán). 1921.

Morales

BERJANO ESCOBAR, D.   *El pintor Luis de Morales (el Divino).* 1921.

El Greco

COSSÍO, M. B.   *El Greco;* 1908. *Lo que se sabe de la vida del Greco.* 1914. *El entierro del conde de Orgaz.* 1914.
BARRÈS, M. AND LAFOND, P.   *Le Greco.* 1911.
LAFOND, P.   *Le Greco.* 1913.
KEHRER, H.   *Die Kunst des Greco.* 3rd ed. München, 1920.
MAYER, A. L.   *El Greco.* München, 1911; *Domenico Theotocopuli, el Greco. Kritisches und illustriertes Verzeichnis des Gesamtwerkes.* München, 1926.
BERITENS, G.   *Aberaciones del Greco cientificamente considerados.* 1913.
SAN ROMÁN, F. DE   *El Greco en Toledo.* 1910.

Ribera

LAFOND, P.   *Ribera et Zurbarán.* 1909.
MAYER, A. L.   *Jusepe de Ribera (Lo Spagnoletto).* 2nd ed. Leipzig, 1923.

Zurbarán

VINIEGRA, S. DE   *Catálogo oficial ilustrado de la Exposición de las obras de Francisco de Zurbarán.* 1905.
CASCALES Y MUÑOZ, J.   *Francisco de Zurbarán, his life and works.* New York. (Privately printed), 1918. Spanish ed. 1911.
KEHRER, H.   *Francisco de Zurbarán.* 1918.
LAFOND, P.   (See *Ribera.*)

Velázquez

JUSTI, C.   *Velázquez und seine Jahrhundert.* 2nd ed. Bonn, 1903. English translation of first German ed. (1888), by A. H. Keane. 1889.
MAYER, A. L.   *Kleine Velásquezstudien.* München, 1913; *Diego Velázquez.* Berlin, 1924.
BERUETE Y MORET, A. DE   *Velázquez.* Translated from the French by H. E. Poynter. 1906.
ALLENDE-SALAZAR, J.   *Velázquez, des Meisters Gemälde.* Einleitung von W. Gensel. 4th ed. Stuttgart (Klassiker der Kunst), 1925.
RICKETTS, C. S.   *The Prado and its masterpieces,* capp. i.-v. 1903.

Carreño de Miranda.

BERJANO ESCOBAR, D.   *El pintor D. Juan Carreño de Miranda (1614-85). Su vida y obras.* (1926.)

Murillo

MAYER, A. L.   *Murillo, des Meisters Gemälde.* Stuttgart (Klassiker der Kunst), 1913.
CALVERT, A.   *Murillo.* 1907.

Valdés Leal

BERUETE Y MORET, A. DE   *Valdés Leal: estudio critico.* 1911.
LAFOND, P.   *Juan de Valdés Leal: essai sur sa vie et son œuvre, suivi d'un catalogue et d'une bibliographie.* 1914.
GESTOSO Y PÉREZ, J.   *Biografia del pintor sevillano, Juan de Valdés Leal.* Sevilla, 1916.

Goya

LOGA, F. VON   *Francisco de Goya.* Berlin. 1903.
STOKES, H.   *Francisco Goya,* 1914.
BERUETE Y MORET, A. DE   *Goya, pintor de retratos.* 3 vols. 1916-18. English translation by S. Brinton. 1922. *Colección de reproducciones de cuadros, dibujos y aguafuertes de Don F. de Goya.* Precedidas de un epistolario del pintor y de las noticias biograficas pubicadas por Don F. de Zapater y Gómez. 1924.
STARKWEATHER, W. E. B.   *Paintings and drawings by F. Goya in the Collection of the Hispanic Society of America.* (Hisp. Soc.). 1916. *Les dessins de F. de Goya y Lucientes au Musee du Prado.* Texte explicatif de P. d'Achiardi, Rome, 1908.
HOFMANN, J.   *F. de Goya. Katalog seines graphischen Werkes.* Wien, 1907.
DELTEIL, L.   *Le peintre-graveur illustré* (vols. XIV, XV). 1922.
BERUETE Y MORET, A. DE   *Goya, pintor de retratos.* Vol. III: *Goya grabador.* 1918.
   Les caprices de Goya. Edition illustrée de reproductions des eaux-fortes, de l'Académie royale de Madrid, Précédee d'une étude . . . par T. Leclère. (1910.)

Modern Schools

TEMPLE, A. G.   *Modern Spanish Painting.* Being a review of some of the painters and paintings of the Spanish school since the time of Goya. 1908.

CÁNOVAS, A.   *Apuntes para un diccionario de pintores malagueños del siglo XIX.* 1908.
    Catálogo dela Exposición de pinturas españoles de la primera mitad del siglo XIX. 1913.

CIERVO. J.   *El arte y el vivir de Fortuny.* 1920 (?)
    Catalogue of paintings by J. Sorolla y Bastida, exhibited by the Hispanic Society of America. With introduction by L. Williams. 1909.

DOMÉNECH, R.   *Sorolla.* 1910.

BERUETE Y MORET, A. DE   *Joaquin Sorolla.* (1920?)

    Exhibition of paintings by Ignacio Zuloaga . . . . With foreword by J. S. Sargent; introductory notes and bibliography by S. Brinton. 1916-17-18. New York, 1916.

VI.—MINIATURES AND PORTRAITS.

EZQUERRA DEL BAYO, J.   *Exposición de la miniatura-retrato en España. Catálogo general.* (Soc. Española de Amigos del Arte). 1916.

EZQUERRA DEL BAYO, J.   *Catálogo de las miniatures y pequeños retratos pertenecientes al Excmo. Sr. Duque de Berwick y de Alba.* (Privately printed.) 1924.
    Catálogo de la Exposición de retratos de mujeres españolas por artistas españoles anteriores á 1850. (Junta de Iconografía Nacional). 1918.
    Exposición de retratos de niño en Espana. Catálogo general. (Soc. Esp. de Amigos del Arte.) 1925.

BARCIA, A. M. DE   *Catálogo de los retratos de personajes españoles, que se conservan en la Sección de Estampas y de Bellas artes de la Biblioteca Nacional.* (Revista de Archivos.) 1901.

ALLENDE SALAZAR, J. AND SÁNCHEZ CANTON, F. J.   *Retratos del Museo del Prado. Identificación y rectificaciones.* (Junta de Icon. Nac.) 1919.

SÁNCHEZ CANTON, F. J.   *Catálogo de las pinturas del Instituto de Valencia de Don Juan.* 1923.

BERWICK AND ALBA, DUKE OF   *Contribución al estudio de la persona de Don Fernando de Toledo, III Duque de Alba.* (Discursos leidos ante la R. Acad. de la Historia.) 1919.

BERWICK AND ALBA, DUKE OF   *El mariscal de Berwick.* 1925.

VII.—DRAWINGS.

BARCIA, A. M. DE   *Catálogo de la colección de dibujos originales de la Biblioteca Nacional.* 1911.

MAYER, A. L.   *Dibujos originales de maestros españoles . . . del siglo XVI hasta el siglo XIX.* 2 vols. Leipzig (for Hispanic Soc. of America). 1920.
    (See also Section V: *Goya.*)

VIII.—SCULPTURE.

LAFOND, P.   *La sculpture espagnole.* 1908.

WEISE, G.   *Spanische Plastik aus sieben Jahrhunderten.* Reutlingen. 1905.

CALVERT. A.   *Sculpture in Spain.* 1912.

DIEULAFOY, M.   *La statuaire polychrome en Espagne.* 1908. *Academie des Inscriptions—Monuments et Memoires.* No. 34. 1903.

GÜELL, CONDE DE   *Escultura policroma religiosa española.* (Una collection.) 1925.

BUSCHBECK, H.   *Der Portico de la Glorja von Santiago de Compostela.* Berlin; Wien. 1919.

MAYER, A. L.   *Mittelalterliche Plastik in Spanien.* München. 1922.

PORTER, A. K.   *Romanesque sculpture of the pilgrimage roads.* Vols. V, VI. Boston. 1923.

ORUETA, R. DE   *La escultura funeraria en España: provincia de Ciudad Real, Cuenca, Guadalajara.* (Junta para Ampl. de Est.) 1919.

DURAN Y CANAMERAS, J.   *La escultura en los paises que formaron la Corona de Aragon, y especialmente en Cataluña, desde el siglo V al XVI.* Barcelona, 1924.

DURAN, F.   *La escultura medieval catalana,* n.d.

SAGARRA Y DE SISCAR F. DE   *Sigillografía catalana.* Barcelona, 1915—

COOK, W. W. S.   *The stucco altar-frontals of Catalonia.* (In " Art Studies, Mediæval, Renaissance and Modern.") Princeton, 1924.

SERRANO FATIGATI, E.   *Escultura en Madrid desde mediados del siglo XVI, precedida de un capitol sobre escultura castellana en general.* 1912.
    Catálogo de la Seccion de Escultura. Museo Provincial de Valladolid. 1916.

OSMA, G. J. DE   *Catalogo de azabaches compostelanos, precedido de apuntes sobre los amulétos, imágenes, y la cofradia de los azabacheros de Santiago.* 1926.

MAYER, A. L.   *Spanische Barock-Plastik.* München. 1923.

AGAPITO Y REVILLA, J.   *Alonso Berruguete; sus obras, su influencia.* Valladolid. 1910.

ORUETA, R. DE   *Berruguete y su obra.* 1917.

AGAPITO Y REVILLA, J.   *La obra de los maestros de la escultura vallisoletana. I. Berruguete—Juni—Jordán.* Valladolid. 1920.

ORUETA, R. DE   *La vida y la obra de Pedro de Mena y Medrano.* (Junta para Ampl. de Est.) 7914.

ORUETA, R. DE   *Gregoria Hernández.* 1920.

TEJERA Y DE QUESADA, S.   *Los grandes escultores. Estudio . . . de Don José Luján Pérez, natural de Ciudad de Guia (Gran Canaria).* Con un prólogo de E. Tormo y Monzó. 1914.

IX.—TEXTILES.

PASCO, J.   *Catalogue de la collection de tissus anciens de D. Francisco Miguel y Badia,* classifiés par D. José Pasco. Barcelona. 1900.
    Museo de Arte decorativo y arqueológico. Barcelona. Catálogo de la sección de tejidos, bordados y encajes. Barcelona. 1906.

ARTIÑANO Y GALDÁCANO, P. M. DE   *Catálogo de la Exposición de tejidos españoles anteriores á la introducción del Jaquard* (Soc. Esp. de Amigos del Arte.) 1917.

WILLIAMS, L.   *The arts and crafts of older Spain.* Vol. II. 1907.

AMADOR DE LOS RIOS, R.   *Trofeos militares de la reconquista. Estudio acerca de las enseñas musulmanas del real monasterio de las Huelgas (Burgos) y de la catedral de Toledo.* 1893.

CASTELLANOS Y DIAZ, M.   *Historia y tecnica ornamental y decorativa de los bordados españoles: siglos XV al XVII.* Apéndice sobre la historia y técnica de los tapices de Goya. 1922.

VALVERDE, MARQUÉS, DE   *Catálogo de la Exposición de lenceria y encajes españoles, del siglo XVI al XIX.* (Soc. de Amigos del Arte.) 1915.

WHISHAW, B. AND E. M.   (See Section III.—Andalusia.)

BURLINGTON MAGAZINE   XVIII, 100 (Nov.) 1910. *Hispano Moresque carpets*—by W. G. THOMSON; XIX, 344 (Sept.) 1911, XX, 124 (Sept.) 1924. *Some fifteenth century Spanish carpets*—by A VAN DE PUT.

VALENCIA DE DON JUAN, CONDE DE   *Tapices de la corona de España.* Reproducción . . . par Hauser y Menet. 2 vols. 1903.

TORMO Y MONZÓ, E.   *Los tapices de la casa del Rey N. S. Notas para el catálogo y para la historia de la colección y de la fabrica* . . . Edición dirigida por P. M. de Artiñano. Traducción francesa de A. Mousset. 1919.

GÓMEZ MARTINEZ, A. AND CHILLÓN SAMPEDRO, B.   *Los tapices de la catedral de Zamora.* Zamora, 1925.

X.—COSTUME.

PALENCIA, I. DE   *El traje regional de España.* 1926.

EZQUERRA DEL BAYO, J.   *Exposición de " El abanico " en España. Catálogo general.* (Soc. esp. de Amigos del Arte), 1920.

XI.—CERAMICS (Early).
I.—GENERAL.

OSMA, G. J. DE.   *Apuntes sobre cerámica morisca: Textos y documentos.* 4 pts. Madrid, 1906-11.

OSMA, G. J. DE.   *Azulejos sevillanos del siglo XIII.* Madrid, 1902.

ARTIÑANO, P. M. DE.   *Resumen de la historia comparada de la cerámica en España. Segunda parte. In " Coleccionismo. Revista mensual,"* V. Madrid, 1917.

KÜHNEL, E.   *Daten zur Geschichte der Spanisch-maurischen Keramik. In " Jahrbuch der asiatischen Kunst,"* II, pt. ii, 170. Berlin, 1925.

BARBER, E. A.   *Hispano-moresque pottery in the collection of the Hispanic Society of America.— Spanish maiolica in the collection (etc.).* 2 vols. New York, 1915.

II.—ANDALUSIA.

VELÁZQUEZ BOSCO, R.   *Arte del Califato de Córdoba: Medina Azzahra y Alamiriya.* Madrid (*Junta para Ampliación de Estudios*), 1912.

SARRE, F.   *Die Spanisch-maurischen Lüsterfayencen des Mittelalters und ihre Herstellung in Malaga. In " Jahrbuch der Kgl. Preussischen Kunstammlungen,"* XXIV, 103. Berlin, 1903.

SECO DE LUCENA, L.   *La Alhambra.* 2 edn. Granada, 1910.

FERRANDIS, J.   *Los vasos de la Alhambra. In " Boletín de la Sociedad española de Excursiones,"* XXXIII, 47. Madrid, 1925.

GESTOSO Y PÉREZ, J.   *Historia de los barros vidriados sevillanos.* Sevilla, 1903.

III.—VALENCIA.

FONT Y GUMÁ, J.   *Rajolas valencianas y catalanas.* Vilanova y Geltrú, 1905.

TRAMOYERES BLASCO, L.   *Cerámica valenciana del siglo XVII. In " Almanaque de ' Las Provincias ' de Valencia,"* 1908.

VAN DE PUT, A.   *Hispano-Moresque ware of the XV century.* London, 1904. *Supplementary studies,* 1911.

FOLCH I TORRES, J.   *Noticia sobre le cerámica de Paterna; i sobre els materials procedents de les excavaciones de 1908 á 1911.* Barcelona (*Junta de Museus*). 1921.

IV.—ALLIED SCHOOLS.

BUTLER, A. J.   *Islamic pottery: a study mainly historical.* 1926.

SARRE, F.   *Die Keramik von Samarra. Unter Mitwirkung von E. Herzfeld, . . . und von H. Arnold.* Berlin, 1925.

BALLARDINI, G.   *The bacini of S. Apollinare Nuovo, Ravenna. In* BURLINGTON MAGAZINE, XXXII, No. 181. London, 1918.

BEYLIÉ, L. DE.   *La Kalaa des Beni-Hammad, une capitale berbère . . . au XIe siècle.* Paris, 1909.

BODE, W. VON.   *Die Anfänge der Majolikakunst in Toscana unter besonderer Berücksichtigung der Florentiner Majoliken.* Berlin, 1911.

BARBER, E. A.   *Mexican maiolica in the collection of the Hispanic Society.* New York, 1915.

CERAMICS (Later).

VACA GONZÁLEZ, D.   *Algunos datos para una historia de la cerámica de Talavera de la Reina. In " Revista de Archivos,"* 3rd series, XXIII-XXV. 1910-11.

PÁRAMO, P.   *La cerámica antigua de Talavera.* 1919.

CASAL, CONDE DE   *Historia de la cerámica de Alcora.* 1919.

PÉREZ-VILLAMIL, M.   *Artes e industries del Buen Retiro: la fábrica de la China (etc.)* 1904. *Catálogo de la colección de porcelana del Buen Retiro del . . . Señor D. F. de Laiglesia.* 1908.

BARBER, E. A.   *Spanish porcelains and terra cottas in the collection of the Hispanic Society of America.* New York (Hispanic Soc.). 1915.

XII.—GLASS.

BARBER, E. A.	*Spanish glass in the collection of the Hispanic Society of America.* (Hisp. Soc.) 1917.
GUDIOL Y CUNILL, J.	*Catàlech dels vidres que integren la coleccio Amattler.* Barcelona (priv. printed), 1925.
SHERRILL, C. H.	*Stained glass tours in Spain and Flanders.* 1924.
SANCHIS Y SIVERA, J.	*Vidriera historiada medieval de la catedral de Valencia.* In "Archivo de Arte valenciano," IV. 1918.

XIII.—FURNITURE, WOODWORK, INTERIORS.

	Catálogo de la Exposición de Mobiliario Español de los siglos XV y XVI, y primera mitad del XVII. (Soc. Esp. de Amigos del Arte.) 1912.
DOMÉNECH, R. AND BUENO, L. P.	*Muebles antiguos españoles.* Barcelona. (1921?)
BYNE, A. AND STAPLEY, M.	*Spanish interiors and furniture.* 3 vols. New York. 1921-25.
BYNE, A. AND STAPLEY, M.	*Decorated wooden ceilings in Spain.* (Hispanic Soc. of America.) 1920.
QUINTERO DE ATAURI, P.	*Sillas de coro. Noticia de los más notables que se conservan en España.* 1908.
MARTORELL, J.	*Interiores. Estructuras autenticas de habitaciones, del siglo XIII al XIX.* Barcelona. 1923.

XIV.—METALWORK.

I.—GOLD AND SILVER.

	Catálogo guía de la Exposición de orfebrería civil española. (Introduction by M. de Artiñano y Galdácano. Soc. Esp. de Amigos del Arte.) 1923.
SENTENACH, N.	*Bosquejo sobre la orfebreria española.* In " Revista de Archivos," 3rd series, XIX, XX. 1908-9.
ROULIN, E.	*Orfèvrerie et émaillerie. Mobilier liturgique d'Espagne.* In " Revue de l'Art chrétien." 1903.
GUDIOL Y CUNILL, J.	*L'orfebrería en l'Exposició Hispano-francesa de Saragosa.* In " Anuari de l'Inst. d'Estudis Catalans." 1908.
DURÁN, F.	*La orfebrería catalana.* In " Revista de Archivos," 3rd series, XXXIII, XXXV. 1915-16.
GUDIOL Y CUNILL, J.	*Les creus d'argenteria a Catalunya.* In " Anuari de l'Inst. d'Est. Cat." 1915-20.
BALSA DE LA VEGA, R.	*Orfebreria gallega.* In " Boletin de la Soc. Esp. de Excursiones," XX. 1912.
RAMÍREZ DE ARELLANO, R.	*Estudio sobre la orfebrería en Córdoba.* In " Colección de documentos inéditos para la historia de España," CVII. 1893.
RAMÍREZ DE ARELLANO R.	*Estudio sobre la historia de la orfebrería toledana.* Toledo. 1915.
GASCON DE GOTOR, A.	*El Corpus Christi y las custodias procesionales de España.* Barcelona. 1916.
SANCHIS Y SIVERA, J.	*El santo cáliz de la Cena (Santo Grial), venerado in Valencia.* Valencia. 1914.
ROULIN, E.	*L'ancien trésor de l'abbaye de Silos.* 1901.
SÁNCHEZ CANTON, F. J.	*Los Arfes, escultores de plata y oro (1501-1603).* 1920.
LEGUINA, E. DE, BARON DE LA VEGA DE HOZ	*Arte antiguo: La plata española.* 1894. *Esmaltes españoles: los frontals de Orense, San Miguel in " Excelsis," Silos y Burgos.* 1909.

II.—IRON, STEEL, ETC.

LABARTA. L.	*Hierros artísticos—Fers artistiques. . . particulièrement castillans et catalans.* 2 vols. Barcelona. 1902.
BYNE, A. AND STAPLEY, M.	*Spanish ironwork.* New York (Hispanic Soc.). 1915.
ORDUÑA Y VIGUERA, E.	*Rejeros españoles.* (R. Academia de San Fernando.) 1915.
ARTIÑANO Y GALDÁCANO M. DE	*Exposición de hierros antiguos españoles.* Catálogo. (Soc. Esp. de Amigos del Arte). 1919.
BYNE, A. AND STAPLEY, M.	*Rejeria of the Spanish Renaissance.* (Hispanic Soc. of America.) 1914.
LEGUINA, E. DE BARON DE LA VEGA DE HOZ	*Arte antiguo: Espadas históricas.* 1898. *Espadas de Carlos V.* 1908. *Obras de bronce.* 1907.
CALVERT, A. F.	*Spanish Arms and Armour: Royal Armoury at Madrid.* 1907.
VALENCIA DE DON JUAN, CONDE DE	*Catálogo histórico-descriptivo de la Real Armería de Madrid.* 1898.
	Museo-Armería de D. José Estruch y Cumilla. Reproducción fototipica. Barcelona. 1896.

XV.—PERIODICALS.

Revista de Archivos, Bibliotecas y Museos.
Boletin de la Sociedad Española de Excursiones.
Cultura Española.
Arte Español. Revista de la Sociedad de Amigos del Arte. Madrid.
Museum: revista mensual de arte español antiguo y moderns.
Archivo Español de Arte y Arqueología. (Junta para Ampliacion de Estudios.)
Gaseta de les Arts. Barcelona (Junta de Museus.)
Coleccionismo: organo de la Asociació Española de Coleccionistas.
Cuadernos de trabajos. Rome (Escuela Española de Arqueologia é Historia.)

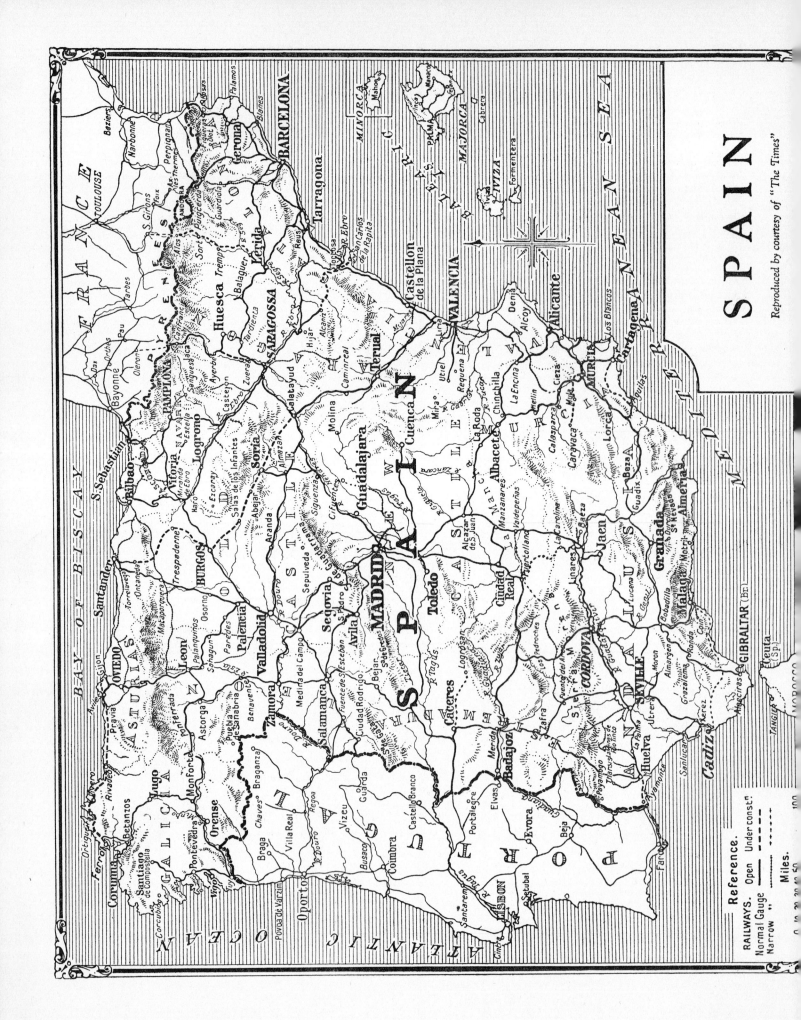

SPAIN

Reproduced by courtesy of "The Times"

Reference.

RAILWAYS. Open Under constⁿ

Normal Gauge — — — —

Narrow "

Miles.

INDEX

The letters before the page numbers indicate the section of the book to which page reference is made. Thus, A means Architecture; C, Ceramics; M, Metalwork; P, Paintings; S, Sculpture; T. Textiles; W, Woodwork

THE FOLLOWING PAGES ARE DEVOTED TO
ANNOUNCEMENTS BY ART DEALERS, MOST
OF WHOM ARE OWNERS OF SPANISH WORKS
OF ART. IT IS HOPED THAT THESE
ANNOUNCEMENTS WILL BE OF INTEREST
AND SERVICE TO READERS, AS CONSTITUT-
ING SOMETHING IN THE NATURE OF AN
INDEX IN WHICH THE NAMES AND
ADDRESSES OF THOSE ABLE TO OFFER
SPANISH AND OTHER WORKS OF ART
FOR SALE MAY BE FOUND. THE PUBLISHERS
HAVE ENCOURAGED ADVERTISERS TO
INSERT PHOTOGRAPHS, MANY OF WHICH
ARE OF UNUSUAL INTEREST AND WHICH,
IT IS HOPED, WILL ADD TO THE GENERAL
ATTRACTIVENESS OF THE BOOK.

OLD MASTERS

B. E. MURILLO. "*The Immaculate Conception.*"

A. L. NICHOLSON

4 ST. ALBAN'S PLACE,

(Behind 14 Regent Street)

LONDON, S.W.1

Cables : Artson, London

Old Panelled Rooms

Antique Furniture and Fine Decoration

WHITE ALLOM & CO.

LONDON   NEW YORK

OLD MASTERS

AND

WORKS OF ART

WANTED

ARTHUR RUCK

GALLERIES: 4 BERKELEY STREET
PICCADILLY ⁊ LONDON ⁊ W. 1

OWNERS OF IMPORTANT OLD MASTERS AND
WORKS OF ART DESIROUS OF SELLING
PRIVATELY SHOULD COMMUNICATE WITH
MR. ARTHUR RUCK, WHO IS IN DIRECT
TOUCH WITH THE CHIEF AMERICAN,
COLONIAL AND EUROPEAN
PURCHASERS

EXAMPLES MUST BE OF THE HIGHEST QUALITY

OLD AND MODERN MASTERS

PORTRAIT OF PHILIP IV OF SPAIN   Canvas Size 20 in. x 15 in.

Certified by Dr. August L. Mayer as having been painted in the studio of Velasquez in the year 1623 or 1624

THE CARROLL GALLERY

10 GEORGE STREET, HANOVER SQUARE, LONDON, W.1

Telegrams : Carolling, London. A.B.C. Code   Telephone : Mayfair 1819

FRANK T. SABIN

OLD MASTERS

ENGRAVINGS AND DRAWINGS

172 New Bond Street, London, W.1

FRENCH & CO.

❧

6 EAST 56TH STREET

NEW YORK

❧

WORKS OF ART,
ANTIQUE TAPESTRIES,
FURNITURE, TEXTILES,
AND
DECORATIONS.

M. KNOEDLER & CO.

Telephone : GERRARD 2514   Telegrams : KNOEDLER, PICCY, LONDON.

GOYA.
Admiral Mazaredo.
$41\frac{1}{4} \times 33$. *Signed on lower right.*

LONDON :   15 Old Bond Street, W.1.
PARIS :   17 Place Vendôme.
NEW YORK   14 East 57th Street.

The Gallery of

P. JACKSON HIGGS

ELEVEN EAST FIFTY-FOURTH STREET
NEW YORK

OLD MASTERS

TAPESTRIES

CHINESE PORCELAINS

BRONZES, SCULPTURE

GREEK AND ROMAN GLASS

*Special attention is called to masterworks by
Rembrandt, Van Dyck, Rubens, Lawrence
Raeburn and Gilbert Stuart*

Cable Address : Pejayaitch

Study of an Old Man's Head. Rembrandt. Panel, 6½ × 8 inches, actual size. The property of Mr. Anthony F. Reyre, 22 Old Bond Street, London, W.1.

LEWIS & SIMMONS

OBJETS D'ART - OLD MASTERS.

Palus Moreelse, 50 x 40.

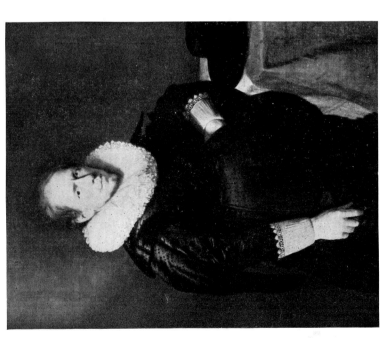

Palus Moreelse, 50 x 40.

730 FIFTH AVENUE, NEW YORK CITY.

Paris : 16 Rue de la Paix, 22 Place Vendôme.

London : 74 South Audley Street, Mayfair.

Chicago : 908 North Michigan Boulevard.

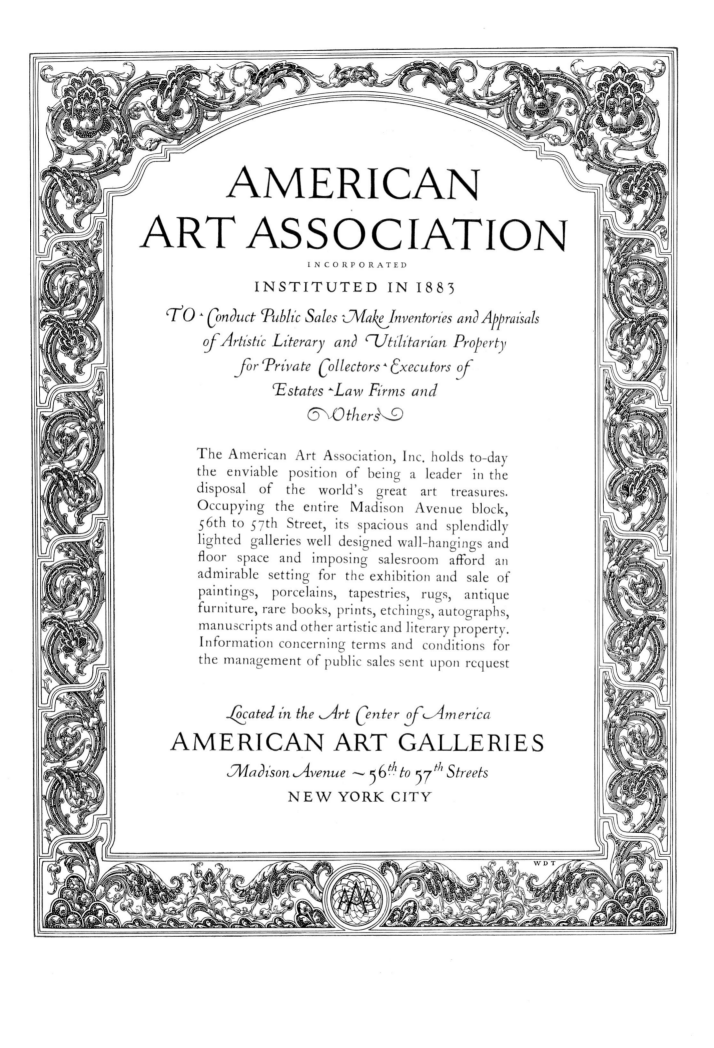

AMERICAN ART ASSOCIATION

INCORPORATED

INSTITUTED IN 1883

TO · Conduct Public Sales · Make Inventories and Appraisals of Artistic Literary and Utilitarian Property for Private Collectors · Executors of Estates · Law Firms and Others

The American Art Association, Inc. holds to-day the enviable position of being a leader in the disposal of the world's great art treasures. Occupying the entire Madison Avenue block, 56th to 57th Street, its spacious and splendidly lighted galleries well designed wall-hangings and floor space and imposing salesroom afford an admirable setting for the exhibition and sale of paintings, porcelains, tapestries, rugs, antique furniture, rare books, prints, etchings, autographs, manuscripts and other artistic and literary property. Information concerning terms and conditions for the management of public sales sent upon request

Located in the Art Center of America

AMERICAN ART GALLERIES

Madison Avenue ~ 56ᵗʰ to 57ᵗʰ Streets

NEW YORK CITY

WDT

A. S. DREY

OLD PAINTINGS
AND
WORKS OF ART

St. Jacobus, by El Greco (0.90 m. x 0.73 m.)

MUNICH: MAXIMILIANSPLATZ 7

Cameron-Smith & Marriott Ltd

THE WORLD'S LEADING EXPERT ART PACKERS

TREASURES in TRANSPORT

WE have a reputation for careful handling and packing of Antiques and Art Treasures. Proof is found in our appointment as Expert Art Packers and Shipping Agents to the **ANDERSON GALLERIES**, Park Avenue and 59th Street, New York City, for whom we have packed and shipped many famous collections including that of the late Viscount Leverhulme.

Offices :

LONDON :
6-10 CECIL COURT, ST. MARTIN'S LANE,
W.C.2

Telephone :
Gerrard 3043

Cablegrams and Telegrams :
'' Kamsmarat, London ''

Case Making and Packing Warehouses :
6, 7 & 8 Whitcher Place, Rochester Road, Camden Town, N.W.1

NEW YORK :
Cameron-Smith & Marriott, Ltd.
Hudson Forwarding and Shipping Co., Inc.
17-19 STATE STREET, NEW YORK CITY

Telephone :
Bowling Green, 10329-10330

Cables :
''Jacberg, New York ''

Also represented in Boston, Philadelphia and principal cities of the world.

MAGGS BROS

❧

RARE BOOKS
PERSIAN INDIAN & EUROPEAN
ILLUMINATED MANUSCRIPTS
AND MINIATURES
ON VIEW AT

❧

34 & 35 CONDUIT STREET, NEW BOND STREET
LONDON, W. 1
130, BOULEVARD HAUSSMANN,
PARIS

A very interesting soft paste Buen Retiro porcelain group, depicting a frightened Arab servant climbing a tree, while at the base there is a Leopard feeding an infant in its cradle. Finely decorated in Polychrome. Circa 1755. 19½ in. high.

XVIth, XVIIth and XVIIIth Century WORKS OF ART

J. NACHEMSOHN

Established 1894

13 OLD BOND STREET, LONDON, W.1

Telephone : Regent 250   Telegrams : "Jachnachem."

OCT 31 '47

DATE DUE
